T0348639

China

CHANDOS
ASIAN STUDIES SERIES

Series Editor: Professor Chris Rowley,
Centre for Research on Asian Management, Cass Business School,
City University, UK; HEAD Foundation, Singapore
(email: *c.rowley@city.ac.uk)*

Chandos Publishing is pleased to publish this major Series of books entitled *Asian Studies: Contemporary Issues and Trends.* The Series Editor is Professor Chris Rowley, Director, Centre for Research on Asian Management, City University, UK and Director, Research and Publications, HEAD Foundation, Singapore.

Asia has clearly undergone some major transformations in recent years and books in the Series examine this transformation from a number of perspectives: economic, management, social, political and cultural. We seek authors from a broad range of areas and disciplinary interests covering, for example, business/management, political science, social science, history, sociology, gender studies, ethnography, economics and international relations, etc.

Importantly, the Series examines both current developments and possible future trends. The Series is aimed at an international market of academics and professionals working in the area. The books have been specially commissioned from leading authors. The objective is to provide the reader with an authoritative view of current thinking.

New authors: we would be delighted to hear from you if you have an idea for a book. We are interested in both shorter, practically orientated publications (45,000+ words) and longer, theoretical monographs (75,000–100,000 words). Our books can be single, joint or multi-author volumes. If you have an idea for a book, please contact the publishers or Professor Chris Rowley, the Series Editor.

Dr Glyn Jones
Chandos Publishing
Email: *g.jones.2@elsevier.com*

Professor Chris Rowley
Cass Business School, City University
Email: *c.rowley@city.ac.uk*
www.cass.city.ac.uk/faculty/c.rowley

Chandos Publishing: Chandos Publishing is an imprint of Elsevier. The aim of Chandos Publishing is to publish books of the highest possible standard: books that are both intellectually stimulating and innovative.

We are delighted and proud to count our authors from such well-known international organisations as the Asian Institute of Technology, Tsinghua University, Kookmin University, Kobe University, Kyoto Sangyo University, London School of Economics, University of Oxford, Michigan State University, Getty Research Library, University of Texas at Austin, University of South Australia, University of Newcastle, Australia, University of Melbourne, ILO, Max-Planck Institute, Duke University and the leading law firm Clifford Chance.

A key feature of Chandos Publishing's activities is the service it offers its authors and customers. Chandos Publishing recognises that its authors are at the core of its publishing ethos, and authors are treated in a friendly, efficient and timely manner. Chandos Publishing's books are marketed on an international basis, via its range of overseas agents and representatives.

Professor Chris Rowley: Dr Rowley, BA, MA (Warwick), DPhil (Nuffield College, Oxford) is Subject Group leader and the inaugural Professor of Human Resource Management at Cass Business School, City University, London, UK, and Director of Research and Publications for the HEAD Foundation, Singapore. He is the founding Director of the multi-disciplinary and internationally networked Centre for Research on Asian Management (*http://www.cass.city.ac.uk/cram/index.html*) and Editor of the leading journal *Asia Pacific Business Review* (*www.tandf.co.uk/journals/titles/13602381.asp*). He is well known and highly regarded in the area, with visiting appointments at leading Asian universities and top journal Editorial Boards in the UK, Asia and the US. He has given a range of talks and lectures to universities, companies and organisations internationally with research and consultancy experience with unions, business and government, and his previous employment includes varied work in both the public and private sectors. Professor Rowley researches in a range of areas, including international and comparative human resource management and Asia Pacific management and business. He has been awarded grants from the British Academy, an ESRC AIM International Study Fellowship and gained a 5-year RCUK Fellowship in Asian Business and Management. He acts as a reviewer for many funding bodies, as well as for numerous journals and publishers. Professor Rowley publishes extensively, including in leading US and UK journals, with over 370 articles, books, chapters and other contributions.

China

Trade, foreign direct investment, and development strategies

YANQING JIANG

AMSTERDAM•BOSTON•CAMBRIDGE•HEIDELBERG•LONDON
NEW YORK•OXFORD•PARIS•SAN DIEGO
SAN FRANCISCO•SINGAPORE•SYDNEY•TOKYO
Chandos Publishing is an imprint of Elsevier

Chandos Publishing
Elsevier Limited
The Boulevard
Langford Lane
Kidlington
Oxford OX5 1GB
UK
store.elsevier.com/Chandos-Publishing-/IMP_207/

Chandos Publishing is an imprint of Elsevier Limited

Tel: +44 (0) 1865 843000
Fax: +44 (0) 1865 843010
store.elsevier.com

First published in 2014

ISBN: 978-1-84334-762-0 (print)
ISBN: 978-1-78063-443-2 (online)

Library of Congress Control Number: 2014931608

British Library Cataloguing-in-Publication Data.
A catalogue record for this book is available from the British Library.

Project management by Neil Shuttlewood Associates, Gt Yarmouth, Norfolk, UK
Printed in the UK and USA

Contents

List of abbreviations

ASEAN	Association of Southeast Asian Networks
COD	Chemical Oxygen Demand
CV	Coefficient of Variation
DEA	Data Envelopment Analysis
FD	First Differencing
FD 2SLS	First Differenced Two Stage Least Squares
FDI	Foreign Direct Investment
GDP	Gross Domestic Product
GMM	Generalized Method of Moments
GRP	Gross Regional Product
HCS	Hoover's Coefficient of Specialization
KSI	Krugman Specialization Index
NBS	National Bureau of Statistics of China
NCEE	National College Entrance Examination
OLS	Ordinary Least Squares
PIM	Perpetual Inventory Method
PRD	Pearl River Delta
PUBL	PUBLications per worker
RE	Random Effects
RD	Relative Demand
RS	Relative Supply
TFP	Total Factor Productivity

About the author

Yanqing Jiang is associate professor at Shanghai International Studies University in Shanghai, China. His recent research is mainly on China's opening up, growth and development. He started his research in this area in 2004 when he was affiliated to the Hanken School of Economics and the Helsinki Centre of Economic Research as a doctoral researcher in Helsinki, Finland. He has published many articles on China in various refereed journals.

Introduction

Abstract: Openness to foreign trade and foreign direct investment plays an important role in shaping China's development strategies. This book explores how openness to foreign trade and foreign direct investment affects development strategies regarding China's processes and patterns of economic restructuring. This introductory chapter introduces the topics, and subsequent chapters enter into theoretical discussions and empirical analyses addressing the many facets of the central theme of the book.

Key words: trade, foreign direct investment, development strategies, China, opening up, regional disparity.

Openness to foreign trade and foreign direct investment (FDI) plays an important role in shaping China's development strategies. It is the development process in China that drives the strong pressure for continuous restructuring of the Chinese economy. This book, *China: Trade, Foreign Direct Investment, and Development Strategies*, explores how openness to foreign trade and FDI affects China's development strategies as they relate to the processes and patterns of economic restructuring. The book aims to provide the reader with insight and findings that shed new light on related issues and problems. This introductory chapter introduces the topics, and subsequent chapters enter into the theoretical discussions and empirical analyses that address the many facets of the central theme of the book. Despite cross-referencing between chapters from time to time, each chapter is sufficiently self-contained and can thus be read on its own, a feature that hopefully improves the usefulness of the book as a text.

Along with China's rapid economic growth in the past few decades, substantial disparities have emerged in productivity and per capita income across different regions in China. In Chapter 2, in preparation for subsequent examinations of regional development and spatial inequality in China, we construct a theoretical framework within which regional growth in total output can be broken down into the growth of its various contributors. As unbalanced growth and development in China can be seen to be a result of the uneven regional growth of productivity and production factors, we then propose a coherent framework, not only to investigate the potential forces shaping the pattern of China's spatial disparities, but also to evaluate their relative importance by quantitatively breaking the imbalance down into its various contributory factors. In sum, the discussions in this chapter constitute an analytic foundation on which our analyses in subsequent chapters can be built.

Different phases in development strategies have generated different forces that affect China's unbalanced development. In Chapter 3, we present facts and trends about the interregional inequality in China, and attempt to establish a linkage between the various forces generated by policy regime switching and the changing pattern of interregionally unbalanced economic development in China. Among other findings, our empirical results suggest that the sharp increase in overall interregional inequality in the early 1990s can largely be attributed to the between-zone contribution of physical capital. Besides the coastal–inland disparity, the variation between coastal regions appears at times to be the dominant factor behind overall interregional inequality in China. Moreover, it can be shown that the process underlying the opening up of China to trade and FDI does account for a substantial share of China's interregional inequality, and the share rises over time.

Chapter 4 is devoted to preliminary discussion of the potential effects of foreign trade on economic development as it relates to the Chinese economy, with a focus on the possible mechanisms through which foreign trade can exert its various impacts on economic development. One such mechanism is technology diffusion. Openness to foreign trade promotes total factor productivity (TFP) growth in China by facilitating technological spillovers from technologically advanced countries. Our preliminary empirical analysis in this chapter is based on a hypothesis positing that, given the level of TFP at the world technology frontier, China's regional TFP growth is a positive function of regional openness to foreign trade and a negative function of the current level of regional TFP. Our regression results show that there exists a significantly positive effect of regional openness on regional TFP growth, and that there is evidence for conditional convergence in TFP across China's regions.

Symmetrical to the preceding chapter, Chapter 5 is devoted to preliminary discussion of the potential effects of openness to FDI on China's economic development. Our focus in this chapter is on potential mechanisms through which openness to FDI can exert its various impacts on China's economic development. FDI inflows not only enhance capital accumulation in China, which in itself is crucial to China's development, but also exert several spillover effects through different channels. The regression results of our preliminary empirical analysis in Chapter 5 suggest that regional openness to FDI tends to promote regional TFP growth and hence regional income growth. Motivated by the preliminary discussions in Chapters 4 and 5, we then proceed to investigate the impacts of openness to foreign trade and FDI on China's economic development from different perspectives in the subsequent chapters of this book.

In Chapter 6 we investigate the effects of international openness, domestic coastal-inland market integration, and human capital accumulation on TFP growth in inland regions in China. By using a variety of panel data regression techniques, we show that human capital accumulation plays an important role in promoting TFP growth in China's inland provinces. Our results support the argument that the most important contribution of human capital to income growth lies not in its static direct effect as an accumulable factor in the production function, but rather in its dynamic role in promoting TFP growth. Our results also provide evidence of the positive role coastal–inland market integration plays in promoting TFP growth in inland regions of China.

Openness to foreign trade and FDI increases the efficiency in the way production factors are allocated by lifting barriers to the mobility of resources across different sectors. In Chapter 7 we empirically analyze the relationship between openness to foreign trade and FDI and China's structural change. Our regression results show just how useful the Lewis model can be at analyzing China's process of industrialization. Our empirical analyses also show that openness to foreign trade and FDI plays an important role in China's structural transformation. The results suggest that regional openness promotes regional structural transformation in terms of labor share shifts from the agricultural to the manufacturing sector, and that structural transformation in poorer regions tends to be faster, demonstrating convergence in per-worker income across the different regions of China.

Chapter 8 focuses on the linkage between change in the pattern of China's comparative advantage and the continuous transformation in economic structure of the country. After formalizing the processes of structural transformation and the shift of comparative advantage across sectors, we use the specialization index to proxy for the intensity of comparative advantage in our empirical analysis. Results show that the specialization index of primary goods has been declining while that of manufactured goods has been climbing over time. They further show that, of the various subdivisions of primary goods, the specialization index of mineral fuels and non-edible raw materials has been falling whereas, of the various subdivisions of manufactured goods, the specialization index of machinery and transport equipment has been rising. To a large degree, the empirical results support the hypothesis of the theoretical model presented in Chapter 8.

Chapter 9 contains a theoretical study concerning transaction efficiency and the patterns of specialization, which has important implications for empirical analysis and policy evaluation with respect to a large developing country such as China. In this theoretical study, we revisit the old Ricardian model of comparative advantage. Following an inframarginal methodology, we build an extended theoretical model based on the concepts of comparative advantage and transaction efficiency to explain development and inequality in developing economies. According to our model, an increase in domestic transaction efficiency reduces inequality within a developing economy while an increase in international transaction efficiency enhances the overall welfare level in a developing economy. The results of our model have important implications for China in its policy-making.

In Chapter 10 we explore issues related to economies of scale and industrial agglomeration, and their linkages to regional development and interregional disparity in China. We focus specifically on an empirical examination of the spatial distribution of manufacturing activity in China in the 2000s, a time of increasing opening up to foreign trade and FDI. We set up our regression model and carry out a regression exercise to empirically examine the effects of openness to foreign trade and FDI on industrial distribution and agglomeration across China's provinces. Our regression results support our claim that openness to foreign trade and FDI indeed plays an important role in shaping the spatial pattern and distribution of industries across China's provinces.

Knowledge as an intangible production input not only promotes economic growth but also facilitates structural change of a developing economy. Education is the major means of knowledge accumulation. Higher education in China plays an important role not only in promoting knowledge accumulation, but also in facilitating human capital mobility in China. Chapter 11 empirically investigates the issue of the relationship between regional disparities, college preferences, and admissions under the National College Entrance Examination (NCEE) system and potential interregional human capital mobility in China.

Our empirical results show that examinees from western provinces tend to have a strong preference for coastal universities, compared with examinees from central provinces. In this sense, we expect college admissions in China under the NCEE system to exert a stronger impact on potential human capital movement from western to coastal regions than from central to coastal regions.

Chapter 12 aims to empirically examine the linkages between pollution emission, output growth, and openness to foreign trade and FDI. Our regression results suggest that the 'gains from openness' hypothesis, which posits that openness to foreign trade and FDI has a positive impact on the environment, dominates the 'race to the bottom' hypothesis as far as China's regions are concerned. Our regressions do not provide evidence to support the 'race to the bottom' hypothesis. As openness to foreign trade and FDI is likely to contribute to a better environment for China, policy-makers should remove barriers to foreign trade and FDI for environmental technology, goods, and services to allow further gains from openness.

Finally, Chapter 13 provides a tentative discussion of the knowledge economy and knowledge-based development in China. Despite its long tradition of respect for knowledge, China's development is still based much more heavily on the advantages of low-cost labor. For China, one central challenge posed by the global knowledge economy is to develop an industrial structure that could better exploit rapidly growing global knowledge to accelerate its own economic development and facilitate its transition toward a knowledge-based economy. For this purpose, China should further leverage its FDI inflows, focusing more on attracting FDI with a higher degree of knowledge content. Foreign trade is another channel through which Chinese enterprises can tap global knowledge and technology. While importing capital goods is a major way of acquiring foreign technology, the management and knowledge support that comes with it are necessary to maximize productivity from technology investment.

2

Regional growth and
its decomposition

Abstract: Along with China's rapid economic growth in the past few decades, substantial disparities have emerged in productivity and per-capita income across the different regions of China. In this chapter, in preparation for subsequent examinations of regional development and spatial inequality in China, we construct a theoretical framework within which regional growth in total output can be broken down into the growth of its various contributors. As unbalanced growth and development in China can be seen to be a result of the uneven regional growth of productivity and production factors, we propose a coherent framework, not only to investigate the potential forces shaping the pattern of China's spatial disparities, but also to evaluate their relative importance by quantitatively breaking the inequality down into its constituent parts. In sum, our discussion in this chapter constitutes an analytic foundation on which our analyses in subsequent chapters can be built.

Key words: economic growth, productivity, inequality, growth decomposition, intensive growth, extensive growth.

JEL classification codes: O47; O57.[1]

Introduction

Before 1978, China had a centrally planned economy, characterized by low productivity, widespread poverty, and very low inequality in income. Thanks to the post-1978 reforms, China has achieved spectacular economic growth in the ensuing 35 years. However, great disparities have emerged in productivity and per-capita income across the different regions of China. The Gini coefficient, for example, which measures economic inequality in society, rose by about 40 percent in total from 0.33 in 1980 to 0.46 in the early 2000s (Sisci, 2005; WB, 2005; Fan and Sun, 2008; Knight, 2008). Such a rate of increase, according to the

World Bank, was the fastest in the world. Spatial income disparities, especially those between urban and rural areas and between coastal and inland regions, have been on the rise and became a prominent issue in China during the country's transition and development (Yin, 2011). By the end of the 1990s, interregional income inequality had exceeded that in any other country, and by 2005 the average per-capita income of the richer coastal regions was at least 2.5 times higher than that of inland regions (Yang, 1999; Zhu et al., 2008). Some researchers claim that the growing inequality may 'threaten the social compact and thus the political basis for economic growth and social development' (Fan et al., 2009).

Why have some regions in China become so much richer than others? In spite of regional preferential policies, there are a number of other factors that may also play a role in shaping interregional income inequality. These factors, often interrelated, may include geographical differences (Demurger et al., 2002), regional infrastructure development (Demurger, 2001), regional openness and the process of globalization (Zhang and Zhang, 2003; Kanbur and Zhang, 2005; Wan et al., 2007), development of the regional industrial mix (Huang et al., 2003), openness and development of regional township and village enterprises (Yao, 1997; DaCosta and Carroll, 2001), the process of marketization (Jian et al., 1996), effects of regional structural shocks and structural transformation (Jiang, 2010), and investment in and accumulation of regional human capital (Fleisher et al., 2010), to name a few.

The influencing factors just listed may contribute to interregional income inequality through their impacts either on regional growth of productivity or on regional accumulation of physical and human capital. Differential rates of regional productivity growth and regional physical and human capital accumulation will lead to different rates of regional output growth and ultimately shape the pattern of the evolution of interregional income inequality across China's different regions. Therefore, in order to empirically examine regional development and interregional inequality in China, we first need to construct a theoretical framework within which regional growth in total output can be broken down into growth of its constituent parts.

A theoretical framework for output decomposition

In this section we apply the Solow growth model and break output growth down theoretically. We can use this framework to empirically examine interregional inequality in China. Moreover, we augment the traditional Solow model by incorporating human capital into the aggregate production function. Specifically, we assume that, at any given point in time, output is produced according to the following function

$$Y = F(K, AH) \tag{2.1}$$

where Y denotes the level of output, K denotes the level of physical capital stock, H denotes the level of human capital–augmented labor used in production, and A denotes the level of productivity (technology), which is, for convenience, assumed to be labor augmenting (Harrod neutral). As A and H enter the production function 2.1 multiplicatively, we refer to AH as effective labor. We further assume that each unit of labor (each worker) is identical within the economy and is trained with E years of education. That is, human capital intensity is determined by

$$h = \exp[\phi(E)] \tag{2.2}$$

where human capital intensity h is defined as per-worker human capital (i.e., $h \equiv H/L$). By assuming $\phi(0) = 0$, the function $\phi(E)$ reflects the relative efficiency of a worker with E years of education compared with one who receives no education (see, for example, Hall and Jones, 1999).

In order to make the model workable, we have to assume that the production function 2.1 exhibits constant returns to scale in its two arguments: physical capital and effective labor.[2] This assumption allows us to work conveniently with the production function in intensive form. We therefore define $\hat{k} \equiv K/(AH)$ and $\hat{y} \equiv Y/(AH)$, and under the assumption of constant returns to scale we have

$$F\left(\frac{K}{AH}, 1\right) = \frac{1}{AH} F(K, AH) \tag{2.3}$$

which can be rewritten in the intensive form as

$$\hat{y} = f(\hat{k}) \tag{2.4}$$

where we define $f(\hat{k}) \equiv F(\hat{k}, 1)$. Thus we can write output per unit effective labor as a function of physical capital per unit effective labor. We assume that $f(\hat{k})$ satisfies $f(0) = 0$, $f'(\hat{k}) > 0$, and $f''(\hat{k}) < 0$, which implies that the marginal product of physical capital is positive, but that it declines as capital (per unit effective labor) rises.

The model distinguishes three sources of variation in per-worker output Y/L: differences in per-worker physical capital K/L, differences in technology A, and differences in per-worker human capital h. It follows directly from Eq. 2.1 that

$$y = F(k, Ah) \tag{2.5}$$

where $y \equiv Y/L$ and $k \equiv K/L$, which are defined as per-worker output and per-worker physical capital, respectively. An accounting approach can thus be applied to account for variation in per-worker output y in terms of per-worker physical capital k, technology A, and per-worker human capital h, provided that the functional form of Eq. 2.1 is specified. If we adopt the well-known Cobb–Douglas functional form $Y = F(K, AH) = K^{\alpha}(AH)^{1-\alpha}$, then

$$y = F(k, Ah) = k^{\alpha}(Ah)^{1-\alpha} \tag{2.6}$$

Taking logs then yields

$$\ln y = \alpha \ln k + (1 - \alpha) \ln h + (1 - \alpha) \ln A \tag{2.7}$$

In terms of growth rates, we have

$$\frac{\dot{y}}{y} = \alpha \frac{\dot{k}}{k} + (1 - \alpha)\frac{\dot{h}}{h} + (1 - \alpha)\frac{\dot{A}}{A} \tag{2.8}$$

where a dot over a variable indicates the first-order derivative with respect to time. Thus the growth rate (or level) of per-worker output can be accounted for by the growth rates (or levels) of technology, per-worker physical capital, and per-worker human capital. However, the growth accounting framework has a serious shortcoming. It ignores the causal linkage between the growth (or level) of technology (or per-worker human capital) and the growth (or level) of per-worker physical capital.

To understand this point, we need to consider the dynamics of the Solow model. We further assume that technology A and human capital–augmented labor H grow exogenously at constant rates

$$\dot{A}/A = g \tag{2.9}$$

$$\dot{H}/H = \rho \tag{2.10}$$

Output can be divided between consumption and investment, where the fraction of output devoted to investment s is assumed to be exogenous and constant, with one unit of output devoted to investment yielding one unit of new physical capital. In addition, existing physical capital depreciates at rate δ. To keep our analysis simple, education is taken not as investment in human capital, but rather as part of consumption. At any given point in time, we have

$$\dot{K} = sY - \delta K \tag{2.11}$$

It follows that

$$\dot{\hat{k}} = \frac{\dot{K}}{AH} - \frac{K}{(AH)^2}(A\dot{H} + \dot{A}H) \tag{2.12}$$

Inserting Eqs. 2.9, 2.10, and 2.11 into Eq. 2.12, we obtain

$$\dot{\hat{k}} = sf(\hat{k}) - (\rho + g + \delta)\hat{k} \tag{2.13}$$

The steady-state value of physical capital per unit effective labor, denoted by $\hat{k}^*$, is determined by

$$sf(\hat{k}^*) = (\rho + g + \delta)\hat{k}^* \tag{2.14}$$

Therefore,

$$\hat{k}^*/f(\hat{k}^*) = s/(\rho + g + \delta) \tag{2.15}$$

Let us define a new function $\chi(\hat{k}) \equiv \hat{k}/f(\hat{k})$, where $\chi(\hat{k})$ is increasing in $\hat{k}$ as $f'(\hat{k}) > 0$ and $f''(\hat{k}) < 0$. Thus $\hat{k}^*$, which is ultimately a function of the four parameters, s, ρ, g, and δ, can be written as

$$\hat{k}^* = \chi^{-1}(s/(\rho + g + \delta)) \tag{2.16}$$

The steady-state value of output per unit effective labor, denoted by $\hat{y}^*$, is then given by

$$\hat{y}^* = f(\hat{k}^*) = f[\chi^{-1}(s/(\rho + g + \delta))] \tag{2.17}$$

Eqs. 2.16 and 2.17 describe a balanced growth path along which the values of $\hat{k}^*$ and $\hat{y}^*$ are determined by the four exogenous parameters s, ρ, g, and δ.

Of the four parameters, investment rate s is the one that policy is most likely to affect. The long-term effect on output of a change in the investment rate allows us to obtain the following partial derivative of $\hat{y}^*$ with respect to s

$$\frac{\partial \hat{y}^*}{\partial s} = f'(\hat{k}^*)\frac{\partial \hat{k}^*}{\partial s} \tag{2.18}$$

As $\hat{k}^*$ is the steady-state value of $\hat{k}$, it must satisfy

$$sf(\hat{k}^*) = (\rho + g + \delta)\hat{k}^* \tag{2.19}$$

As Eq. 2.19 holds for all values of s, we take the derivative on both sides with respect to s, which yields

$$sf'(\hat{k}^*)\frac{\partial \hat{k}^*}{\partial s} + f(\hat{k}^*) = (\rho + g + \delta)\frac{\partial \hat{k}^*}{\partial s} \tag{2.20}$$

Rearranging Eq. 2.20 gives

$$\frac{\partial \hat{k}^*}{\partial s} = \frac{f(\hat{k}^*)}{(\rho + g + \delta) - sf'(\hat{k}^*)} \tag{2.21}$$

Inserting Eq. 2.21 back into Eq. 2.18, we obtain

$$\frac{\partial \hat{y}^*}{\partial s} = \frac{f'(\hat{k}^*)f(\hat{k}^*)}{(\rho + g + \delta) - sf'(\hat{k}^*)} \tag{2.22}$$

Using Eq. 2.19 to substitute for s in Eq. 2.22, we end up with the following elasticity form

$$\frac{s}{\hat{y}^*}\frac{\partial \hat{y}^*}{\partial s} = \frac{\hat{k}^* f'(\hat{k}^*)/f(\hat{k}^*)}{1 - \hat{k}^* f'(\hat{k}^*)/f(\hat{k}^*)} = \frac{\chi(\hat{k}^*)f'(\hat{k}^*)}{1 - \chi(\hat{k}^*)f'(\hat{k}^*)} \tag{2.23}$$

where $\hat{k}^* f'(\hat{k}^*)/f(\hat{k}^*)$ is the elasticity of output with respect to physical capital at $\hat{k} = \hat{k}^*$.

However, though a change in investment rate s changes an economy's balanced growth path and thus the level of output per worker at any point in time, it does not affect the growth rate of output per worker as far as the balanced growth rate is concerned. This becomes clear when we consider Eq. 2.5, according to which output per worker (at a given point in time) on the balanced growth path is determined by

$$y^* = F(k^*, Ah) = F[Ah \cdot \chi^{-1}(s/(\rho + g + \delta)), Ah] \tag{2.24}$$

where $k^* = \hat{k}^* Ah = Ah \cdot \chi^{-1}(s/(\rho + g + \delta))$, which shows that investment rate s has only a level effect – not a long-term growth effect on k^*, as the long-term (balanced path) growth of k^* depends only on the growth of Ah over time. We further assume that labor L grows exogenously at a constant rate n, that is

$$\dot{L}/L = n \tag{2.25}$$

Using Eqs. 2.10 and 2.25, we see that human capital intensity h grows at a constant rate $(\rho - n)$, that is

$$\dot{h}/h = \rho - n \tag{2.26}$$

Since by construction $k = \hat{k}Ah$, we have the following decomposition

$$\frac{\dot{k}}{k} = \frac{\dot{\hat{k}}}{\hat{k}} + \frac{\dot{A}}{A} + \frac{\dot{h}}{h} \tag{2.27}$$

Inserting Eqs. 2.9, 2.13, and 2.26 into Eq. 2.27 yields

$$\frac{\dot{k}}{k} = s\frac{f(\hat{k})}{\hat{k}} - (n + \delta) \tag{2.28}$$

Using Eq. 2.14 to substitute for s in Eq. 2.28, coupled with a little rearrangement, we obtain

$$\frac{\dot{k}}{k} = \left(\frac{\chi(\hat{k}^*)}{\chi(\hat{k})} - 1\right)(n + \delta) + \frac{\chi(\hat{k}^*)}{\chi(\hat{k})}(g + \rho - n) \qquad (2.29)$$

where we remember that $\chi(\hat{k}) \equiv \hat{k}/f(\hat{k})$, a function that is increasing in $\hat{k}$. It is clear from Eq. 2.29 that a change in investment rate s affects the growth dynamics of physical capital per worker (and hence output per worker) by shifting the steady-state level of physical capital per unit effective labor $\hat{k}^*$. Since Eq. 2.29 shows investment rate s having no more than a level effect – not a long-run growth effect on per worker physical capital (or hence on per-worker output) because in the long run (i.e., on the balanced growth path), where $\hat{k} = \hat{k}^*$, physical capital per worker would grow at a rate equal to $(g + \rho - n)$, which is obviously independent of investment rate s.

The important point to note from all this is that Eq. 2.24 reveals that per-worker output on a balanced growth path is dependent on A and h through two different channels. As seen from Eq. 2.24, A and h affect y^* not only directly, but also indirectly through (per-worker) physical capital accumulation (i.e., k^* is dependent on A and h). This means the growth accounting decomposition in Eq. 2.8 failed to take this into account and would thus mistakenly attribute (a part of) contributions of A and h to physical capital accumulation.

For growth accounting decomposition to be properly carried out in this chapter, we need to apply the Cobb–Douglas functional form to the aggregate production function, so that $Y = K^\alpha(AH)^{1-\alpha}$ or, equivalently, $y = k^\alpha(Ah)^{1-\alpha}$ as in Eq. 2.6. Using this Cobb–Douglas functional form and rearranging the mathematics, we obtain the following equation

$$y = \left(\frac{K}{Y}\right)^{\alpha/(1-\alpha)} Ah = \left(\frac{k}{y}\right)^{\alpha/(1-\alpha)} Ah \qquad (2.30)$$

On a balanced growth path, where K and Y (or k and y) grow at the same rate, per-worker output (at a given point in time) can be written specifically as

$$y^* = \left(\frac{s}{\rho + g + \delta}\right)^{\alpha/(1-\alpha)} Ah \qquad (2.31)$$

where $K^*/Y^* = k^*/y^* = \hat{k}^*/\hat{y}^* = s/(\rho + g + \delta)$ has been applied.

In order to study interregional disparities in China, we are now in a position to perform an output decomposition exercise for China's different regions, based on the idea expressed by Eqs. 2.30 and 2.31. We assume that for any region (province) i in China, its aggregate production function takes the Cobb–Douglas form, that is

$$Y_i = K_i^{\alpha}(A_iH_i)^{1-\alpha} \tag{2.32}$$

Therefore, for region i, the relationship in Eq. 2.30 applies

$$y_i = \left(\frac{K_i}{Y_i}\right)^{\alpha/(1-\alpha)} A_ih_i \tag{2.33}$$

Using Eq. 2.33, differences in y across China's different regions can be broken down into differences in K/Y, in A, and in h. There are two main reasons this decomposition is performed in terms of the capital–output ratio (K/Y) rather than the capital–labor ratio (K/L). First, as discussed above, the capital–output ratio (K/Y) along a balanced growth path is proportional to the investment rate, so that this form of decomposition has a natural interpretation (see Eq. 2.15, see also Klenow and Rodriguez Clare, 1997; Hall and Jones, 1999). Second and more importantly, this decomposition credits A for variations in K/L generated by differences in A.

The decomposition in Eq. 2.33 enables us to calculate A_i as a residual once data on y_i, K_i/Y_i, and h_i are obtained. We further define $X_i \equiv (K_i/Y_i)^{\alpha/(1-\alpha)}h_i$ and, according to Eq. 2.33, we also have $\ln y_i = \ln A_i + \ln X_i$, which leads to the following variance decomposition

$$1 = \frac{\mathrm{Var}(\ln y_i)}{\mathrm{Var}(\ln y_i)} = \frac{\mathrm{Cov}(\ln y_i, \ln A_i)}{\mathrm{Var}(\ln y_i)} + \frac{\mathrm{Cov}(\ln y_i, \ln X_i)}{\mathrm{Var}(\ln y_i)} \tag{2.34}$$

Later in this chapter, we will come back to variance as broken down by Eq. 2.34 to examine the relative contributions of productivity, physical capital, and human capital to regional per-worker output.

Productivity growth

In order to study regional growth and interregional inequality in China, it is crucial, first of all, to investigate the relationship between regional productivity growth and regional output (GDP) growth in China. The issue surrounding contributions of productivity growth to output growth has been an interesting and hotly debated topic among researchers. Conceptually, researchers follow the traditional definition of productivity growth and treat it as the difference between growth in output and combined growth in inputs. Empirically, however, two broad methods have been adopted to estimate productivity growth. In the first method, productivity growth and technological progress are treated as synonymous, with productivity growth usually being measured by applying the traditional growth accounting framework. In the second method, technological progress is considered as just one component of productivity growth, whereas productivity growth can also include technological progress, technical efficiency change, and the scale efficiency effect (Wu, 2011).

The literature shows the role played by productivity in China's growth and development processes has been extensively studied. A large number of studies are concerned with the contributions of productivity to output growth – at various levels from the economy-wide, industry, region, or firm level. Early studies focusing on the agricultural sector, where the first wave of China's economic reform took place, have looked into the impacts of rural reforms on agricultural productivity and output growth. One common conclusion of those studies is that economic reforms at the early stage substantially boosted productivity growth in the Chinese agricultural sector.[3] However, findings regarding other areas are controversial (Wu, 2011). Some studies find the role played by productivity growth in China's output growth insignificant while others are more positive about the contributions of productivity growth to output growth in China.[4] Empirical estimations of levels or growth rates of productivity depend crucially on capital stock data. As data on capital stock series are not directly available from China's official statistical system, researchers are forced to produce their own capital stock series, applying different methods based on different capital depreciation rates and initial capital stock levels. Assumed depreciation rates and initial capital stock values can vary substantially from study to study,[5] which directly leads to significantly different estimates of levels and growth rates of productivity.

This seems a prime area for application of a meta-analysis to examine the way in which different empirical estimates of productivity levels or growth rates have been associated with the characteristics of different studies. The meta-analysis of Wu (2011) surveys 74 studies, where 151 estimates of productivity growth rates at the economy or sector levels are reported. Wu Yanrui finds that the mean productivity growth rate in the 151 estimates is 3.62%, which accounts for about 36% of China's average output growth during 1978–2007. Overall, the estimated productivity growth rates are fairly spread around their mean with the exception of a few outliers (Wu, 2011).[6]

Wu (2011) applies regression analysis in which the dependent variable represents estimates of productivity growth rates and the independent variables capture the characteristics of the empirical studies surveyed.

Variables on the right-hand side are all designed as dummy variables covering such characteristics of the studies as time periods, methods, data types, estimation techniques, and the publication formats. They also include whether the studies are written in English or Chinese, whether control variables such as human capital, education and information, and communications technology are considered and whether the traditional concept of productivity (where productivity growth and technological progress are treated synonymously) or the frontier concept of productivity (where technological progress is only part of productivity growth) is adopted. The meta-analysis shows that the application of data envelopment analysis (DEA) is likely to produce lower estimates of productivity growth rates, and that studies using production function approaches tend to report low rates of productivity growth. In addition, estimates for the economy nationwide and for the agricultural sector, and those based on a period covering the 1990s up to today tend to be lower than others. Moreover, studies focusing on state-owned enterprises or those published in academic journals are more likely to report low estimates of productivity growth rates while studies written in English seem to generate higher rates of productivity growth.

Failure to take into acount the considerable variations in the rates of capital depreciation across different regions or sectors can distort estimations of productivity levels and growth rates. Wu (2009), who uses a simulation approach to derive region-specific and sector-specific rates of capital depreciation, finds that the capital depreciation rate is generally high in more developed regions and low in less developed ones, and that Beijing, Tianjin, and Shanghai have relatively low capital depreciation rates – probably because these cities have relatively large service sectors where the rates of depreciation are lower than those of manufacturing sectors. In view of such a complication, Wu (2011) suggests that future work emphasize heterogeneity at a more disaggregate level.

We study 28 Chinese provincial-level divisions over the period 1996–2011. These 28 provincial-level divisions include provinces, ethnic minority autonomous regions, and municipalities in mainland China. Owing to incomplete data, three regions, Tibet, Chongqing and Hainan, are not included in our sample. The data were mostly obtained from the annual editions of the *China Statistical Yearbook* (1996–2012) published by the state. As mentioned earlier, *China Statistical Yearbooks* do not directly record data on regional physical capital stock for the nation's regions. In order to calculate the levels of regional physical capital stock, we follow the perpetual inventory procedure of Wu (2008), who extends his own (Wu, 2004) method by adopting different rates of capital depreciation for different regions in China.[7] The different values of the rates of physical capital depreciation for different regions, obtained by following a simulation process, are listed in table A1 of Wu (2008). Generally, the rate of depreciation tends to be high in more developed regions, and low in less developed regions and the three municipalities of Beijing, Tianjin, and Shanghai. What is more, as Wu (2008) has noted, it is interesting to see that the mean regional rate of depreciation is about 4%, close to that used by the World Bank (WB, 1997). Therefore, according to Wu (2008), the adoption of a uniform capital depreciation rate of 7% in his 2004 book or that of 9.6% in Zhang (2008) would lead to an underestimation of China's regional physical capital stock levels.

Let us now follow Hall and Jones (1999) and Aiyar and Feyrer (2002) to calculate regional human capital intensity. We assume that h is related to educational attainment by Eq. 2.2, where E denotes the average years of education (schooling) attained by a worker in the labor force. Therefore, by assuming $\phi(0) = 0$, the function $\phi(E)$ in Eq. 2.2 reflects the relative efficiency of a worker with E years of schooling compared with one who receives no schooling. The derivative $d\phi(E)/dE$ is the return to schooling estimated in a Mincerian wage regression (Mincer, 1974). In Hall and Jones (1999) and Aiyar and Feyrer (2002), $\phi(E)$ is assumed to be piecewise linear, with the rates of return being 13.4, 10.1, and 6.8 percent, respectively, for schooling of the first four years, the second four years, and that beyond the eighth year. These rates of return are all based on Psacharopoulos (1994)'s survey of evidence from many countries on return-to-schooling estimates. The rate for the first four years, 13.4 percent, corresponds to the average return to an additional year of schooling in sub-Saharan Africa. The rate for the second four years, 10.1 percent, is the average return to an additional year of schooling worldwide, while that for schooling above the eighth year, 6.8 percent, is taken from the average return to an additional year in the OECD.

Let us now follow the author's previous work (Jiang, 2012) to construct the regional levels of human capital intensity. Our measure of real human capital intensity h_{it} (for region i in year t) is constructed as follows

$$h_{it} = \left(\frac{h_{it}^* L_{it}}{\sum_i h_{it}^* L_{it}} \cdot NH_t \right) \bigg/ L_{it} = h_{it}^* \cdot \frac{NH_t}{\sum_i h_{it}^* L_{it}} \qquad (2.35)$$

where $h_{it}^* = (h^a \cdot L_{it}^a + h^b \cdot L_{it}^b + h^c \cdot L_{it}^c + h^d \cdot L_{it}^d + h^e \cdot L_{it}^e)/L_{it}^*$, with L^* being the sum of the L^j's ($j = a, b, c, d, e$). NH_t in Eq. 2.35 denotes the level of China's national real human capital stock as calculated by Li et al. (2009). h_{it}^* is the unadjusted provincial human capital intensity, which we will later adjust along the time dimension to take account of significant changes in the quality of education over time. L_{it}^* denotes province i's population aged 6 and above at time t, which we divide into five groups by educational attainment: group a through group e, where L_{it}^a denotes the total number of people aged 6 and above who have received zero schooling, and L_{it}^b through L_{it}^e, respectively, denote the total number of people aged 6 and above who have received schooling up to primary school level, junior secondary school level, senior secondary school level, and college (and higher) level. Human capital intensity in each of the five groups is represented, respectively, by h^a through h^e.

Data on these (L_{it}^j/L_{it}^*)'s for the 28 Chinese provinces for each year between 1996 and 2011 can be found in the annual editions of the *China Statistical Yearbook* (1996–2012). The key to constructing h_{it}^* is to determine the value of each of the h^j's. Necessarily $h^a = 1$ by construction. In addition, we set $h^b = 2$, $h^c = 2.6$, $h^d = 3.2$, and $h^e = 4.4$ for all provinces in each year during 1996–2011. These h^j values are calculated exactly according to the aforementioned piecewise linear rates of return to schooling based on Psacharopoulos (1994)'s survey. For simplicity, we assume relative marginal returns to education (expressed as a percentage) do not vary across provinces or over time.

Having obtained the levels of physical capital stock and per-worker human capital stock for the 28 regions as above, we are now able to calculate the values of regional productivity as a residual by applying Eq. 2.33. What we need is to assume an appropriate value for the structural parameter α in the production function in order to calculate the levels of regional productivity. We thus follow Chow and Li (2002), Chow (2008), Zheng et al. (2009b), Brandt and Zhu (2010), and Jiang (2011, 2012) and assume that α is 0.5 for these regions. By applying data on regional physical capital and regional human capital intensity, and by inserting the assumption $\alpha = 0.5$ into Eq. 2.33, we can thus obtain the time series of regional productivity levels for each of the 28 regions over our sample period 1996–2011.

From Eq. 2.34 we can gain an idea of how much of the variation in per-capita output is attributable to variations in productivity and how much is due to variations in factor accumulation. The decomposition in Eq. 2.34 is equivalent to looking at OLS coefficients from separate regressions of $\ln A_i$ and $\ln X_i$ on $\ln y_i$, respectively. Therefore, this decomposition shows how much higher the conditional expectation of A_i (and X_i) would be if y_i were 1 percent higher. The results show that the split between contributions of productivity and production inputs remained fairly stable over the sample period. Roughly, variations in productivity accounted for about 70–75 percent of the total variations in y_i across the provinces. We can thus conclude that differences in productivity explain most static differences in per-capita output across the Chinese provinces for our sample period. As a result, the growth in regional productivity accounted for most of the growth of regional per-capita output over our sample period.

Extensive versus intensive growth

Since the early 1980s, when the various economic reforms were initiated, China has become one of the fastest growing countries in the world. By 2025 China is likely to surpass the United States and become the world's largest economic power by almost any standard (Holz, 2008). However, economists are now increasingly referring to China's growth as 'extensive growth', which cannot be sustained in the long run as it is fueled by increased production inputs rather than increased productivity (Zheng et al., 2009b). Researchers have raised concerns over the sustainability of China's growth in light of a slowdown in measured productivity growth. Generally, extensive growth refers to a growth strategy focusing on increasing the quantity of output by increasing the quantities of inputs (Irmen, 2005). If we rewrite Eq. 2.33 as the following

$$Y_i = \left(\frac{K_i}{Y_i}\right)^{\alpha/(1-\alpha)} A_i h_i L_i \tag{2.36}$$

We could then roughly define 'extensive growth' as the growth of Y_i due to the growth of labor input L_i and/or the growth of the capital–output ratio K_i/Y_i, and 'intensive growth' as the growth of Y_i due to growth of productivity A_i and/or the growth of human capital intensity h_i.

According to various recent studies, the main reason for China's economic growth has been increased investment (extensive growth); there has also been a marginal increase in productivity. Although China's growth before the late 1990s was less dependent on the growth of labor and capital than other fast-growing Asian economies (WB, 1997), suggesting that factors other than labor and investment were important determinants of output growth during the early reform period, studies have shown that a slowdown in productivity growth started to emerge in 2000. For example, Zheng and Hu (2006) find that productivity growth dramatically declined during the period 1995–2001: productivity rose by 3.2–4.5 percent annually before 1995, but rose by only 0.6–2.8

percent per year after 1995. Owing to the fall in the rate of productivity growth that started in the mid-1990s, annual productivity growth averaged 3.7 percent during 1978–2003 but slowed down to 2.8 percent by the end of that period (OECD, 2005; *The Economist*, 2005).

Applying the traditional growth accounting method, Zheng et al. (2009b) find that the contribution of productivity growth to China's output growth has declined in recent years. For 1978–1995, the average annual growth rates of output and total factor productivity were 10.11 and 3.80 percent, respectively, but for 1995–2007, the rates were 9.25 and 1.45 percent, respectively. This implies that productivity growth's contribution to output growth declined from 37.6 percent in the former period to 15.7 percent in the latter period. By contrast, the average growth rate of physical capital stock rose from 9.12 percent in 1978–1995 to 12.81 percent in 1995–2007, which implies that physical capital accumulation's contribution to output growth increased from 45.1 percent in the former period to 69.2% in the latter period. Based on these findings, Zheng et al. (2009b) argue that China's growth pattern is 'extremely extensive', with physical capital stock growth exceeding output growth by 3.56 percentage points during 1995–2007. If China's recent growth strategies remain unchanged, the investment–output ratio would need to reach unprecedented levels in the next two decades to maintain annual growth of real GDP of 8 percent (Kuijs and Wang, 2006; Zheng et al., 2009b).[8] Following this argument, a timely shift from 'extensive growth' to 'intensive growth' is imperative for China if it is to sustain its high growth rates in the decades to come. The importance of productivity growth cannot therefore be overemphasized.

Interregional inequality

The analysis above shows that unbalanced growth and development in China can be viewed in terms of the uneven regional growth of productivity and production factors. We are now in a position to propose a coherent framework not only to investigate the potential forces shaping the pattern of interregional disparities, but also to evaluate their relative importance by quantitatively breaking interregional inequality down into its constituent parts. More specifically, we can follow the idea of Tsui (2007) and let $I(\mathbf{y})$ be some measure of interregional inequality, with $\mathbf{y}$ being a vector of regional GDP per capita (or per worker). As long as regional output and factor inputs can be captured by the regional production function, the rate of change in interregional inequality over time, $dI(\mathbf{y})/dt$, may be expressed as a function of regional growth rates. Applying our decomposition framework discussed above, we can then break the growth of regional GDP per capita down into individual contributions from the growth of productivity and the accumulation of factor inputs such as physical and human capital. The rate of change in interregional inequality $dI(\mathbf{y})/dt$ may thus be traceable to the changing pattern in the interregional (spatial) allocation of investment captured by the interregional differential growth in physical and human capital as well as the impact of institutional improvements reflected by the growth of productivity (Tsui, 2007).[9]

The aggregate trend of interregional inequality and unbalanced development can be arrived at as a result of the convergence of a variety of different forces some having a reinforcing effect and others a counteracting effect. We need to look deeper than simply observing the aggregate trend in interregional inequality to understand the dynamics of the underlying factors at play. These factors may, for example, include the changing spatial pattern of physical investment and the spread of education. The spatial distribution of resources incurred by different institutional arrangements may have important implications for comparative advantages and economies of scale inducing higher productivity at the aggregate level. Overcoming the shortcomings of previous studies such as those of Tsui (1991, 1996) and Naughton (2002), which lacked an adequate means of isolating the effects of the different forces on interregional inequality, Tsui (2007) introduces a framework to examine more precisely the different forces shaping interregional inequality. This is a framework for the decomposition of changes in interregional inequality, in which the rate of change in interregional inequality, $dI(\mathbf{y})/dt$, is broken down into five components. The first three components each capture the contributions made by growth in productivity, in physical capital, and in human capital to change in interregional inequality. The fourth component captures the effect of population growth on interregional inequality as, for example, faster population growth in a poor region, other things being equal, would lead to an increase in interregional inequality. Finally, the fifth component captures the effect a changing population has on interregional inequality.

The gap between coastal regions and inland regions is a prominent feature of interregional inequality in China. An important dimension of

China's economic reform is the open-door policy as manifested by the huge influx of foreign direct investment (FDI), the spatial distribution of which is skewed towards coastal regions. An issue of interest is thus how different degrees of regional openness shape interregional inequality through their effect on regional economic growth. The spatial reshuffling of industries is another factor that affects interregional inequality. As economic reform has progressed, the spatial flows of investments have increasingly conformed to regional comparative advantages and economies of scale. On the one hand, increasing industrial agglomeration in coastal regions due to economic reform tends to induce coastal–inland inequality. On the other hand, local protectionism, by posing barriers to resource mobility across local jurisdictions, may have weakened the effect of agglomeration and economies of scale on regional inequality.

The literature as exemplified by Tsui (2007) suggests that the different policy environments of the Maoist and reform era were the catalyst for different changes in the interregional distribution of growth in production factors and in productivity, often with opposing impacts on interregional inequality. The late 1970s represented a dividing line where the roles played by productivity growth and capital accumulation began to be reversed. The inequality-decreasing effect of productivity growth more than offset the inequality-increasing effect of capital accumulation, resulting in the decline of interregional inequality in the 1980s. However, the decreasing effect of productivity growth began to fade, only to be replaced by the increasing effect of capital accumulation in the 1990s. In addition, industrial reshuffling in the 1980s seems not only to have induced a decline in both within-zone and between-zone inequality, but was so powerful that it overrode the other inequality-increasing forces, leading to an overall decrease in interregional inequality.[10] According to Tsui (2007), the inequality-decreasing between-zone effect of capital accumulation pre economic reform was more than offset by the increase in the between-zone contribution of productivity growth. Since the mid-1970s, changing spatial patterns of investment have been the major factor shaping between-zone inequality. The sharp increase in overall interregional inequality in the early 1990s was mostly due to the increase in the between-zone contribution of physical capital.

The roles of education and human capital have been much less discussed in the literature. Some researchers argue that investment in education pre economic reform laid the foundations for the remarkable economic growth in the reform era. Studies such as Tsui (2007) suggest that the contribution of education first increased and then reduced interregional inequality. As school age children in less developed regions entered the labor force only gradually in the 1970s, the inequality-reducing effect of education seems to be a consequence of the expansion of basic education pre economic reform. Moreover, the contribution of quality-adjusted labor to growth is small compared with that of productivity and physical capital.

Figures 5–11 of Tsui (2007) provide an excellent summary of how the contributions of the different components to overall interregional inequality changed. The cumulative contribution of physical capital – the dominant factor and focus of many studies – unambiguously declined until 1972 and started to climb thereafter. The initial decline was due to the fall in both within-zone and between-zone contributions of physical capital (though the magnitude of the latter was much larger). The fall in the between-zone contribution coincided with the 'third front campaign', a time when massive amounts of state investment were directed to inland provinces. Increase in the trend toward cumulative contribution of physical capital can be largely explained by the widening gap between coastal, central, and western regions. By the 1990s, this increasing trend was entirely propelled by the between-zone contribution of physical capital, which was the major force driving interregional inequality upward in the reform era. The reform marked the start of an era in which new sources of investment funds, such as self-raised funds or foreign capital, were made possible. Under the open-door and preferential policies, the major part of these funds went to the richer coastal regions. The spatial distribution of investment funds in the reform era has thus been increasingly skewed in favor of richer regions, which explains the increase in the between-zone contribution of physical capital. The cumulative contribution of productivity growth (before deducting the impacts of FDI and industrial restructuring) to interregional inequality was equally if not more important in certain sub-periods. FDI initially contributed to an increase in interregional inequality but its effect diminished from the mid-1980s onwards. Over time, the within-zone contribution of FDI showed a one-off decrease followed by an upward trend while the between-zone contribution of FDI did not follow any discernible trend. Industrial restructuring since the 1970s contributed to a reduction in overall interregional inequality, but the effect began to diminish in the 1990s. The downward trend is shown to be largely due to the within-zone effect of industrial restructuring. Industrial restructuring reduced interregional inequality by newly industrializing the less developed regions in the early stages of the reform era.

Concluding remarks

This chapter can serve as a foundation on which to build the related analyses in subsequent chapters. Along with China's rapid economic growth in the past few decades, substantial disparities have emerged in terms of productivity and per-capita income across China's different regions. The factors shaping the spatial pattern of income inequality in China either impact regional productivity growth or the regional accumulation of physical and human capital. In preparation for subsequent empirical examinations of regional development and interregional inequality in China, in this chapter we have constructed a theoretical framework within which regional growth in total output can be broken down into growth of its constituent parts. Such a framework allows us to study regional productivity growth and regional factor accumulation, as well as their relative importance to output growth in China's regions. As unbalanced growth and development in China can be seen to be the result of uneven regional growth of productivity and production factors, we propose a coherent framework, not only to investigate the potential forces shaping the pattern of China's spatial disparities, but also to evaluate their relative importance by quantitatively breaking the inequality down into its various contributory components. In sum, all the discussions in this chapter constitute an analytic foundation on which our analyses in the subsequent chapters can be built.

Notes

1. Works on economics are often classified according to JEL classification codes, a system set up by the *Journal of Economic Literature*.
2. This assumption can be thought of as combining two assumptions. The first is that the economy is so big that the gains from specialization have been exhausted. The second is that inputs other than physical capital, human capital–augmented labor, and technology are relatively unimportant (Romer, 2006).
3. See, for example, McMillan et al. (1989), Fan (1991), Lin (1992), and Fan and Zhang (2002).
4. See, for example, Borensztein and Ostry (1996) and Hu and Khan (1997).

5. For example, Hu and Khan (1997) adopt an annual capital depreciation rate that is 3.6 percent while Maddison (1998) adopts one that is 17.0 percent. Most studies usually apply an annual capital depreciation rate of 4–10 percent. Some examples include WB (1997), which uses 4 percent, Perkins (1988), Woo (1998), Meng and Wang (2000), and Wang and Yao (2003), who use 5 percent, Chow and Li (2002), who use 5.4 percent, Young (2003), who uses 6.0 percent, Wu (2004), who uses 7.0 percent, and Zhang (2008), who uses 9.6 percent. The latter two, Wu (2004) and Zhang (2008), are regional studies. See, for example, Wu (2009, 2011) for a summary of the capital depreciation rates and initial capital stock levels used in different studies.
6. See table 1 of Wu (2011) for a full list of the 74 studies surveyed. See figure 1 of Wu (2011) for a histogram of the estimates. Also, see table 2 of Wu (2011) for summary information about the estimates.
7. This is the first such attempt in the literature.
8. See also the study of Zheng et al. (2009a).
9. This section draws essentially on the results of Tsui (2007). In Tsui (2007), a population-weighted version of Theils's entropy measure is constructed (see eq. (1) of Tsui, 2007), and is then broken down into measures of within-region and between-region inequality.
10. China's zones comprise the eastern zone (eastern provinces), central zone (central provinces), and western zone (western provinces).

References

Aiyar, S.; and Feyrer, J. (2002) *A Contribution to the Empirics of Total Factor Productivity* (Dartmouth College Working Paper No. 02-09), Hanover, NH: Dartmouth College.

Borensztein, E.; and Ostry, J.D. (1996) 'Accounting for China's growth performance,' *American Economic Review*, 86(2), 224–8.

Brandt, L.; and Zhu, Xiaodong (2010) *Accounting for China's Growth* (Working Papers tecipa-394), Toronto, Canada: Department of Economics, University of Toronto.

Chow, G.C. (2008) 'Another look at the rate of increase in TFP in China,' *Journal of Chinese Economic and Business Studies*, 6(2), 219–24.

Chow, G.C.; and Li, Kui-Wai (2002) 'China's economic growth: 1952–2010,' *Economic Development and Cultural Change*, 51(1), 247–56.

DaCosta, M.; and Carroll, W. (2001) 'Township and village enterprises, openness and regional economic growth in China,' *Post-communist Economist*, 13(2), 229–41.

Demurger, S. (2001) 'Infrastructure development and economic growth: an explanation for regional disparity in China?' *Journal of Comparative Economics*, **29**(1), 95–117.

Demurger, S.; Sachs, J.; Woo, W.T.; Bao, S.; Chang, G.; and Mellinger, A. (2002) 'Geography, economic policy and regional development in China,' *Asian Economic Papers*, **1**(1) 146–97.

Fan, C.C.; and Sun, Mingjie (2008) 'Regional inequality in China, 1978–2006,' *Eurasian Geography and Economics*, **49**(1), 1–20.

Fan, Shenggen (1991) 'Effects of technological change and institutional reform on production growth in Chinese agriculture,' *American Journal of Agricultural Economics*, **73**(2), 266–75.

Fan, Shenggen; and Zhang, Xiaobo (2002) 'Production and productivity growth in Chinese agriculture: new national and regional measures,' *Economic Development and Cultural Change*, **50**(4), 819–38.

Fan, Shenggen; Kanbur, R.; and Zhang, Xiaobo (2009) 'Regional inequality in China: an overview,' in Shenggen Fan, R. Kanbur and Xiaobo Zhang (Eds.), *Regional Inequality in China: Trends, Explanations and Policy Responses*, London: Routledge.

Fleisher, B.; Li, H.; and Zhao, M.Q. (2010) 'Human capital, economic growth, and regional inequality in China,' *Journal of Development Economics*, **92**(2), 215–31.

Hall, R.E.; and Jones, C.I. (1999) 'Why do some countries produce so much more output per worker than others?' *Quarterly Journal of Economics*, **114**, 83–116.

Holz, C.A. (2008) 'China's economic growth 1978–2025: what we know today about China's economic growth tomorrow,' *World Development*, **36**(10), 1665–91.

Hu, Z.F.; and Khan, M.S. (1997) 'Why is China growing so fast?' *IMF Staff Papers*, **44**(1), 103–31.

Huang, J.T.; Kuo, C.C.; and Kao, A.P. (2003) 'The inequality of regional economic development in China between 1991 and 2001,' *Journal of Chinese Economic and Business Studies*, **1**(3), 273–85.

Irmen, A. (2005) 'Extensive and intensive growth in a neoclassical framework,' *Journal of Economic Dynamics and Control*, **29**(8), 1427–48.

Jian, T.; Sachs, J.D.; and Warner, A.M. (1996) 'Trends in regional inequality in China,' *China Economic Review*, **7**(1), 1–21.

Jiang, Yanqing (2010) 'An empirical study of structural factors and regional growth in China,' *Journal of Chinese Economic and Business Studies*, **8**(4), 335–53.

Jiang, Yanqing (2011) 'Understanding openness and productivity growth in China: an empirical study of the Chinese provinces,' *China Economic Review*, **22**(3), 290–8.

Jiang, Yanqing (2012) 'Technology diffusion, spatial effects and productivity growth in the Chinese provinces,' *International Review of Applied Economics*, **26**(5), 643–56.

Kanbur, R.; and Zhang, X. (2005) 'Fifty years of regional inequality in China: a journey through central planning, reform, and openness,' *Review of Development Economics*, **9**(1), 87–106.

Klenow, P.; and Rodriguez-Clare, A. (1997) 'The neoclassical revival in growth economics: has it gone too far?' *NBER Macroeconomics Annual*, **12**, 73–103.

Knight, J. (2008) 'Reform, growth and inequality in China,' *Asian Economic Policy Review*, **3**(1), 140–58.

Kuijs, L.; and Wang, Tao (2006), 'China's pattern of growth: moving to sustainability and reducing inequality,' *China and World Economy,* **14**(1), 1–14.

Li, Haizheng; Fraumeni, B.M.; Liu, Zhiqiang; and Wang, Xiaojun (2009) *Human Capital in China* (NBER Working Paper 15500), Cambridge, MA: National Bureau of Economic Research.

Lin, J.Y. (1992) 'Rural reforms and agricultural growth in China,' *American Economic Review,* **82**(1), 34–51.

Maddison, A. (1998) *Chinese Economic Performance in the Long Run,* Paris: OECD Development Centre.

McMillan, J.; Whalley, J.; and Zhu, L. (1989) 'The impact of China's economic reforms on agricultural productivity growth,' *Journal of Political Economy,* **97**(4), 781–807.

Meng, L.; and Wang, X. (2000) *Assessment of the Reliability of China's Economic Growth Statistics* (Monograph), Beijing, China: National Economic Research Institute.

Mincer, J. (1974) *Schooling, Experience, and Earnings,* New York: Columbia University Press.

Naughton, B. (2002) 'Provincial economic growth in China: causes and consequences of regional differentiation,' in M.F. Renard (Ed.), *China and Its Regions: Economic Growth and Reform in Chinese Provinces,* Cheltenham, U.K.: Edward Elgar, pp. 57–86.

OECD (2005) *OECD Economic Surveys: China,* Paris: Organisation for Economic Co-operation and Development.

Perkins, D. (1988) 'Reforming China's economic system,' *Journal of Economic Literature,* **26**, 601–45.

Romer, D. (2006) *Advanced Macroeconomics,* Third Edition, New York: McGraw-Hill.

Psacharopoulos, G. (1994) 'Returns to investment in education: a global update,' *World Development,* **22**, 1325–43.

Sisci, F. (2005) 'Is China headed for a social red alert?' *Asia Times Online,* 20 October 2005. Available from: *http://www.atimes.com/atimes/China_Business/GJ20Cb01.html*

The Economist (2005) 'The OECD on China's economy: a model of reform,' *The Economist,* 15 September 2005. Available from: *http://www.economist.com/node/4407973*

Tsui, Kai-yuen (1991) 'China's regional inequality, 1952–85,' *Journal of Comparative Economics,* **15**, 1–21.

Tsui, Kai-yuen (1996) 'Economic reform and interprovincal inequalities in China,' *Journal of Development Economics,* **50**(2), 353–68.

Tsui, Kai-yuen (2007) 'Forces shaping China's interprovincial inequality,' *Review of Income and Wealth,* **53**(1), 60–92.

Wan, G.; Lu, M.; and Chen, Z. (2007) 'Globalization and regional income inequality: empirical evidence from within China,' *Review of Income and Wealth,* **53**(1), 35–59.

Wang, Y.; and Yao, Y.D. (2003) 'Sources of China's economic growth 1952–1999: incorporating human capital accumulation,' *China Economic Review,* **14**, 32–52.

WB (1997) *China 2020: Development Challenges in the New Century,* Washington, D.C.: World Bank.

WB (2005) *World Development Report 2006: Equity and Development.* New York: Oxford University Press.

Woo, W.T. (1998) 'China's total factor productivity: contributions of reallocation of rural labor,' *Journal of Economic Studies (Jingjin Yanjiu)*, **3**, 31–9.

Wu, Yanrui (2004) *China's Economic Growth: A Miracle with Chinese Characteristics*, London: Routledge Curzon Press.

Wu, Yanrui (2008) 'The role of productivity in China's growth: new estimates,' *Journal of Chinese Economic and Business Studies*, **6**(2), 141–56.

Wu, Yanrui (2009) 'Capital stock estimates by region and sector,' in Chen, Chunlai (Ed.), *China's Integration with the Global Economy: WTO Accession, Foreign Direct Investment and International Trade*, Cheltenham, U.K.: Edward Elgar, pp. 37–52.

Wu, Yanrui (2011) 'Total factor productivity growth in China: a review,' *Journal of Chinese Economic and Business Studies*, **9**(2), 111–26.

Yang, D.T. (1999) 'Urban-biased policies and rising income inequality in China,' *American Economic Review Papers and Proceedings*, **89**(2), 306–10.

Yao, S. (1997) 'Industrialization and spatial income inequality in rural China, 1986–92,' *Economics of Transition*, **5**(1), 97–112.

Yin, Heng (2011) 'Characteristics of inter-regional income disparities in China,' *Social Sciences in China*, **32**(3), 123–44.

Young, A. (2003) 'Gold into base metals: productivity growth in the People's Republic of China during the reform period,' *Journal of Political Economy*, **111**(6), 1220–61.

Zhang, Jun (2008) 'Estimation of China's provincial capital stock (1952–2004) with applications,' *Journal of Chinese Economic and Business Studies*, **6**(2), 177–96.

Zhang, X.; and Zhang, K. (2003) 'How does globalization affect regional inequality with a developing country? Evidence from China,' *Journal of Development Studies*, **39**(4), 47–67.

Zheng, Jinghai; and Hu, Angang (2006) 'An empirical analysis of provincial productivity in China (1979–2001),' *Journal of Chinese Economic and Business Studies*, **4**(3), 221–39.

Zheng, Jinghai; Bigsten, A.; and Hu, Angang (2009a) 'Can China's growth be sustained: a productivity perspective?' *World Development*, **37**(4), 874–88.

Zheng, Jinghai; Hu, Angang; and Bigsten, A. (2009b) 'Measuring potential output in a rapidly developing economy: the case of China in comparison with the US and EU,' *Federal Reserve Bank of St. Louis Review*, July/August, 317–42.

Zhu, Shujin; Lai, Mingyong; and Fu, Xiaolan (2008) 'Spatial characteristics and dynamics of provincial total factor productivity in China,' *Journal of Chinese Economic and Business Studies*, **6**(2), 197–217.

3

Unbalanced development in China

Abstract: In this chapter we present the facts and trends of interregional inequality in China, and attempt to establish a linkage between the various forces generated by policy regime switching and the changing pattern of interregionally unbalanced economic development in China. Among other findings, our empirical results suggest that the sharp increase in overall interregional inequality in the early 1990s can largely be attributed to the between-zone contribution of physical capital. Besides the coastal–inland disparity, variation within coastal regions is a dominant factor in overall interregional inequality in China. Moreover, it can be shown that the process by which China opened up to trade and FDI can account for a large part of China's interregional inequality, a part that is continually increasing.

Key words: economic development, interregional inequality, decomposition, within-zone contribution, between-zone contribution, policy regime.

JEL classification codes: F41; O11; O57.[1]

Introduction and background

Economic reform and the opening up of China during the past 35 years have led to three big closely related events: a gradualist transition from central planning towards a market system, a remarkable rate of economic growth, and a dramatic rise in income inequality (Knight, 2008).[2] The tradeoff between economic growth and income equality, however, is a longstanding world issue. Worldwide, the experience of the past century shows that policy-makers have struggled to cope with the challenge of bringing about economic growth that leads to balanced human development. Over the decades, two different approaches to addressing this challenge have been developed. One is the interventionist approach, which argues that social disparities will never disappear; rather, they will widen with economic development. Since the market allocates resources unequally when it is left to its own devices, China's government strives to organize the economy in such a way that distribution of the benefits of economic development could be done more equitably. However, the outcome is usually equality in poverty. Any attempt to suppress the market mechanism has the effect of delinking contributions and benefits and thus removes the incentives of micro agents to make contributions to economic development. This is exactly what happened in pre-1980 China under the centrally planned system.

The other approach is the liberal approach, proponents of which believe that social and economic inequalities have to be taken for granted because they can never be eliminated. Therefore, the primary aim of government policy should be to create a level playing field so that everyone has equal opportunities to contribute to economic growth and draw benefit from it. However, proponents of this view are aware that even a level playing ground is an artifice, some will still contribute more and benefit more than others as some are more apt to seize opportunities than others. Thus one problem with this approach is that the fruits of economic growth may initially become so unevenly distributed and the disparities may grow so wide that the level playing ground as such ceases to exist. Serious inequalities may then emerge. In such a case, it becomes morally and politically imperative for the government to intervene to support the less fortunate members of society. In the last quarter of the twentieth century, governments almost everywhere embraced the liberal point of view as this approach seemed at least to promote economic growth and social development, despite the possibility of it also widening the social gaps between different groups (UN, 2001).

All in all, it is challenging if not completely impossible for governments to make policies to generate economic growth, on the one hand, and distribute the benefits of social development evenly, on the other hand. Disparities between different groups of people such as those between urban and rural areas or across different geographical regions may stem from natural differences, sociocultural conditions, and policy decisions. Although it is difficult to remove all the disparities completely, it is possible and necessary to reduce at least man-made obstacles like policy decisions or social constraints that prevent people or areas from developing their full potential (UN, 2001). The creation of equal opportunities (i.e., a level playing field) for everyone is necessary to achieve balanced economic and social development.

In China there are serious disparities across different geographical regions as well as between urban and rural areas. Taking interregional inequality as an example, we can see that regional development strategies in China in the last four decades passed through a number of phases, and brought about forces that ultimately resulted in unbalanced development across China's regions. Pre the reform era, the Chinese government saw it as one of its major political goals to reduce the gap between coastal and interior regions. The apparatus of central planning gave the Chinese government a handle to mobilize resources to do so, as witnessed by state appropriations becoming the dominant source of investment funds (Lardy, 1978; Naughton, 2002; Tsui, 2007). However, efficiency considerations such as comparative advantages and economies of scale were usually irrelevant in determining the spatial allocation of investment funds. A case in point was the 'third front campaign', a defense-related program to relocate industries to inland regions in the mid-1960s and the early 1970s (Naughton, 1988). Such a massive plan to transfer industrial capacities to less developed regions, regardless of their infrastructure and comparative advantages, turned out to be a recipe for economic waste (Tsui, 2007). The effect of favoring inland provinces with additional investment was thus offset by all the other forces that undercut efficiency and productivity.

The reform era represented a policy break with the past. With the retreat of central planning and the initiation of a market system, the government's role in allocating investment diminished in importance. The economic reform unleashed new forces that led to spatial restructuring of industries, by fundamentally changing the spatial allocation of investment funds. Specifically, fiscal decentralization allowed local governments, administrative agencies, and state-owned enterprises to retain more of the revenue generated within their jurisdictions and opened up more opportunities to boost their fiscal intake. As a result, there emerged an explosion of self-raised funds, the distribution of which was highly skewed in favor of the richer coastal regions (Tsui, 2007). In addition, market forces began to channel industries to regions according to their comparative advantages and economies of scale – not to politically motivated strategies that could be detrimental to economic efficiency. Besides inducing changes in the spatial distribution patterns of investment and industries, economic reforms also set off a series of productivity-enhancing institutional innovations that were often localized with spatially differentiated effects. Some of the institutional innovations benefited poorer inland regions, others enhanced productivity in richer coastal regions. Coastal regions also experienced a faster pace of market reforms and opening up to the outside world, reinforcing the effects of the new spatial distribution patterns of investment and industries.

It is important to note that the different policy regimes adopted in the last four decades unleashed various forces that exerted different and at times opposing effects on interregional disparities (Tsui, 2007). Different policy regimes have shaped the spatial distribution of production factors such as physical and human capital, which in turn has led to differential rates of regional economic growth. In addition, development strategies and the institutional environment have also exerted spatially different impacts on regional productivity. Under the influences of the various shaping forces, the dynamics of spatial inequality become complex and do not follow monotonic change over time (Tsui, 2007). Therefore, this chapter looks at the facts and trends of interregional inequality in China. This chapter is organized as follows. In the chapter's second section 'An analytical framework', we present a framework that lays the foundation for our empirical analysis. In the third section 'Empirical evidence', we analyze and present the basic results. In the fourth section 'The persistence of interregional inequality', we further discuss the persistence of interregional inequality in China.

An analytical framework

If we are to study unbalanced development across China's regions, we first need an analytical framework to empirically measure and examine interregional inequality in the country. As already discussed in Chapter 2, if we let $I(\mathbf{y})$ be some measure of overall interregional inequality, where $\mathbf{y}$ is a vector of regional GDP per capita (or per worker), in so far as regional output and factor inputs are captured by the regional production function, the rate of change in interregional inequality over time, $dI(\mathbf{y})/dt$, can then be expressed as a function of regional growth rates. Employing the decomposition framework discussed in Chapter 2, we are able to break the growth of regional GDP per capita down into individual contributions of the growth in total factor productivity and the accumulation of such production inputs as physical and human capital. The rate of change in interregional inequality $dI(\mathbf{y})/dt$ can then be attributed to the changing pattern of spatial allocation in investment captured by interregional differential growth in physical and human capital as well as to the impact of institutional improvements reflected in the growth of total factor productivity (see Tsui, 2007).

In this connection, we follow Tsui (2007) to construct a population-weighted version of Theil's entropy as our measure of interregional inequality, which is

$$I(\mathbf{y}) = \sum_{g=1}^{G} \sum_{n=1}^{Ng} \lambda_{g,n} \ln\left(\frac{\bar{y}}{y_{g,n}}\right) \tag{3.1}$$

where $\bar{y}$ is defined as $\bar{y} = \sum_{g=1}^{G} \sum_{n=1}^{Ng} \lambda_{g,n} y_{g,n}$. G is the total number of geographical zones in China and Ng is the total number of divisions (provincial level) in the gth geographical zone. $\mathbf{y} = (\mathbf{y}_1, \ldots, \mathbf{y}_G)$ is a vector of regional GDP per capita, where $\mathbf{y}_g = (y_{g,1}, \ldots, y_{g,Ng})$. $\lambda_{g,n}$ is defined as $\lambda_{g,n} = M_{g,n} / \sum_{g=1}^{G} \sum_{k=1}^{Ng} M_{g,k}$, in which the letter M stands for population. In the present study China's regions are grouped into the eastern, central, and western zones so that G is equal to 3. Eq. 3.1 can be applied to examine how overall interregional inequality in China has changed over time.

To help us focus on the income gap between coastal and inland regions, we can further decompose the overall inequality measure in Eq. 3.1 into two components, within-zone inequality and between-zone inequality, respectively

$$I(\mathbf{y}) = I^W(\mathbf{y}) + I^B(\mathbf{y}) \tag{3.2}$$

The former, within-zone inequality, is defined as

$$I^W(\mathbf{y}) = \sum_{g=1}^{G} \lambda_g I(\mathbf{y}_g) \tag{3.3}$$

with $\lambda_g = \sum_{n=1}^{Ng} M_{g,n} / \sum_{g=1}^{G} \sum_{n=1}^{Ng} M_{g,n}$, while the latter, between-zone inequality, is defined as

$$I^B(\mathbf{y}) = \sum_{g=1}^{n} \lambda_g \ln\left(\frac{\bar{y}}{\bar{y}_g}\right) \tag{3.4}$$

where $\bar{y}_g = \sum_{n=1}^{Ng} Y_{g,n} / \sum_{n=1}^{Ng} M_{g,n}$.

With the measures of inequality properly defined as above, we can now proceed to set up an analytical framework to break overall change in inequality down into its different elements. We start with the regional production function

$$Y_{g,n} = A_{g,n} F_{g,n}(K_{g,n}, H_{g,n}) \tag{3.5}$$

where $Y_{g,n}$ is the level of GDP of the nth region in the gth zone.[3] On the right-hand side $A_{g,n}$ and $F_{g,n}$ enter the expression multiplicatively. $F_{g,n}$ is a function whose two arguments, $K_{g,n}$ and $H_{g,n}$, are increasing. $K_{g,n}$ is the stock of physical capital while $H_{g,n}$ denotes the amount of human capital (quality-adjusted labor). Further, $H_{g,n} = h_{g,n}L_{g,n}$, where $L_{g,n}$ is the amount of raw labor (e.g., the number of workers), while $h_{g,n}$ is labor-augmenting human capital intensity, which is in turn supposed to be related to the general level of education of the labor force. $A_{g,n}$ is the term that captures the level of total factor productivity (TFP).

Differentiating Eq. 3.5 with respect to time yields the following

$$\dot{Y}_{g,n} = \dot{A}_{g,n}F_{g,n}(K_{g,n}, H_{g,n}) + A_{g,n}\left(\frac{\partial F_{g,n}}{\partial K_{g,n}}\dot{K}_{g,n} + \frac{\partial F_{g,n}}{\partial H_{g,n}}\dot{H}_{g,n}\right) \quad (3.6)$$

where a dot over a variable is shorthand for the first-order derivative with respect to time. Dividing both sides of Eq. 3.6 by $Y_{g,n}$ gives

$$\frac{\dot{Y}_{g,n}}{Y_{g,n}} = \frac{\dot{A}_{g,n}}{A_{g,n}} + \frac{K_{g,n}}{F_{g,n}}\frac{\partial F_{g,n}}{\partial K_{g,n}}\frac{\dot{K}_{g,n}}{K_{g,n}} + \frac{H_{g,n}}{F_{g,n}}\frac{\partial F_{g,n}}{\partial H_{g,n}}\frac{\dot{H}_{g,n}}{H_{g,n}} \quad (3.7)$$

which immediately implies that per-capita growth of regional GDP can be broken down into the growth of four elements

$$\frac{\dot{y}_{g,n}}{y_{g,n}} = \frac{\dot{A}_{g,n}}{A_{g,n}} + \alpha^K_{g,n}\frac{\dot{K}_{g,n}}{K_{g,n}} + \alpha^H_{g,n}\frac{\dot{H}_{g,n}}{H_{g,n}} - \frac{\dot{M}_{g,n}}{M_{g,n}} \quad (3.8)$$

where $\alpha^K_{g,n}$ and $\alpha^H_{g,n}$ are defined as

$$\alpha^K_{g,n} = \frac{K_{g,n}}{F_{g,n}}\frac{\partial F_{g,n}}{\partial K_{g,n}} \quad \text{and} \quad \alpha^H_{g,n} = \frac{H_{g,n}}{F_{g,n}}\frac{\partial F_{g,n}}{\partial H_{g,n}},$$

respectively. Therefore, different growth rates in TFP, physical capital, human capital, and population all contribute to different growth rates in regional output per capita. Any change in our inequality index $I(\mathbf{y})$ may thus ultimately depend on changes in all the four elements: TFP, physical capital, human capital, and population.

Differentiating Eq. 3.1 with respect to time, we obtain the following

$$\frac{dI(\mathbf{y})}{dt} = \sum_{g=1}^{G}\sum_{n=1}^{Ng}(s_{g,n} - \lambda_{g,n})\frac{\dot{y}_{g,n}}{y_{g,n}} + \sum_{g=1}^{G}\sum_{n=1}^{Ng}(s_{g,n} - \lambda_{g,n}\ln y_{g,n})\frac{\dot{\lambda}_{g,n}}{\lambda_{g,n}} \quad (3.9)$$

where $s_{g,n} = Y_{g,n}/\sum_{g=1}^{G}\sum_{k=1}^{Ng}Y_{g,k}$.[3] There are two terms on the right-hand side of Eq. 3.9. The first term captures the impact of differential growth rates across regions on interregional inequality while the second term captures the impact of changes in a region's share of the population. As noted by Tsui (2007), the direction taken by the impact of $\dot{y}_{g,n}/y_{g,n}$ on interregional inequality hinges on the sign of the term $(s_{g,n} - \lambda_{g,n})$. This conforms to the implicit ethical judgment that whenever a region's income share lags behind its population share, then transferring more income to the region should reduce inequality. This ethical judgment is analogous to the Pigou–Dalton transfer principle on inequality measurement.[5]

Then, inserting Eq. 3.8 into Eq. 3.9 yields the following decomposition, from which we see the change in interregional inequality depends on the growth of TFP and factor inputs

$$\frac{dI(\mathbf{y})}{dt} = \delta_A + \delta_K + \delta_H + \delta_M + \delta_\lambda \qquad (3.10)$$

where

$$\delta_A = \sum_{g=1}^{G} \sum_{n=1}^{Ng} (\varepsilon_{g,n} - \lambda_{g,n}) \frac{\dot{A}_{g,n}}{A_{g,n}}$$

$$\delta_K = \sum_{g=1}^{G} \sum_{n=1}^{Ng} (s_{g,n} - \lambda_{g,n}) \alpha_{g,n}^K \frac{\dot{K}_{g,n}}{K_{g,n}}$$

$$\delta_H = \sum_{g=1}^{G} \sum_{n=1}^{Ng} (s_{g,n} - \lambda_{g,n}) \alpha_{g,n}^H \frac{\dot{H}_{g,n}}{H_{g,n}}$$

$$\delta_M = -\sum_{g=1}^{G} \sum_{n=1}^{Ng} (s_{g,n} - \lambda_{g,n}) \frac{\dot{M}_{g,n}}{M_{g,n}}$$

$$\delta_\lambda = \sum_{g=1}^{G} \sum_{n=1}^{Ng} (s_{g,n} - \lambda_{g,n} \ \mathbf{In} \ y_{g,n}) \frac{\dot{\lambda}_{g,n}}{\lambda_{g,n}}$$

The first three components, δ_A, δ_K, and δ_H can naturally be interpreted as the contributions of growth in TFP, physical capital, and human capital to the change in interregional inequality. The fourth component, δ_M, captures the effect of population growth on interregional inequality. Fast growth of the population in poor regions tends to result in an increase in interregional inequality. The fifth component, δ_λ, is associated with the effect that changes in population shares have on interregional inequality.

One of the main objectives of this chapter is to measure and examine the trend of the income gap between China's coastal regions and inland regions. It is necessary to conceptually distinguish between within-zone inequality and between-zone inequality, as the two may exhibit quite divergent trends over time and mixing them together may produce misleading results. The terms in Eq. 3.10 can be further broken down into within-zone and between-zone contributions. The change of within-zone inequality over time can be written as

$$\frac{dI^W(\mathbf{y})}{dt} = \delta_A^W + \delta_K^W + \delta_H^W + \delta_M^W + \delta_\lambda^W \qquad (3.11)$$

in which the individual components are defined as follows

$$\delta_A^W = \sum_{g=1}^{G} \lambda_g \left(\sum_{n=1}^{Ng} (s_{g,n}^g - \lambda_{g,n}^g) \frac{\dot{A}_{g,n}}{A_{g,n}} \right)$$

$$\delta_K^W = \sum_{g=1}^{G} \lambda_g \left(\sum_{n=1}^{Ng} (s_{g,n}^g - \lambda_{g,n}^g) \alpha_{g,n}^K \frac{\dot{K}_{g,n}}{K_{g,n}} \right)$$

$$\delta_H^W = \sum_{g=1}^{G} \lambda_g \left(\sum_{n=1}^{Ng} (s_{g,n}^g - \lambda_{g,n}^g) \alpha_{g,n}^H \frac{\dot{H}_{g,n}}{H_{g,n}} \right)$$

$$\delta_M^W = -\sum_{g-1}^{G} \lambda_g \left(\sum_{n-1}^{Ng} (s_{g,n}^g - \lambda_{g,n}^g) \frac{\dot{M}_{g,n}}{M_{g,n}} \right)$$

$$\delta_\lambda^W = \sum_{g=1}^{G} \lambda_g \left(\sum_{n=1}^{Ng} (s_{g,n}^g - \lambda_{g,n}^g \ln y_{g,n}) \frac{\dot{\lambda}_{g,n}^g}{\lambda_{g,n}^g} + I(\mathbf{y}_g) \frac{\dot{\lambda}_g}{\lambda_g} \right)$$

where $s_{g,n}^g = Y_{g,n} / \sum_{k=1}^{Ng} Y_{g,k}$ and $\lambda_{g,n}^g = M_{g,n} / \sum_{k=1}^{Ng} M_{g,k}$. Likewise, for the change of between-zone inequality over time, we have the following decomposition

$$\frac{dI^B(\mathbf{y})}{dt} = \delta_A^B + \delta_K^B + \delta_H^B + \delta_M^B + \delta_\lambda^B \tag{3.12}$$

in which

$$\delta_A^B = \sum_{g=1}^{G} \sum_{n=1}^{Ng} (s_{g,n} - \lambda_g s_{g,n}^g) \frac{\dot{A}_{g,n}}{A_{g,n}}$$

$$\delta_K^B = \sum_{g=1}^{G} \sum_{n=1}^{Ng} (s_{g,n} - \lambda_g s_{g,n}^g) \alpha_{g,n}^K \frac{\dot{K}_{g,n}}{K_{g,n}}$$

$$\delta_H^B = \sum_{g=1}^{G} \sum_{n=1}^{Ng} (s_{g,n} - \lambda_g s_{g,n}^g) \alpha_{g,n}^H \frac{\dot{H}_{g,n}}{H_{g,n}}$$

$$\delta_M^B = -\sum_{g=1}^{G} \sum_{n=1}^{Ng} (s_{g,n} - \lambda_g s_{g,n}^g) \frac{\dot{M}_{g,n}}{M_{g,n}}$$

$$\delta_\lambda^B = \sum_{g=1}^{G} \left(\sum_{n=1}^{Ng} \left(s_{g,n} \frac{\dot{\lambda}_{g,n}}{\lambda_{g,n}} - \lambda_g s_{g,n}^g \frac{\dot{\lambda}_{g,n}^g}{\lambda_{g,n}^g} \right) - \lambda_g \ln \bar{y}_g \frac{\dot{\lambda}_g}{\lambda_g} \right)$$

where $\bar{y}_g = \sum_{n=1}^{Ng} \lambda_{g,n}^g y_{g,n}$. Note that $s_{g,n}^g$ and $\lambda_{g,n}^g$ are defined with respect to a zone. In the case of the between-zone contribution, $(s_{g,n} - \lambda_g s_{g,n}^g)$ equals $s_{g,n}^g (s_{g,n}/s_{g,n}^g - \lambda_g)$ and the term $s_{g,n}/s_{g,n}^g$ is actually the share of income accruing to region g, so $(s_{g,n}/s_{g,n}^g - \lambda_g)$ is the difference between the income share and the population share of the gth region.

Empirical evidence

In order to make our empirical analysis manageable, we need to specify a functional form for the regional production function in Eq. 3.5. We therefore assume a Cobb–Douglas production function of the form

$$Y_{g,n} = A_{g,n}K_{g,n}^{\alpha}H_{g,n}^{1-\alpha} \tag{3.13}$$

Such a form of the Cobb–Douglas production function assumes constant returns to scale of K and H, which can be thought of as combining two assumptions. One is that inputs other than physical capital K and human capital H as well as knowledge (or technology, as captured by A) are relatively unimportant. In particular, here we temporarily neglect land and other natural resources as important factors of production. The other assumption is that the regional economy is big enough that further gains from specialization have been exhausted. The structural parameter α has been assumed to be the same across regions and over time. Obviously, in reality there may exist structural differences in the regional production function so that the value of α may differ across regions and/or over time.[6] However, owing to a lack of convincing evidence in the literature concerning the heterogeneous values of α, here we simply make the more usual assumption that China's regions share a common value of α, which remains constant across regions and over time.

Therefore, we have to make an assumption about the specific value of this common α. As discussed in Chapter 2, some cross-country studies such as those by Hall and Jones (1999) and Aiyar and Feyrer (2002) assume a common $\alpha = 1/3$ worldwide when choosing a likely value of α. However, Chow and Li (2002), Chow (2008), Zheng et al. (2009), and Brandt and Zhu (2010) have provided further evidence for the likely value of the structural parameter α. Zheng et al. (2009) point out that α is about 0.3 for the United States (see CBO, 2001), about 0.4 for the EU (see Musso and Westermann, 2005), and for China it can be as high as 0.6 (see Chow and Li, 2002 and Chow, 2008). Based on national income accounts and national input–output tables constructed by the National Bureau of Statistics of China, α is roughly 0.5 in the non-agricultural sector, about 0.3 in the agricultural sector, and about 0.40–0.42 for the entire Chinese economy (Brandt and Zhu, 2010). However, Brandt and Zhu (2010) argue that the high-factor share of labor in agriculture (about 0.7) is inconsistent with estimates based on household data, which suggest a labor share in the vicinity of 0.5. Therefore, Brandt and Zhu (2010) assume that α is 0.5 for all three sectors in their study throughout the sample period (Jiang, 2012). In our present study, we follow Brandt and Zhu (2010) and assume a universal value $\alpha = 0.5$ for all China's regions throughout our sample time.

We study 28 provincial-level divisions in mainland China over the period 1996–2011.[7] China's mainland is divided into three geographical zones: the eastern coastal zone, the central zone, and the western zone. These zones exhibit systematic differences not only in such aspects as climate and resource endowment, but also in others like culture, policy, and exposure to foreign trade and foreign direct investment (Wei, 2002). Therefore, each of our 28 regions is classified as either a coastal province, a central province, or a western province.

Our data principally come from annual editions of the *China Statistical Yearbook* (1996–2012), an official publication of the state, where a series of nominal GDP, GDP indices, total population, and the total number of employed persons (workers) for each region are directly available. This facilitates calculation of a series of real regional GDP and real regional GDP per capita. As mentioned in Chapter 2, the annual editions of the *China Statistical Yearbook* do not directly record data on regional physical capital stock for China's regions. We follow the perpetual inventory procedure of Wu (2008) to obtain the data series of regional capital stock for each region.[8] Wu (2008) extends his previous method (Wu 2004) by adopting different rates of capital depreciation for China's different regions, which is the first such exercise ever in the literature. The different rates are derived by following a simulation process through which estimated depreciation values converge with actual depreciation values given in the *China Statistical Yearbook*. In general, the depreciation rate is high in more developed regions, and low in less developed regions and the three municipalities Beijing, Tianjin, and Shanghai. Moreover, as Wu (2008) has noted, it is interesting to see that the mean regional rate of depreciation is about 4%, close to the one used by the World Bank (WB, 1997).

To get a data series of regional human capital, we follow the same method as described in Jiang (2012) and in Chapter 2: we first construct the levels of human capital intensity and then calculate the levels of regional human capital stock by multiplying the former by the corresponding size of the regional labor force.[9] Measuring human capital has always been a weak point in growth empirics (Gundlach, 1997). Researchers have been forced to devise various measures to proxy for the flow or stock of human capital. For example, in a regional growth study of China Gundlach (1997) uses publications per worker ($PUBL$) as a measure of the stock of regional human capital. Gundlach argues that the regional supply of written information correlates with the regional quantity of human capital. As the amount of written information is likely to be dominated by newspapers, $PUBL$ will more or less reflect the consumption of newspapers per worker at the regional level. Therefore, this measure may reflect differences in literacy rates across different regions in China, which, in turn, may turn out to be more plausible measures of exogenous interregional differences in human capital than reported schooling rates. However, owing to incomplete data on regional publications, we stick to the method described in Chapter 2 to calculate regional human capital. By applying data on physical and human capital derived in this way, the levels of regional TFP can then be calculated as a residual based on Eq. 3.13.

Although we have deviated somewhat from the method used by Tsui (2007), our empirical results basically conform with Tsui's. The major objective of the discussion in this chapter is to establish a linkage between the various forces generated by policy regime switching and the changing pattern of interregionally unbalanced economic development in China. Our empirical results suggest that the sharp increase in overall interregional inequality in the early 1990s can largely be attributed to the between-zone contribution of physical capital. Besides the coastal–inland disparity, variation within coastal regions contributes, sometimes dominantly, to overall interregional inequality. An interesting but much less studied aspect of interregional inequality is education and human capital. There exist huge disparities in terms of education resources and human capital stocks across China's different regions. Probably owing to the incomplete measure of human capital, our results show that the contribution of human capital to growth is small compared with productivity and physical capital.

The persistence of interregional inequality: further discussion

Persistent interregional inequality within a country is at odds with neoclassical theory, which posits that when the economy is functioning well, all interregional inequality should be eliminated by factor mobility, trade, or arbitrage (Candelaria et al., 2013). The real reason for the prevalent phenomenon of interregional inequality has still not been found even though a large body of the literature has been devoted to this topic (Magrini, 2007). In this section we further discuss the patterns and causes of persistent interregional inequality in China.

World Bank estimates show that China is a country of severe inequality, with its income Gini coefficient far exceeding that of other Asian countries such as India, Pakistan, and Bangladesh. Income disparities in China exist both within and between regions. Even though intraregional differences (such as urban–rural income gaps within regions) in China have been the focus of much research, there sems to be no end to the discussions that have recently emerged on interregional inequality across different regions in China. For example, Kanbur and Zhang (2005) find that the evolution of China's interregional inequality matches the phases of China's history remarkably well and can be explained at different times by the share of heavy industry in total output, the level of decentralization, and the degree of openness. Their discussion suggests that the process of decentralization affected interregional inequality during China's economic transition from a planned to a market economy, and that greater openness led to greater interregional inequality in China. Yao and Zhang (2001) show that there exists divergence in real per capita income across different groups of Chinese provinces. Wan et al. (2007) point out that the processes of increasing opening up, uneven domestic capital formation, and privatization all contribute to interregional inequality in China. Xia et al. (2013) show that urban income inequality across China's different regions is affected by reforms in the public sector.

Candelaria et al. (2013) have recently attempted to come up with the reasons for persistent interregional inequality in China. Their measure of interregional inequality is across-region variation in regional real wages, where they use regional average wages adjusted by region-specific consumer price indexes. By using the number of college graduates and real government expenditure on education as proxy variables for the level of education in the labor force, the study finds that higher levels of education are associated with higher average real wages. Rich provinces generally have higher wages and more government expenditure on education. Moreover, the higher shares of the manufacturing and service sectors, which tend to have higher labor productivity, are associated with higher real wages and can account for over 50% of interregional variation in regional real wages. The higher shares of agricultural sector are associated with lower regional wages and can account for about 40% of total variation in real wages across China's regions. Finally, provinces with larger commercial ports, as measured by berth capacity, are associated with higher real wages. All these factors jointly account for over 80% of interprovincial variation in real wages across China's provinces. In sum, Candelaria et al. (2013) found that the major sources of interregional inequality in China were long-term and structural factors such as labor quality, industry mix, and geographical location. In addition, they also found that interregional mobility of labor and other production factors failed to offset interregional wage inequality during the sample period. Therefore, they concluded that the current situation of interregional inequality in China is likely to persist and will not be substantially ameliorated in the near future.

One issue of particular interest is how globalization and China's opening up affect the pattern of interregional inequality in China. Wan et al. (2007) point out that globalization can account for a substantial share of China's interregional inequality and that the share rises over time. Further globalization and opening up will lead to even higher interregional inequality in China unless concerted efforts are made to enhance trade and inflows of FDI to China's interior regions. Geographic and market considerations mean the less developed regions find themselves in a disadvantageous situation when it comes to conducting foreign trade and absorbing inflows of FDI. Preferential policies promoting trade and FDI that were given to coastal provinces but are now being gradually phased out should be restored in China's interior provinces.

Concluding remarks

Economic reform and the opening up in China during the past few decades have led to three big and closely related events: the gradualist transition from a planned toward a market system, the remarkable rate of economic growth, and the dramatic rise in income inequality. This chapter presents facts and trends relating to interregional inequality in China, and establishes the linkage between the various forces generated by policy regime switching and the changing pattern of interregionally unbalanced economic development in China. Among other findings our empirical results suggest that the sharp increase in overall interregional inequality in the early 1990s can largely be attributed to the between-zone contribution of physical capital. Besides the coastal–inland disparity, variation within coastal regions contributes, sometimes dominantly, to overall interregional inequality. Recent research further suggests that the major sources of interregional inequality in China were long-term and structural factors such as labor quality, industry mix, and geographical location, and that the current situation of interregional inequality in China is likely to persist and will not be substantially improved in the near future. One issue of particular interest is the way in which China's opening up affects interregional inequality in China. Research suggests that the very act of China opening up to trade and FDI may well account for a substantial share of China's interregional inequality, a share that is increasing as time goes by.

Notes

1. Works on economics are often classified according to JEL classification codes, a system set up by the *Journal of Economic Literature*.
2. For recent discussions of interregional inequality in China, see also Yang (1999), Sisci (2005), WB (2005), Fan and Sun (2008), Zhu et al. (2008), Fan et al. (2009), and Yin (2011).
3. We omit the time subscript to avoid cluttering the notation.
4. To save space we omit details on how Eq. 3.9 is derived. The interested reader is directed to appendix B of Tsui (2007) for the details.
5. The Pigou–Dalton transfer principle says that a transfer of income from a richer to a poorer person, so long as that transfer does not reverse the ranking of the two, will lead to a fall in inequality.
6. See, for example, Gollin (2002), who provides evidence showing the sense of assuming a heterogeneous share of capital in the production function.
7. As in the previous chapter, the 28 provincial-level divisions include provinces, ethnic minority autonomous regions, and municipalities in mainland China. Owing to incomplete data, Tibet, Chongqing, and Hainan are not included in our sample.
8. See Chapter 2 for more details.
9. See Chapter 2 for more details.

References

Aiyar, S.; and Feyrer, J. (2002) *A Contribution to the Empirics of Total Factor Productivity* (Dartmouth College Working Paper No. 02-09), Hanover, NH: Dartmouth College.

Brandt, L.; and Zhu, Xiaodong (2010) *Accounting for China's Growth* (Working Papers tecipa-394), Toronto, Canada: Department of Economics.

Candelaria, C.; Daly, M.; and Hale, G. (2013) *Persistence of Regional Inequality in China* (Working Paper 2013-06), Federal Reserve Bank of San Francisco.

CBO (2001) 'CBO's method for estimating potential output: an update,' August 2001. Available from: *http://www.cbo.gov/ftpdocs/30xx/doc3020/PotentialOutput.pdf* [Congressional Budget Office].

Chow, G.C. (2008) 'Another look at the rate of increase in TFP in China,' *Journal of Chinese Economic and Business Studies*, 6(2), 219–24.

Chow, G.C.; and Li, Kui-Wai (2002) 'China's economic growth: 1952–2010,' *Economic Development and Cultural Change*, 51(1), 247–56.

Fan, C.C.; and Sun, Mingjie (2008) 'Regional inequality in China, 1978–2006,' *Eurasian Geography and Economics*, 49(1), 1–20.

Fan, Shenggen; Kanbur, R.; and Zhang, Xiaobo (2009) 'Regional inequality in China: an overview,' in Shenggen Fan, R. Kanbur and Xiaobo Zhang (Eds.), *Regional Inequality in China: Trends, Explanations and Policy Responses*, London: Routledge.

Gollin, D. (2002) 'Getting income shares right,' *Journal of Political Economy*, 110, 458–75.

Gundlach, E. (1997) 'Regional convergence of output per worker in China: a neoclassical interpretation,' *Asian Economic Journal*, 11, 423–42.

Hall, R.E.; and Jones, C.I. (1999) 'Why do some countries produce so much more output per worker than others?' *Quarterly Journal of Economics*, 114, 83–116.

Jiang, Yanqing (2012) 'Technology diffusion, spatial effects and productivity growth in the Chinese provinces,' *International Review of Applied Economics*, 26(5), 643–56.

Kanbur, R.; and Zhang, X. (2005) 'Fifty years of regional inequality in China: a journey through central planning, reform, and openness,' *Review of Development Economics*, 9(1), 87–106.

Knight, J. (2008) 'Reform, growth and inequality in China,' *Asian Economic Policy Review*, 3(1), 140–58.

Lardy, N. (1978) *Economic Growth and Distribution in China*, Cambridge, U.K.: Cambridge University Press.

Magrini, S. (2007) 'Regional (di)convergence,' *Handbook of Regional and Urban Economics*, Vol. 4, Amsterdam, The Netherlands: Elsevier B.V., pp. 2741–96.

Musso, A.; and Westermann, T. (2005) *Assessing Potential Output Growth in the Euro Area: A Growth Accounting Perspective* (ECB Occasional Paper No. 22), Frankfurt, Germany: European Central Bank.

Naughton, B. (1988) 'The third front: defence industrialization in the Chinese interior,' *The China Quarterly*, 115, 351–86.

Naughton, B. (2002) 'Provincial economic growth in China: causes and consequences of regional differentiation,' in M.F. Renard (Ed.), *China and Its Regions: Economic Growth and Reform in Chinese Provinces*, Cheltenham, U.K.: Edward Elgar, pp. 57–86.

Sisci, F. (2005) 'Is China headed for a social red alert?' *Asia Times Online*, 20 October 2005. Available from: *http://www.atimes.com/atimes/China_Business/GJ20Cb01.html*

Tsui, Kai-yuen (2007) 'Forces shaping China's interprovincial inequality,' *Review of Income and Wealth*, 53(1), 60–92.

UN (2001) *Reducing Disparities: Balanced Development of Urban and Rural Areas and Regions within the Countries of Asia and the Pacific*, New York: United Nations Publications.

Wan, G.; Lu, M.; and Chen, Z. (2007) 'Globalization and regional income inequality: empirical evidence from within China,' *The Review of Income and Wealth*, **53**(1), 35–59.

WB (1997) *China 2020: Development Challenges in the New Century*, Washington, D.C.: The World Bank.

WB (2005) *World Development Report 2006: Equity and Development*, New York: Oxford University Press.

Wei, Shang-Jin (2002) 'China as a window to the world: trade openness, living standards and income inequality,' *G-20 Workshop on Globalisation, Living Standards and Inequality: Recent Progress and Continuing Challenges, 2002*, sponsored by the Reserve Bank of Australia and the Australian Treasury.

Wu, Yanrui (2004) *China's Economic Growth: A Miracle with Chinese Characteristics*, London: Routledge Curzon Press.

Wu, Yanrui (2008) 'The role of productivity in China's growth: new estimates,' *Journal of Chinese Economic and Business Studies*, **6**(2), 141–56.

Xia, Q.; Song, L.; Shi, L.; and Appleton, S. (2013) *The Effects of the State Sector on Wage Inequality in Urban China: 1988–2007* (IZA Discussion Paper No. 7142), Bonn, Germany: Institute for the Study of Labor.

Yao, Shujie and Zhang, Zongyi (2001) 'Regional growth in China under economic reforms,' *Journal of Development Studies*, **38**(2), 167–86.

Yin, Heng (2011) 'Characteristics of inter-regional income disparities in China,' *Social Sciences in China*, **32**(3), 123–44.

Yang, D.T. (1999) 'Urban-biased policies and rising income inequality in China,' *American Economic Review Papers and Proceedings*, **89**(2), 306–10.

Zheng, Jinghai; Hu, Angang; and Bigsten, A. (2009) 'Measuring potential output in a rapidly developing economy: the case of China in comparison with the US and EU,' *Federal Reserve Bank of St. Louis Review*, July/August, 317–42.

Zhu, Shujin; Lai, Mingyong; and Fu, Xiaolan (2008) 'Spatial characteristics and dynamics of provincial total factor productivity in China,' *Journal of Chinese Economic and Business Studies*, **6**(2), 197–217.

4

Potential effects of foreign trade on development

Abstract: This chapter discusses in a preliminary way the potential effects of foreign trade on Chinese economic development, and focuses on the possible mechanisms through which foreign trade impacts economic development. One such mechanism is technology diffusion. Openness to foreign trade promotes total factor productivity (TFP) growth in China by facilitating technological spillovers from technologically advanced countries. Our preliminary empirical analysis in this chapter is based on a hypothesis positing that, given the level of TFP at the world technology frontier, China's regional TFP growth is a positive function of regional openness to foreign trade and a negative function of the current level of regional TFP. Our regression results show that regional openness has a significantly positive effect on regional TFP growth, and that there is evidence for conditional convergence in TFP across China's regions.

Key words: foreign trade, exports, imports, development, regional openness, total factor productivity.

JEL classification codes: F41; O11; O57.[1]

Introduction

China's foreign trade has experienced spectacular expansion in line with the country's dramatic economic growth and development. The causal linkages between foreign trade, economic growth, and development have long been a subject of great interest among academic researchers as well as government policy-makers. A major finding from the extensive literature on this subject shows that internationally active countries tend to be more productive than those that mainly produce for their domestic markets. Foreign trade expansion may positively influence economic growth and development because it is known to increase capacity utilization and the efficiency of resource allocation, allow a country to take advantage of economies of scale, and promote technical change and overall productivity (Tyler, 1981; Balassa, 1985, 1988).

Empirical studies show that foreign trade positively affects economic growth and development by promoting technological progress, capital accumulation, industrial structure upgrading, and institutional advancement (Sun and Heshmati, 2010). Specifically, increased imports of capital and intermediate goods may lead to productivity growth in domestic manufacturing (Lee, 1995). Exporting exposes domestic firms to intense international competition, which forces them to improve productivity to enhance their international competitiveness (Wagner, 2007). Learning by doing occurs more rapidly in the export industry because of spillovers of knowledge and technology. Before the 1960s, research on the effects of foreign trade was limited to a few specific countries. As modern econometric techniques have advanced, so more complicated methodologies to analyze the relationship between foreign trade and economic development have arisen. To date, research in this area can be roughly divided into two categories. One focuses on the causal relationship between openness to foreign trade and economic development while the other mainly examines the contribution of foreign trade to economic growth and development (Sun and Heshmati, 2010).

In particular, the linkage between foreign trade, economic growth, and development seems to be strong in developing countries. Take China as an example, its foreign trade experienced very rapid growth as the country transformed from central planning to a market system. By the 2000s, the total value of China's foreign trade had exceeded U.S.$500 billion. Its foreign trade achieved an average annual growth of 15 percent since 1978, remarkably higher than its average annual GDP growth of 9.5 percent in the same period. Studies on the relationship between foreign trade and economic development for developing countries have attracted a great deal of research with consensus on export-led growth first emerging in the 1980s, following the success stories of the newly industrialized economies (Feder, 1983; Krueger, 1990; Sun and Parikh, 1999). The export-led growth hypothesis posited that exports unidirectionally promote economic growth and development (Tyler, 1981). The hypothesis further shaped the development policies of a number of countries and the World Bank (WB, 1987). However, while the newly industrialized economies of Asia are broadly seen as successful examples of export-led growth and development, there is much less consensus on the effects of exports on economic growth and development for other economies, particularly when these economies are large and in transition from a centrally planned to a market system like China (Sun and Parikh, 1999).

For a large developing transitional economy like China, empirical research often leads to mixed results. Some studies, on the one hand, find either that the export expansion and open-door policy in China has had positive effects on China's economic growth (Li and Leung, 1994; Kwan and Kwok, 1995; Lardy, 1995; Xue, 1995; Demurger, 1996), or that there is a bidirectional causal relationship between China's foreign trade and its economic growth and development (Liu et al., 1997; Shan and Sun, 1998). Moreover, Shen and Li (2003) find that there exists a significant positive relationship between the share of exports in total output and per-capita GDP, and that capital accumulation and institutional transitions are the two important channels through which foreign trade impacts per-capita GDP. Zhang et al. (2005) point out that foreign demand (exports) contributes positively to China's total output level, while foreign supply (imports) has a negative impact on the the country's total output level, but the two have different multiplier effects. Even if the volume of total exports exactly equals that of total imports, the net effect of foreign trade would still be a positive contribution to China's economic growth. On the other hand, however, Yang and Shu (1998) show that China's growth has been fueled mainly by the increasing accumulation of physical capital, and that there does not necessarily exist a positive relationship between exports and economic growth in China. The FTPPT (1999) concluded, 'The contribution of net exports is very limited ... except for a few years (like 1990 and 1994), when the foreign trade surplus increased dramatically. Only in those few years, was net exports' contribution relatively large (more than three percentage) ...' Zhu (1998) argues that China's economic development is mainly propelled by domestic demand instead of exports. Yang (1998) and Li et al. (2004) believe that foreign trade has differential impacts on economic growth in different regions across China. Shen (1999) and Zhao et al. (2001) find that there exists a short-run causality between China's exports and output, but there is no stable long-run equilibrium relationship between the two. Zhang and Hu (1999) find that China's foreign trade balance and GDP growth are negatively related: in years that see a high GDP growth rate, the estimated contribution of net exports is usually low. Sun (2000) finds no significant causal relationship between foreign trade and economic growth in China.

The mixed results provided by these studies can be traced back to two shortcomings. First, whether the studies focus on the causal relationship between openness to foreign trade and economic development, or specifically on the contribution of the former to the latter, they generally lack thorough analysis when it comes to the mechanisms or channels through which a unidirectional or bidirectional causal relationship can be established between openness to foreign trade and economic development. Second, the studies usually fail to distinguish the differential impacts of foreign trade on economic development in the context of the stage of development in China's different regions or sectors. However, discussion of the mechanisms or channels through which openness to foreign trade may have effects on economic growth and development is, to put it mildly, challenging, as the two may be so intricately linked. This is the reason economic research separates trade from growth when developing economic models. Incorporating foreign trade into growth models or including temporal dynamics in trade models is clearly not easy.

Despite the difficulties, the remainder of this chapter discusses the potential mechanisms through which foreign trade may affect economic development. The remaining sections are organized as follows. In the second section 'China's foreign trade', we summarize the way in which China's foreign trade policy and foreign trade performance have evolved. In the third section 'Basic approaches and their implications', we discuss different approaches to studying the relationship between foreign trade and economic development, focusing on the empirical implications of these approaches. In the fourth section 'A preliminary empirical analysis', we look at regional openness to foreign trade and regional economic growth across China's provinces.

China's foreign trade: a summary of policy and performance

In this section we draw on previous research, such as Sun and Heshmati (2010), to summarize the evolution of China's foreign trade policy and foreign trade performance.

As is well known, before 1978 China had a centrally planned economic system and an inward-oriented policy, which rendered foreign trade subordinate to the national economy. At that time, China had only minimal trade with the rest of the world, importing goods such as strategic minerals and other necessities not available from domestic production, and paying for these goods by exporting surplus raw materials and simple manufactured goods. The central-planning system and import substitution policy encouraged the growth of domestic industries pre the nation's opening up, and thus fostered economic growth by establishing a number of important national industries. However, owing to a lack of international openness, domestic producers were not able to enjoy the dynamic benefits of foreign trade, such as efficiency, competition, and technological spillover.

China's open-door policy was initiated in 1978, after which China underwent unprecedented trade liberalization. Opening up gradually permeated from coastal provinces to inland provinces. Enormous benefits were gained as a result of the country's integrating with the global market. Continuous development of China's economic structure and increased income presented a great need for foreign trade, which in turn made an increasingly important contribution to China's economic development. In the early 1980s, import tariffs were imposed on many products by the state to check the flow of foreign goods into China's domestic market. The Chinese government terminated its import substitution list in the 1980s with a view to allowing market forces to predominate so that resource allocation could be made efficient. With less intervention from the government, the value of imports exceeded that of exports at the end of the 1980s. Energy, raw materials, machinery, electronics, and light industrial and textile products made up a large proportion of imports. Between 1989 and 1992, the value of imports dropped below that of exports, with imports at that time mainly comprising energy, oil, and petrochemicals. Various foreign trade policies also targeted the enhancement of science of technology. China's Ministry of Science and Technology and the former Ministry of Foreign Trade and Economic Cooperation launched 'Trade Vitalization through Science and Technology' in 1999, a strategy that boosted trade in high-technology goods and promoted the adoption of high technology by domestic industries.

Membership of the WTO was a strategic decision made by the Chinese government in an era of globalization. China's accession to the WTO contributed to narrowing the technological gap between China and the developed countries. Fully embracing the rule-based spirit of the WTO was arguably the most profound impact brought about by China's accession. By embracing this spirit, China has abolished, revised, and promulgated more than 3000 laws and regulations at the central government level and 190,000 at the local government level. Since WTO accession, China has taken great strides to reducing trade barriers. As of 2008 the average tariff rate dropped below 10%, and in the meantime China agreed to eliminate other non-tariff barriers. By 2010 China's exports and imports of merchandise grew, reaching six times the 2001 levels. Trade growth brought with it diversification of China's trade relations. China's exports and imports of merchandise in 2010 to and from the U.S., the EU, and Japan declined by about ten percentage points, compared with 2001. This implied potentially greater economic stability worldwide was the result of more widespread trade relations. Following China's accession to the WTO, the country's growth accelerated, which helped transform the economy and enabled China to reduce poverty by an unprecedented extent. Foreign trade and open markets played a crucial role in the transformation. The WTO system provided a stable international regime with open and predictable international markets for a growing China to manage the vast changes required during its transformation.

Basic approaches and their implications

In this section we discuss different approaches to studying the mechanisms through which openness to trade impacts economic development. Different approaches have different underlying assumptions and theoretical implications. The first broad approach is based on the neoclassical theory of growth, which relates to the supply side of the economy. As is usually captured by an aggregate production function, the growth of output is either due to accumulation of any of the various production inputs or to the growth of so-called total factor productivity (TFP), which may in turn indicate improvements in technology or in technical efficiency. The supply-side approach regards openness to foreign trade as a mechanism through which domestic resources can be better allocated. The approach further regards foreign trade as a mechanism facilitating technological spillovers, a channel through which technological improvements can be facilitated or other factors associated with technical or economic efficiency can be positively influenced. There are several ways to incorporate openness to foreign trade into an aggregated production function. Although not theoretically sound, some researchers have used simplistic methods of directly including an openness variable in the aggregate production function in addition to TFP and other production inputs such as labor, land, and physical and human capital. Such a treatment tends to blur the boundary between the effects of openness to foreign trade and those of TFP, and neither reveals or assumes the causal relationship between openness to foreign trade and TFP. Therefore, some researchers opt for a two-step method, one that assumes openness to foreign trade is an important underpinning factor that actively influences TFP. Once the level or growth of TFP is taken as the residual of the accounting framework and estimated using an accounting or regression procedure (the first step), then the empirical relationship between openness to foreign trade and the level (or growth) of TFP can be established and examined. The effect of the former on the latter can thus be estimated (the second step).

Some researchers use more sophisticated methods to model the contribution made by openness to foreign trade to economic growth and development. For example, the whole economy can be divided into two sectors: one that conducts foreign trade (the export sector) and one that produces for the domestic market (the domestic sector). As the export sector has regular access to foreign producers and customers, it enjoys technological spillovers from abroad and thus is able to become more productive than the domestic sector. For example, by capturing the diffusion process of knowledge and technology, Feder (1983) incorporates the output of the export sector (i.e., total exports) into the production function of the domestic sector as a factor that influences the efficiency of the domestic sector.

Another broad approach has a different focus. This focuses on the demand side of the economy and thus studies the contributions of foreign trade, including both exports and imports, to economic growth from the perspective of aggregate demand of the economy. This broad approach is often named 'demand-oriented analysis' or 'post-Keynesian analysis'. As is familiar to those who have taken an introductory macroeconomics course, based on traditional Keynesian theory, an increase in the demand for exports, *ceteris paribus*, leads to an increase in net exports (exports minus imports), which is one of the various factors which, through the well-known multiplier effect, can create a magnified increase in the equilibrium aggregate level of an economy's total output . Proponents of the demand-oriented approach believe that major constraints to modern economic growth, especially in the case of developing countries, lie on the demand side of the economy – not on the supply side (McCombie and Thirlwall, 1994; Lin and Li, 2001).[2]

In the remaining chapters of this book, we will follow the broad framework of the supply-oriented approach. This is because we find that the demand-oriented approach is unsatisfactory, because of its major limitations, when applied to study the potential effects of foreign trade on economic development.

One limitation of the demand-oriented approach is that the approach tends to consider the individual effects of exporting and importing in isolation by failing to treat both sides of foreign trade in a single unified theoretical framework. For example, many empirical studies of China are only concerned with the unidirectional relationship between China's exports and its economic growth. Such studies usually focus on net exports. The idea behind such studies is that, according to Keynesian theory, an increase in net exports – induced by foreign demand, say – immediately leads to an increase in aggregate expenditure, which, in turn, through the multiplier effect, causes an increase in the equilibrium level of an economy's aggregate output. However, analyses that only consider net exports (i.e., the difference between total exports and total imports) can be misleading or at least incomplete.[3] Such analyses simply ignore the welfare-increasing effect of international specialization and trade, the long-term effect of foreign trade on economic development called the 'reallocation' effect, through which foreign trade promotes economic development by allowing more efficient allocation of production resources at the world level.[4]

Another limitation of the demand-oriented approach is that it is rather difficult to model and examine the indirect effects that openness to foreign trade (or exports) has on economic growth or development through other components of aggregate demand within such an analytic framework as the Keynesian model. This can be seen by writing the familiar Keynesian macroeconomic equilibrium condition as follows

$$Y = C + I + G + (X - M) \tag{4.1}$$

where Y, C, I, G, X, and M represent, respectively, national income, consumption, investment, government purchases, exports, and imports. Eq. 4.1 above implies the following growth relation

$$\frac{\dot{Y}}{Y} = \frac{\dot{C}}{C} \cdot \frac{C}{Y} + \frac{\dot{I}}{I} \cdot \frac{I}{Y} + \frac{\dot{G}}{G} \cdot \frac{G}{Y} + \frac{\dot{NX}}{NX} \cdot \frac{NX}{Y} \tag{4.2}$$

where a dot over a variable stands for its time derivative, and the variable of net exports is defined as $NX \equiv X - M$. The last term on the right-hand side of Eq. 4.2, $(\dot{NX}/NX)(NX/Y)$, captures that part of economic growth (growth in Y) which is due to growth in net exports. The problem stems from the fact that the term $(\dot{NX}/NX)(NX/Y)$ is often chosen as a measure of the impact of (net) exports on income growthby the many empirical studies that apply this demand-oriented approach. Needless to say, the term $(\dot{NX}/NX)(NX/Y)$ only captures the direct effect of net exports on income growth and completely ignores possible indirect effects of net exports on income growth via domestic consumption, investment, and government purchases. Many empirical studies suffering from this limitation tend to give unrealistically low estimations of the effect of net exports on economic growth. Some studies even find a negative relationship between China's net exports and its GDP growth. The 'discovery' of the negative relationship between net exports and output level (or growth) has challenged the theoretical foundation of the estimation method (Lin and Li, 2001). In fact, the seemingly puzzling result is a consequence of isolating net exports from the other components of aggregate expenditure. In other words, it is inappropriate to consider the isolated effect of net exports on income growth without considering the interrelationship between net exports and all the other components of aggregate expenditure. According to the Keynesian model, the output level must equal the sum of consumption, investment, government purchases, and net exports in equilibrium. Therefore, the observed negative relationship between net exports and total output may come from the interrelationship between the different components of aggregate expenditure. For example, decreased net exports may come from increased imports that may, in turn, be induced by an exogenous increase in investment or in autonomous consumption (for whatever reason), which, on the whole, still leads to an increase in the level of total output.

Another limitation of the demand-oriented approach is associated with the direction of causality between (net) exports and income growth. The causality can run both ways. On the one hand, it is possible that an exogenous increase in foreign demand for domestic goods (exports) widens net exports, which in turn leads to an increase in the level of total output in equilibrium via the multiplier effect. On the other hand, it is also possible that an exogenous increase in domestic investment or autonomous consumption induces an increase in domestic demand for foreign goods (imports), thus decreasing net exports but increasing the level of total output on the whole. In this sense, the demand-oriented approach fails to reveal the true direction of causality between (net) exports and output growth. Yet another limitation of the demand-oriented approach is that it is only suitable for analysis within a short-term time horizon. In other words, it is more suitable for studying short-run growth than long-run development. This is obvious because the Keynesian model, on which the demand-oriented approach is based, is basically a theoretical model about macroeconomic equilibrium in the short run. For developing countries, especially one as large and unevenly developed as China, the focus of study on long-run development is much more interesting and important than that on short-run growth only.

In view of these limitations inherent in the demand-oriented approach, we will apply the supply-oriented approach throughout the rest of this book. According to the supply-oriented approach, which is based on the neoclassical theory of economic growth, output growth is neither due to the accumulation of various production inputs nor to the growth of TFP. As mentioned earlier, the supply-side approach regards openness to foreign trade as a channel through which resources can be better allocated. This approach further regards foreign trade as a mechanism for technological spillovers, a channel to facilitate technological improvements or to positively influence other factors associated with technical or economic efficiency.

A preliminary empirical analysis

In this section we present a preliminary empirical analysis of the effect of openness to foreign trade on TFP growth in China's provinces. We set up our regression model along the lines of the basic method proposed by Jiang (2011). This method incorporates a model of productivity growth similar to that of Lucas (2009) which transforms it into a model of per-worker output growth similar to that of de la Fuente and Doménech (2001).

Let us assume a Cobb–Douglas form of the aggregate production function in which TFP for China's regions is Hicks neutral. That is, for province i in China at time t, we assume

$$Y_{it} = A_{it}K_{it}^{\alpha}L_{it}^{1-\alpha} \tag{4.3}$$

where Y is total provincial output, K is the stock of physical capital, L is the number of workers, and A is Hicks-neutral TFP. Eq. 4.3 implies

$$y_{it} = A_{it}k_{it}^{\alpha}$$

where $y \equiv Y/L$ and $k \equiv K/L$ are defined as output per worker and physical capital stock per worker, respectively. Taking logs of Eq. 4.4 yields

$$\ln y_{it} = \alpha \ln k_{it} + \ln A_{it} \tag{4.5}$$

which implies

$$\Delta \ln y_{it} = \alpha\Delta \ln k_{it} + \Delta \ln A_{it} \tag{4.6}$$

where Δ denotes growth over the time interval $(t, t+1)$.

In line with the spirit of Lucas (2009), we assume that growth of TFP is governed by

$$\frac{A_{i,t+1}}{A_{it}} = \exp(\xi_i)F_{it}^{\theta}\left(\frac{W_t}{A_{it}}\right)^{\lambda} \tag{4.7}$$

where ξ_i captures assumed time-constant province heterogeneity, F_{it} is a measure of the degree of regional openness to foreign trade, and W_t stands for the level of frontier TFP in the world at time t, so that the term $(W_t/A_{it})^\lambda$ captures the tendency of China's provinces to catch up in TFP, where the parameter λ ($\lambda > 0$) measures the speed of (conditional) convergence in provincial TFP. Eq. 4.7 can be rewritten in log form as

$$\Delta \ln A_{it} = \xi_i + \theta \ln F_{it} + \lambda(\ln W_t - \ln A_{it}) \qquad (4.8)$$

Inserting Eq. 4.5 into Eq. 4.8, we get

$$\Delta \ln A_{it} = \xi_i + \theta \ln F_{it} + \lambda \ln W_t - \lambda \ln y_{it} + \lambda\alpha \ln k_{it} \qquad (4.9)$$

which we insert back into Eq. 4.6 to obtain the following

$$\Delta \ln y_{it} = \xi_i + \theta \ln F_{it} + \lambda \ln W_t - \lambda \ln y_{it} + \lambda\alpha \ln k_{it} + \alpha\Delta \ln k_{it} \qquad (4.10)$$

Finally, we specify our panel data regression model based on Eq. 4.10 as

$$\Delta \ln y_{it} = \eta_t + \theta \ln F_{it} - \lambda \ln y_{it} + \lambda\alpha \ln k_{it} + \alpha\Delta \ln k_{it} + \xi_i + u_{it} \qquad (4.11)$$

where η_t is the time intercept and u_{it} is the zero-mean idiosyncratic error term.

Our sample comprises 28 Chinese provincial-level divisions and covers the period 1986–2011.[5] We use five-year-interval data so that the entire sample period can be divided into five equal time spans of five years: 1986–1991, 1991–1996, 1996–2001, 2001–2006, and 2006–2011. For $\Delta \ln y_{it}$ for example, $t = 1, 2, 3, 4$, and 5 relates to growth of per-worker output during the five time spans, respectively. In practice, four time dummy variables are included in the regression equation to take care of the time intercept η_t. Series of real gross regional product (GRP) for each region can be computed from series of nominal GRP and constant price GRP indexes available from the 1986–2012 issues of the officially published *China Statistical Yearbook*. Real per-worker output is computed as real GRP divided by the number of total employed people for each province, data on the latter are likewise available from these issues of the *China Statistical Yearbook*. Real provincial per-worker capital stocks can be computed as real provincial capital stocks divided by the total number of employed people for each province, where annual data on real provincial capital stocks are obtained in the same way as in Chapter 2. The openness variable F_{it} is constructed as $F_{it} \equiv 1 + \bar{T}_{it}$, which measures the average degree of regional openness to foreign trade of province i over the corresponding time span, where $\bar{T}_{it}$ is computed as the ratio of total value of foreign trade to provincial GRP of the same year, averaged over the corresponding time span.

Owing to the existence of a nonlinear constraint on the parameters of the variables in our regression model (Eq. 4.11), a nonlinear least squares method similar to that used by de la Fuente and Doménech (2001) is required. The parameter λ measures the speed of (conditional) convergence in TFP across China's provinces. We expect a positive value of λ because we expect the diffusion of technology to have a catch-up effect for backward regions in China. The parameter θ measures the effect of provincial openness to foreign trade on provincial TFP growth, and hence on provincial per-worker output growth.

Tables 4.1 and 4.2 summarize the results of nonlinear least squares regressions based on Eq. 4.11. In Table 4.1 we temporarily drop the time-constant province heterogeneity term ξ_t from Eq. 4.11. This assumes that time-constant province-specific factors only affect the (initial) level of TFP – not the growth rate of TFP. In Table 4.1 the estimate of the coefficient α on $\Delta \ln k_{it}$ is significantly positive (at the usual 5 percent significance level), which is 0.429 with a 95 percent interval estimate of (0.332, 0.525). Point and interval estimates of α, the output elasticity of capital, are reasonably close to its traditionally accepted values for China (i.e., in the vicinity of 0.5).[6] The estimated value of the convergence parameter λ is 0.030, which has the expected sign (but is not significant) if it is true that technologically backward provinces do indeed enjoy a catch-up advantage over technologically more advanced provinces. The estimated value of θ is 0.181, which has the expected sign and is significantly positive.

Table 4.1   Estimated parameters from Eq. 4.11 without the ξ_i term

Number of observations: 140				
			95% confidence interval	
Parameter	Estimate	Standard error	Lower	Upper
α	0.4287	0.0488	0.3320	0.5254
λ	0.0302	0.0209	−0.0112	0.0717
θ	0.1810	0.0496	0.0826	0.2794
Adjusted R-squared	0.7173			

We use a time dummy variable for each time span to take care of the time intercept in Eq. 4.11. For brevity the estimated coefficients on the time dummy variables are not reported in the table.

Table 4.2 Estimated parameters from Eq. 4.11 with the ξ_i term

Number of observations: 140				
			95% confidence interval	
Parameter	Estimate	Standard error	Lower	Upper
α	0.4471	0.0652	0.3472	0.5470
λ	0.8241	0.0954	0.6341	1.0141
θ	0.4366	0.0972	0.2431	0.6302
Adjusted R-squared	0.8322			

We use a time dummy variable for each time span and a province dummy variable for each province to take care of the time intercept and province heterogeneity in Eq. 4.11. For brevity the estimated coefficients on the time and province dummy variables are not reported in the table.

We are now in a position to include the province heterogeneity term ξ_i in our regression. Estimated results are shown in Table 4.2. Estimated values of the three parameters α, λ, and θ all have the expected positive sign and are significant. The estimated value of α is now 0.447 with a 95 percent interval estimate of $(0.347, 0.547)$. These point and interval estimates of α are closer to 0.5 than those from the previous regression in Table 4.1. The estimated value of the convergence parameter λ is now 0.824, much higher than that obtained from the previous regression, which was only 0.030.[7] The estimated value of θ in this regression is now 0.437, more than twice its estimate from the previous regression.

Concluding remarks

This chapter discusses in a preliminary way the potential effects of openness to foreign trade on China's economic development. We focus on the possible mechanisms and channels through which openness to foreign trade can impact economic development. One such mechanism is technology diffusion. Openness to foreign trade promotes TFP growth in China by facilitating technological spillovers from technologically advanced countries. This chapter's preliminary empirical analysis is based on a hypothesis positing that, given the level of TFP at the world technology frontier, China's regional TFP growth is a positive function of regional openness to foreign trade and a negative function of the current level of regional TFP. This hypothesis is then supported by our regression results, which have shown that there exists a significantly positive effect of regional openness on regional TFP growth, and that there is evidence for conditional convergence in TFP across China's regions. In the remainder of this book we discuss from various perspectives other potential mechanisms and channels via which openness impacts China's economic development.

Notes

1. Works on economics are often classified according to JEL classification codes, a system set up by the *Journal of Economic Literature*.

2. Kaldor (1972) pointed out, 'contrary to the traditional view which attributed the rate of industrial development in England to the rate of saving and capital accumulation and to the rate of technical progress due to invention and innovation, more recent evidence tends to suggest that Britain's industrial growth was "export-led" from a very early date.' Kaldor also pointed out that, 'there can be little doubt that throughout the nineteenth century and also in the present century, right up to the Second World War, Great Britain's economic growth was closely dependent on the growth of her exports. Given the fact that her share of the world market was bound to decline on a continual basus ... 'It was quite inevitable that both the growth of production and the accumulation of capital should be much lower in Britain than in the countries that were subsequently industrialized ...' (see also Lin and Li, 2001).

3. To illustrate this point let us suppose there are two otherwise identical countries, A and B. Country A is completely self-sufficient, with zero exports and zero imports, and therefore zero net exports, while Country B has a large total value of exports and also an equally large total value of imports, and therefore zero net exports too. However, despite having the same zero exports, the two countries may differ greatly in output and welfare levels. In other words, keeping zero exports throughout, a country can undergo significant economic development as it moves from complete autarky to a certain degree of free trade. In this case, it is foreign trade (i.e., exports and imports taken and considered together) that allows economic

development. The level of net exports (i.e., the difference between exports and imports) is quite simply irrelevant.

4. Needless to say, net exports do have certain effects on an economy's short-run growth, but these effects are neither regarded as interesting or important from a long-run perspective. Some other empirical studies focus on the effect total exports, rather than net exports, have on economic development. These studies are even more problematic. This is because imports are completely ignored in these studies. As a result, these studies fail to consider, measure, and examine the possible countereffect of imports. Suppose such a study, without considering imports, has concluded that increasing foreign demand (i.e., exports) stimulates domestic economic growth. This conclusion may not be true because it may well be increasing domestic demand for imports that is causing the economy to grow and, at the same time, causing exports to expand. In other words, it may actually be increasing domestic demand for foreign goods (imports), rather than increasing foreign demand for domestic goods (exports), that is fueling the growth of the domestic economy in this case.

5. These regions include provinces, ethnic minority autonomous regions, and province-level municipalities, but for convenience sake we call them all 'provinces'. Owing to missing data, three regions – Tibet, Chongqing, and Hainan – are not included in our sample.

6. See, for example, Zheng et al. (2009) and Brandt and Zhu (2010). See also Chow and Li (2002), Chow (2008), CBO (2001), and Musso and Westermann (2005).

7. The big difference is unsurprising because the different convergence rates in TFP implied by the two regressions pertain to two different convergence processes each conditional on a different set of control variables: the second regression controls for the whole set of province dummies – not just trade openness.

References

Balassa, B. (1985) 'Exports, policy choices, and economic growth in developing countries after the 1973 oil shocks,' *Journal of Development Economics*, **18**, 23–35.

Balassa, B. (1988) 'The lessons of East Asian development: an overview,' *Economic Development and Cultural Change*, **36**(3), S273–S290.

Brandt, L.; and Zhu, Xiaodong (2010) *Accounting for China's Growth* (Working Papers tecipa-394), Toronto, Canada: Department of Economics, University of Toronto.

CBO (2001) 'CBO's method for estimating potential output: an update,' August 2001. Available from: *http://www.cbo.gov/ftpdocs/30xx/doc3020/PotentialOutput.pdf* [Congressional Budget Office].

Chow, G.C. (2008) 'Another look at the rate of increase in TFP in China,' *Journal of Chinese Economic and Business Studies*, 6(2), 219–24.

Chow, G.C.; and Li, Kui-Wai (2002) 'China's economic growth: 1952–2010,' *Economic Development and Cultural Change*, 51(1), 247–56.

de la Fuente, A.; and Doménech, R. (2001) 'Schooling data, technological diffusion and the neoclassical model,' *American Economic Review*, 91(2), 323–7.

Demurger, S (1996) 'Openness and industrial growth in Chinese cities,' *Revue Economique*, 47(3), 841–50.

Feder, G. (1983) 'On export and economic growth,' *Journal of Development Economics*, 12, 59–73.

FTPPT (1999) 'Contribution of foreign trade to economic growth and the basic orientation in adjusting foreign trade support policy,' *Finance and Trade Economics*, June, 49–59 [Foreign Trade Policy Project Team].

Jiang, Yanqing (2011) 'Economic environment, technology diffusion, and growth of regional total factor productivity in China,' *Journal of Chinese Economic and Business Studies*, 9(2), 151–61.

Kaldor, N. (1972) 'The irrelevance of equilibrium economics,' *Economic Journal*, 82, 1237–55.

Krueger, A.O. (1990) *Perspectives on Trade and Development*, Chicago, IL: University of Chicago Press.

Kwan, A.C.C.; and Kwok, B. (1995) 'Exogeneity and the export-led growth hypothesis: the case of China,' *Southern Economic Journal*, 61, 1158–66.

Lardy, N.R. (1995) 'The role of foreign trade and investment in China's economic transformation,' *The China Quarterly*, 144, 1065–82.

Lee, J.W. (1995) 'Capital goods import and long-run growth,' *Development Economics*, 48(1), 91–110.

Li, Jianchun; Luo, Yan; and Zhang, Zongyi (2004) 'Regional differentiation in China's export-oriented growth,' *Reform*, 2004(5) [in Chinese].

Li, K.W.; and Leung, W.S.C. (1994) 'Causal relationships among economic aggregates in China,' *Applied Economics*, 26, 1189–96.

Liu, Xiaming; Song, Haiyan; and Romilly, P. (1997) 'An empirical investigation of the causal relationship between openness and economic growth in China,' *Applied Economics*, 29(12), 1679–87.

Lin, Yifu; and Li, Yongjun (2001) 'Export and economic growth in China: a demand-oriented analysis,' *China Economic Quarterly*, 2(4), 779–94.

Lucas, R.E. (2009) 'Trade and the diffusion of the industrial revolution,' *American Economic Journal: Macroeconomics*, 1(1), 1–25.

McCombie, J.; and Thirlwall, A. (1994) *Economic Growth and the Balance of Payments Constraint*, London: St. Martins.

Musso, A.; and Westermann, T. (2005) *Assessing Potential Output Growth in the Euro Area: A Growth Accounting Perspective* (ECB Occasional Paper No. 22), Frankfurt, Germany: European Central Bank.

Shan, J.; and Sun, F. (1998) 'On the export-led growth hypothesis: the econometric evidence from China,' *Applied Economics*, **30**, 1055–65.

Shen, Chenxiang (1999) 'An empirical analysis of China's export-oriented economic growth: 1977–1988,' *The Journal of World Economy*, **1999**(12) [in Chinese].

Shen, Kunrong; and Li, Jian (2003) 'An empirical study on the influencing mechanism of China's trade development and economic growth,' *Economic Research Journal*, **2003**(5) [in Chinese].

Sun, Haishun; and Parikh, A. (1999) *Export and Economic Growth in China* (Working Paper Series 9905), Melbourne, Australia: School of Economics, Deakin University.

Sun, Peng; and Heshmati, A. (2010) *International Trade and Its Effects on Economic Growth in China* (IZA Discussion Papers No. 5151), Bonn, Germany: Institute for the Study of Labor.

Sun, Yanlin (2000) 'An empirical analysis of China's exports and economic growth,' *Journal of International Trade*, **2000**(?) [in Chinese].

Tyler, W.G. (1981) 'Growth and export expansion in developing countries: some empirical evidence,' *Journal of Development Economics*, **9**, 121–30.

Wagner, J. (2007) 'Exports and productivity: a survey of the evidence from firm level data,' *The World Economy*, **30**(1), 60–82.

WB (1987) *World Development Report 1987*, New York: Oxford University Press [World Bank].

Xue, J. (1995) 'The export-led growth model and its application in China,' *Hitotsubashi Journal of Economics*, **36**, 189–206.

Yang, Quanfa (1998) 'An analysis of the output effect of China's regional exports,' *Economic Research Journal*, **1998**(7) [in Chinese].

Yang, Quanfa; and Shu, Yuan (1998) 'The effect of China's exports on economic growth,' *World Economics and Politics*, **1998**(8) [in Chinese].

Zhang, He; Liu, Jinquan; and Gu, Hongmei (2005) 'An empirical study of the effect of foreign aggregate demand and supply on China's economic growth,' *The Journal of World Economy*, **2005**(4) [n Chinese].

Zhang, X.; and Hu, J. (1999) 'Behind free trade: import and China's economic development,' *Intertrade*, **209**, April, 1–16.

Zhao, Ling; Song, Shaohua; and Song, Hongming (2001) 'An empirical study of China's export-oriented economic growth,' *The Journal of World Economy*, **2001**(8) [in Chinese].

Zheng, Jinghai; Hu, Angang; and Bigsten, A. (2009) 'Measuring potential output in a rapidly developing economy: the case of China in comparison with the US and EU,' *Federal Reserve Bank of St. Louis Review*, July/August, 317–42.

Zhu, W. (1998) 'The puzzle of China's export-oriented development strategy,' *Strategy and Management*, **30**, May.

5

Potential effects of foreign direct investment on development

Abstract: This chapter is closely related to the previous chapter and discusses in a preliminary way the potential effects of openness to FDI on China's economic development. This chapter focuses on the potential mechanisms through which openness to FDI can impact China's economic development. FDI inflows not only enhance capital accumulation in China, which in itself is crucial to China's development, but also exert several spillover effects through different channels. The regression results of our preliminary empirical analysis in this chapter suggest that regional openness to FDI tends to promote regional total factor productivity (TFP) growth and hence regional income growth. Motivated by the preliminary discussions in this and the preceding chapter, we then proceed to investigate the impacts of openness to foreign trade and FDI on China's economic development from a number of different perspectives in the subsequent chapters of this book.

Key words: foreign direct investment, spillover effect, economic development, regional total factor productivity, state-owned enterprises, marketization.

JEL classification codes: F41; O11; O57.[1]

Introduction

This chapter investigates the potential effects of foreign direct investment (FDI) on economic development in China. FDI in China began in 1979. Before 1979, there were virtually no foreign-owned firms operating in China, nor did China have many external loans. What FDI there was came from small and medium-sized enterprises in Hong Kong and Guangdong Province. The production from foreign-invested firms was overwhelmingly export oriented and interacted little with domestic markets. However, China began to shift its FDI policies in the early 1980s from restrictive to permissive, then to policies encouraging FDI in general in the mid-1980s, and to policies encouraging more high-tech and capital-intensive FDI projects in the mid-1990s (Fung et al., 2004). FDI in China took off in 1992. Since 1993 China could boast the largest inflow of FDI of the developing world. By the end of 2003, China had accumulated U.S.$500 billion of FDI from foreign-owned enterprises, joint ventures, and cooperative enterprises. FDI played an important role in contributing to China's trade and economic development, and the effects of FDI became prominent in many important aspects.[2]

However, FDI in China is highly unevenly distributed across different geographical regions (Yin, 2011). The highly uneven spatial distribution of FDI, substantially different levels of trade openness, and huge income inequality across China's regions stand out as prominent features during its economic transition.[3] FDI in China started in four special economic zones in the early 1980s and gradually penetrated other coastal and inland regions. As of 2000 FDI can be found in every part of China except Tibet. The spatial feature of FDI distribution that stands out most is the fact that the coastal provinces have by far the larger share of the total inflow of FDI, compared with China's interior provinces (Cheung and Lin, 2004). The broad spatial pattern of FDI distribution has remained fairly stable over time, with the share of the eastern coastal provinces being as large as 85 percent.

China's spectacular economic takeoff and the huge influx of FDI since the 1980s have stimulated much discussion.[4] The focus has been the effects of FDI on China's economic development. Despite an increasing body of literature, systematic treatments of the role played by FDI in China's economic development are quite limited. The purpose of this chapter is to conduct some preliminary empirical analysis to motivate discussions in subsequent chapters. This chapter is structured as follows. In the second section 'Effects of FDI and the mechanisms', we discuss the potential effects and channels through which FDI exerts its impacts. In the third section 'A preliminary model', we present a theoretical framework for our subsequent empirical analysis. In the fourth section 'Preliminary empirical analysis and results', we present our regression results.

Effects of FDI and the mechanisms

There have been many positive effects of FDI on China's economic development. For example, FDI enhances capital formation. China needs capital to boost its economy and promote its transformation. In this regard FDI has made a substantial contribution. In addition, the employment opportunities brought about by the inflow of FDI, either directly or indirectly, have had a major influence on China's economy (OECD, 2000; Madariaga and Poncet, 2007). OECD (2000) reported foreign-invested enterprises in China employing up to 3 percent of the total workforce by the end of the 1990s. FDI has also been at the core of China's export expansion. Foreign-invested enterprises have not only enlarged China's total exports, but also upgraded the country's export structure (Zhang, 2006). Compared with domestic capital, FDI not only contributes to capital accumulation, but also brings about knowledge and technology. Therefore, labor utilization in FDI enterprises tends to be more efficient than in domestic firms. In addition, compared with domestic firms, foreign-invested enterprises are more likely to be concentrated in fast-growing or newly developed industries while domestic firms have a greater presence in conventional capital-intensive industries.

FDI has been decisive in China's participation in the worldwide market segmentation of the production process, and has played an important role in transforming China's industrial structure, diversifying its exports of labor-intensive products, and strengthening China's competitiveness in fast-growing international markets. Moreover, FDI has helped China transition from a centrally planned system to a market-oriented one. This is because of the role played by FDI in stimulating China's move toward marketization by promoting the formation of a market-oriented institutional framework, contributing to changes in the ownership structure toward privatization by facilitating competition and accelerating reforms of state-owned enterprises, and promoting China's economic integration into the world (Zhang, 2006).

However, some researchers point out that FDI can impact China's economy negatively (Fung et al., 2004). FDI may actually lower domestic savings and investment, rather than closing the gap between the two. FDI may also have a negative effect on the local economy by leading to balance-of-payment deficits as a result of rising equity repayment obligations. In the long run, foreign-invested enterprises may suppress domestic firms by using their technological advantage to drive out local competitors. The activities of foreign-invested firms may reinforce China's dualistic economic structure and worsen income disparities owing to their uneven impact on economic development (Zhang and Zhang, 2003). Furthermore, foreign-invested firms may affect government policies in a way that is unfavorable to China's economic development as a result of receiving preferential treatment in the form of tax rebates, investment allowances, prime factory sites and advantageous social services (Zhang, 2006).

In addition to these direct impacts, researchers have identified several spillover mechanisms of FDI.[5] Greater inflows of FDI imply greater exposure to new products imported by foreign firms. Imitating the new technology embodied in new products is an important mechanism for technology transmission, one that improves domestic technology and leads to increased productivity in domestic firms. Furthermore, competition promotes technology spillovers. New competition brought about by foreign-invested firms compels domestic firms to make use of technology spillovers in order to survive. Competition thus raises the productivity of local firms. FDI also brings a number of special resources that are beneficial to the host country such as management skills and access to international production networks and established brand names. Moreover, export spillovers are also sources of productivity gain. To lower the fixed costs of exporting and penetrate new markets, domestic firms can imitate multinational corporations by implementing exporting strategies that involve distribution networks, transport infrastructure, consumer tastes, and so on. Domestic productivity gains can also be realized through vertical spillovers. Foreign-invested enterprises can expand the demand for FDI from local upstream suppliers and thereby spill technology and management skills over to local firms (Rodriguez-Clare, 1996). Spillovers may also occur through the movement of human capital from foreign-invested firms to local firms. Foreign-invested enterprises invest more in technology and staff training, so that labor turnover from foreign-invested enterprises to local firms can bring about increases in productivity in local firms.

A preliminary model

In this section we set up a preliminary model to empirically examine the effects of FDI on China's economic growth and development. This model will then be used for our subsequent analyses. In this preliminary model, we adopt the simplest Cobb–Douglas production function. That is, for province i at time t in China, we assume an aggregate production function of the form

$$Y_i(t) = A_i(t)K_i(t)^\alpha L_i(t)^{1-\alpha} \qquad (5.1)$$

where Y is output, K is physical capital stock (which includes FDI stock), L is the number of workers, and A is our measure of technology (total factor productivity). The functional form in Eq. 5.1 is basically the same as that in

Eq. 4.3, the only conceptual difference being that we are considering FDI here and include it in physical capital stock K. Therefore, in per-worker terms, the intensive form is written as

$$y_i(t) = A_i(t)k_i(t)^\alpha \qquad (5.2)$$

where y and k are per-worker output and per-worker physical capital stock, respectively, $y \equiv Y/L$ and $k \equiv K/L$. Taking logs of Eq. 5.2 gives

$$\ln y_i(t) = \alpha \ln k_i(t) + \ln A_i(t) \qquad (5.3)$$

Our focus here is on the possible effect of FDI on the economy through the impact of per-worker output on TFP. Therefore, we need to model how TFP grows over time. Based on the spirit of Lucas (2009) and following Aiyar and Feyrer (2002), we assume that the growth of TFP is governed by

$$\frac{d \ln A_i(t)}{dt} = \lambda[\ln A_i^*(t) - \ln A_i(z)] \qquad (5.4)$$

where $A^*(t)$ denotes the potential (target) level of TFP in province i at time t, and λ is the rate of convergence of TFP. Eq. 5.4 formally hypothesizes that the rate of change of TFP in a Chinese province is positively related to the size of the gap between its actual TFP at a point in time and its potential TFP at the same moment in time. We further assume that the potential (target) level of TFP is determined in turn by

$$A_i^*(t) = F_i S_i(t)^\phi T(t) \qquad (5.5)$$

where F_i is a province-specific index that is fixed for any specific province over time but varies across different provinces, $T(t)$ is an index of world frontier technology that grows exogenously over time, $S_i(t)$ stands for the spillover effect of FDI for province i at time t, and the parameter ϕ represents the elasticity of potential TFP with respect to the spillover effect of FDI.

Substituting Eq. 5.5 into Eq. 5.4, and rearranging terms, we obtain the following

$$\frac{d \ln A_i(t)}{dt} + \lambda \ln A_i(t) = \lambda[\ln F_i + \phi \ln S_i(t) + \ln T(t)] \qquad (5.6)$$

Multiplying Eq. 5.6 throughout by $e^{\lambda t}$, it then follows that

$$\int_{t_1}^{t_2} e^{\lambda t} \left[\frac{d \ln A_i(t)}{dt} + \lambda \ln A_i(t) \right] dt$$

$$= \ln F_i \int_{t_1}^{t_2} \lambda e^{\lambda t} \, dt + \phi \int_{t_1}^{t_2} \lambda e^{\lambda t} \ln S_i(t) \, dt + \int_{t_1}^{t_2} \lambda e^{\lambda t} \ln T(t) \, dt$$

Assuming $S_i(t)$ remains constant throughout the interval $[t_1, t_2]$, integrating in Eq. 5.7, and multiplying throughout by $e^{-\lambda t_2}$, we obtain the following

$$\ln A_i(t_2) = e^{-\lambda \tau} \ln A_i(t_1) + \phi(1 - e^{-\lambda \tau}) \ln S_i(t_1) + (1 - e^{-\lambda \tau}) \ln F_i$$

$$+ e^{-\lambda t_2} \int_{t_1}^{t_2} \lambda e^{\lambda t} \ln T(t)\, dt \qquad (5.8)$$

where $\tau = t_2 - t_1$. Eq. 5.8 can then be rewritten as

$\ln A_i(t_2) - \ln A_i(t_1)$

$$= -\rho \ln A_i(t_1) + \phi\rho \ln S_i(t_1) + \rho \ln F_i + e^{-\lambda t_2} \int_{t_1}^{t_2} \lambda e^{\lambda t} \ln T(t)\, dt \quad (5.9)$$

where we have defined $\rho \equiv (1 - e^{-\lambda \tau})$. Combining Eqs. 5.3 and 5.9 yields

$$\ln y_i(t_2) - \ln y_i(t_1) = \alpha[\ln k_i(t_2) - \ln k_i(t_1)] - \rho \ln y_i(t_1) + \rho\alpha \ln k_i(t_1)$$

$$+ \phi\rho \ln S_i(t_1) + \rho \ln F_i + e^{-\lambda t_2} \int_{t_1}^{t_2} \lambda e^{\lambda t} \ln T(t)\, dt$$

$$(5.10)$$

This equation will represent the foundation for our empirical analysis in the next section. It can now be rewritten in panel data regression format using its conventional notation

$$\Delta \ln y_{it} = \eta_t + \theta \ln S_{it} - \rho \ln y_{it} + \rho\alpha \ln k_{it} + \alpha\Delta \ln k_{it} + \xi_i + u_{it} \quad (5.11)$$

where $\theta \equiv \phi\rho$, Δ pertains to the time interval between t_2 and t_1, the time intercept η_t captures the term $e^{-\lambda t_2} \int_{t_2}^{t_1} \lambda e^{\lambda t} \ln T(t)\, dt$, the province heterogeneity ξ_i absorbs the term $\rho \ln F_i$, and u_{it} has been added to the equation as the zero-mean idiosyncratic error term.

Preliminary empirical analysis and results

Based on the regression specification in Eq. 5.11, in this section we carry out some preliminary empirical analysis and present the results. Our sample consists of 28 provinces (province-level divisions) in mainland China over the period 1996–2011.[6] Most data needed for our regression analysis were taken from the 1996–2012 issues of the *China Statistical Yearbook*. The total number of the workforce of the 28 provinces in 1996–2011 were likewise available from these issues, so that data on L_{it} could be obtained. Series of nominal provincial GDP and GDP indexes were also available from the *Yearbook*, so that the values of real provincial GDP could also be calculated. The values of y_{it} were calculated as real provincial GDP divided by the number of persons employed provincially. Real provincial per-worker capital stocks can be computed as real provincial capital stocks divided by the total number of those in work for each province, where annual data on real provincial capital stocks can be obtained by adopting the same method used in Chapter 2. The S_{it} variable in Eq. 5.11 is proxied for by per-worker regional FDI stock, and can be calculated by the same method employed for total provincial capital stock. To see how interregional disparity in per-worker FDI stock evolves over time, see Figure 5.1, which shows the levels of the coefficient of variation of provincial per-worker FDI stock across our sample over the period 1996–2011. We can see that the it rose gradually during 1996 2001 and then dropped steadily during 2001–2008.

The regression specification in Eq. 5.11 implies that the growth of per-worker output within a certain time period relies not only on the growth of per-worker capital stock within the same time period, but also on the initial levels of per-worker output, per-worker capital stock, and per-worker FDI stock when the period starts. Owing to the nonlinear restriction involved in the coefficient of the $\ln k_{it}$ term, we choose to use a nonlinear least squares method to estimate the parameters involved. This nonlinear least squares method is similar in structure to those used by de la Fuente and Doménech (2001) and Jiang (2011).

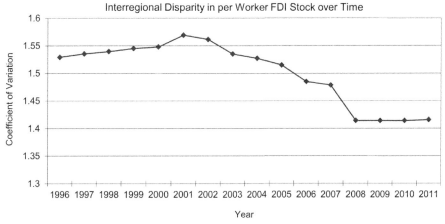

Figure 5.1 **Interregional disparity in per-worker FDI stock over time**

Note: Values of the coefficient of variation are depicted on the vertical axis

Table 5.1 Estimated parameters from Eq. 5.11 without the ξ_i term

Number of observations: 420				
			95% confidence interval	
Parameter	Estimate	Standard error	Lower	Upper
α	0.3621	0.0242	0.3145	0.4096
ρ	0.0062	0.0042	−0.0021	0.0145
θ	0.0042	0.0014	0.0014	0.0069
Adjusted R-squared	0.5239			

We use a time dummy variable for each year to take care of the time intercept in Eq. 5.11. For brevity the estimated coefficients on the time dummy variables are not reported in the table.

Table 5.2 Estimated parameters from Eq. 5.11 with the ξ_i term

Number of observations: 420				
			95% confidence interval	
Parameter	Estimate	Standard error	Lower	Upper
α	0.3632	0.0252	0.3136	0.4128
ρ	−0.0135	0.0230	−0.0586	0.0317
θ	0.0314	0.0112	0.0092	0.0535
Adjusted R-squared	0.6000			

We use a time dummy variable for each year and a province dummy variable for each province to take care of the time intercept and province heterogeneity in Eq. 5.11. For brevity the estimated coefficients on the time and province dummy variables are not reported in the table.

We summarize the results of nonlinear least squares regressions based on Eq. 5.11 in Tables 5.1 and 5.2. In Table 5.1 we temporarily drop the time-constant province heterogeneity term ξ_i from Eq. 5.11. We do this merely for comparison purposes. Dropping the province heterogeneity from the regression specification implies that time-constant province-specific factors affect only the initial level of provincial per-worker output, but not its subsequent growth rate. In Table 5.1 the estimated value of the coefficient α on $\Delta \ln k_{it}$ is significantly positive (at the usual 5 percent significance level), which is 0.362 with the 95 percent interval estimate of (0.315, 0.409). The point and interval estimates of α, the output elasticity of capital, are somewhat lower than its empirically accepted value for China, which is in the vicinity of 0.50.[7] The convergence parameter ρ is estimated at 0.006, which is insignificant but has the expected positive sign. This result is mildly suggestive that poorer provinces have a catch-up advantage over richer provinces in terms of productivity growth. The estimated partial effect of per-worker FDI stock (i.e., the estimated value of θ) is 0.004. Small as it is, it too has the expected positive sign and is statistically significant.

Next we include the time-constant province heterogeneity term ξ_i in our regression to see what effect it has on the results. We show the new estimation results in Table 5.2. The estimated value of α is 0.363, with a 95 percent interval estimate of (0.314, 0.413). The point and interval estimates of α are very close to those obtained from our previous regression in Table 5.1. The value of the convergence parameter ρ is now estimated as negative and insignificant. This implies that the convergence hypothesis is not supported when province heterogeneity is controlled for during regression analysis. The estimated partial effect of per-worker FDI stock, the value of θ, is now 0.031, which is significant and larger than the estimate from our previous regression.

Concluding remarks

This chapter is closely related to the previous chapter and discusses in a preliminary way the potential effects of openness to FDI on China's economic growth and development. Our focus is on the potential mechanisms and channels through which openness to FDI can impact economic development. Not only do inflows of FDI enhance capital accumulation in China, which is in itself a crucial factor in China's economic growth, but FDI also creates employment opportunities and brings about knowledge, technology, export expansion, and more market competition. FDI has been decisive in China's participation in the worldwide market segmentation of the production process. FDI also stimulates China's move toward marketization by facilitating the formation of market-oriented institutions, promoting domestic and international market competition, motivating reforms of state-owned enterprises, and accelerating China's economic integration into the world.

The diffusion of technology is the focus of our preliminary empirical analysis in this chapter. Openness to FDI promotes TFP growth, and hence output growth in China, by facilitating technological spillovers from technologically advanced countries. This analysis is based on a hypothesis stating that China's regional TFP growth is a positive function of regional openness to FDI and a negative function of the current level of regional TFP. This convergence hypothesis is mildly supported by our regression results, which further suggest that regional openness to FDI promotes regional TFP growth and hence regional income growth. In the remaining chapters of this book we consider from various perspectives the other potential mechanisms and channels via which openness (to foreign trade and FDI) impacts China's economic development.

Notes

1. Works on economics are often classified according to JEL classification codes, a system set up by the *Journal of Economic Literature.*
2. Foreign trade and FDI in China are always closely related to each other. Over 50 percent of total exports and 60 percent of total imports in China can be accounted for by foreign-invested enterprises. See, for example, Whalley and Xin (2010) for a recent discussion of the link between FDI inflows and foreign trade in China.
3. By 1999 interregional income inequality in China had exceeded that in any other country (Yang, 1999), and by 2005 per-capita income in the richer coastal provinces was 2.5 times higher than that of the inland provinces (Zhu et al., 2008).
4. Some examples are Zhang (1999), Demurger (2000), DaCosta and Carroll (2001), Yao and Zhang (2001), Bao et al. (2002), Demurger et al. (2002), Hu and Owen (2003), Wang and Gao (2003), Zhang (2006), Madariaga and Poncet (2007), Ouyang (2009), Whalley and Xin (2010), and Jiang (2011).
5. This paragraph draws on Madariaga and Poncet (2007)'s summary of Görg and Greenaway (2004)'s discussion.
6. Mainland China is divided into province-level divisions that include provinces, ethnic minority autonomous regions, and municipalities. For the sake of brevity, however, we term them all 'provinces'. Three

of these regions – Tibet, Chongqing, and Hainan – are not included in our sample because data are not available.

7. See Chapter 4. See also Zheng et al. (2009) and Brandt and Zhu (2010). See also CBO (2001), Chow and Li (2002), Musso and Westermann (2005), and Chow (2008).

References

Aiyar, S.; and Feyrer, J. (2002) *A Contribution to the Empirics of Total Factor Productivity* (Dartmouth College Working Paper No. 02-09), Hanover, NH: Dartmouth College.

Bao, S.; Chang, G.H.; Sachs, J.D.; and Woo, W.T. (2002) 'Geographic factors and China's regional development under market reforms, 1978–98,' *China Economic Review*, **13**(1), 89–111.

Brandt, L.; and Zhu, Xiaodong (2010) *Accounting for China's Growth* (Working Paper tecipa-394), Toronto, Canada: Department of Economics, University of Toronto.

CBO (2001) 'CBO's method for estimating potential output: an update,' August 2001. Available from: *http://www.cbo.gov/ftpdocs/30xx/doc3020/PotentialOutput. pdf* [Congressional Budget Office].

Cheung, K.; and Lin, Ping (2004) 'Spillover effects of FDI on innovation in China: evidence from the provincial data,' *China Economic Review*, **15**(1), 25–44.

Chow, G.C. (2008) 'Another look at the rate of increase in TFP in China,' *Journal of Chinese Economic and Business Studies*, **6**(2), 219–24.

Chow, G.C.; and Li, Kui-Wai (2002) 'China's economic growth: 1952–2010,' *Economic Development and Cultural Change*, **51**(1), 247–56.

DaCosta, M.; and Carroll, W. (2001) 'Township and village enterprises, openness and regional economic growth in China,' *Post-communist Economist*, **13**(2), 229–41.

de la Fuente, A.; and Doménech, R. (2001) 'Schooling data, technological diffusion and the neoclassical model,' *American Economic Review*, **91**(2), 323–7.

Demurger, S. (2000) *Economic Opening and Growth in China*, Paris: OECD Development Centre Studies.

Demurger, S.; Sachs, J.; Woo, W.T.; Bao, S.; Chang, G.; and Mellinger, A. (2002) 'Geography, economic policy and regional development in China,' *Asian Economic Papers*, **1**(1), 146–97.

Fung, K.C.; Iizaka, H.; and Tong, S. (2004) 'FDI in China: policy, recent trend and impact,' *Global Economic Review*, **33**(2), 99–130.

Görg, H.; and Greenaway, D. (2004) 'Much ado about nothing? Do domestic firms really benefit from foreign direct investment?' *World Bank Research Observer*, **19**, 171–97.

Hu, A.; and Owen, R.F. (2003) 'Gravitation at home and abroad: openness and imbalanced regional growth in China,' paper presented at *Fourth International Conference on Chinese Economy: The Efficiency of China's Economic Policy*, Clermont-Ferrand, France: CERDI, Université d'Auvergne.

Jiang, Yanqing (2011) 'Economic environment, technology diffusion, and growth of regional total factor productivity in China,' *Journal of Chinese Economic and Business Studies*, **9**(2), 151–61.

Lucas, R.E. (2009) 'Trade and the diffusion of the Industrial Revolution,' *American Economic Journal: Macroeconomics*, **1**(1), 1–25.

Madariaga, N.; and Poncet, S. (2007) 'FDI in Chinese cities: spillovers and impact on growth,' *The World Economy*, **30**(5), 837–62.

Musso, A.; and Westermann, T. (2005) *Assessing Potential Output Growth in the Euro Area: A Growth Accounting Perspective* (ECB Occasional Paper No. 22), Frankfurt, Germany: European Central Bank, January.

OECD (2000) *Main Determinants and Impacts of Foreign Direct Investment on China's Economy* (Working Paper on International Investment No. 4), Paris: Organisation for Economic Co-operation and Development.

Ouyang, P. (2009) *Economic Growth, Industrial Development and Inter-Regional Spillovers from Foreign Direct Investment: Evidence from China* (Working Paper), New York: Department of Economics, Syracuse University.

Rodriguez-Clare, A. (1996) 'Multinationals, linkages and development,' *American Economic Review*, **86**(4), 852–73.

Wang, Yuwei; and Gao, Ting (2003) '*Openness, Income and Growth in China* (Working Paper), Columbia, MO: Department of Economics, University of Missouri-Columbia.

Whalley, J.; and Xin, Xian (2010) 'China's FDI and non-FDI economies and the sustainability of future high Chinese growth,' *China Economic Review*, **21**(1), 123–35.

Yang, D.T. (1999) 'Urban-biased policies and rising income inequality in China,' *American Economic Review Papers and Proceedings*, **89**(2), 306–10.

Yao, Shujie; and Zhang, Zongyi (2001) 'Regional growth in China under economic reforms,' *Journal of Development Studies*, **38**(2), 167–86.

Yin, H. (2011) 'Characteristics of inter-regional income disparities in China,' *Social Sciences in China*, **32**(3), 123–44.

Zhang, K.H. (1999) 'How does FDI interact with economic growth in a large developing country? The case of China,' *Economic Systems*, **23**(4), 291–303.

Zhang, K.H. (2006) 'Foreign direct investment and economic growth in China: a panel data study for 1992–2004,' paper presented at *Conference of WTO, China and Asian Economies*, University of International Business and Economics, Beijing, China.

Zhang, Xiaobo; and Zhang, K. (2003) 'How does globalisation affect regional inequality within a developing country? Evidence from China,' *Journal of Development Studies*, **39**(4), 47–67.

Zheng, Jinghai; Hu, Angang; and Bigsten, A. (2009) 'Measuring potential output in a rapidly developing economy: the case of China in comparison with the US and EU,' *Federal Reserve Bank of St. Louis Review*, July/August, 317–42.

Zhu, S.; Lai, M.; and Fu, X. (2008) 'Spatial characteristics and dynamics of provincial total factor productivity in China,' *Journal of Chinese Economic and Business Studies*, **6**(2), 197–217.

6

Interregional disparity and the development of inland regions

Abstract: In this chapter we investigate the effects of international openness, domestic coastal–inland market integration, and human capital accumulation on TFP growth in inland regions of China. By using a variety of panel data regression techniques, we show that human capital accumulation plays an important role in promoting TFP growth in China's inland provinces. Our results support the argument that the most important contribution of human capital to income growth lies not in its static direct effect as an accumulable factor in the production function, but rather in its dynamic role in promoting TFP growth. Our results also provide evidence for the positive role coastal–inland market integration plays in promoting TFP growth in China's inland regions.

Key words: total factor productivity, openness, market integration, human capital, interregional disparity, total factor productivity.

JEL classification codes: F41; O11; O57.[1]

Introduction

Since the start of economic reform in the 1980s, China has achieved remarkable growth in the past three decades. However, China's rapid growth has been accompanied by growing inequality that 'threatens the social compact and thus the political basis for economic growth and social development' (Fan et al., 2009). The Gini coefficient, which measures economic inequality in society, was 0.33 in 1980 and later rose by about 40 percent to around 0.46 in the early 2000s (Sisci, 2005; WB, 2005; Fan and Sun, 2008). Such a rate of increase, according to the World Bank, was the fastest in the world. Spatial income disparities, especially those between coastal and inland regions, have been on the rise and became a prominent issue in China during the country's growth and transition (Yin, 2011). In the present study we focus on the relatively backward inland regions of China. Specifically, we examine the potential effects of three factors – international openness, domestic coastal–inland market integration, and human capital accumulation – on TFP (total factor productivity) growth in China's inland provinces.

Growth and development theories suggest that openness to foreign trade and FDI (foreign direct investment) promote the income growth of a country (or region) by raising the level of domestic (or local) productivity. For example, foreign trade opens up access to new technology embodied in imported goods, enlarges the market faced by domestic producers so that they can increase their returns from innovations, and motivates the country's specialization in research-intensive production (Harrison, 1996). It has been widely argued that China's impressive economic takeoff can be attributed, to a large extent, to the country's radical initiatives encouraging openness to foreign trade and inward flows of FDI. However, the degree of participation in foreign trade varies greatly from one Chinese region to another, and FDI inflows are also highly unevenly distributed across different regions. How does this uneven openness affect the income gap between inland and coastal regions of China? To answer this question, the role of openness in promoting regional TFP growth in China, especially TFP growth in inland regions, needs to be thoroughly analyzed.

Another important factor affecting TFP growth in China's inland regions is coastal–inland market integration. China is a very large country characterized by striking economic disparities across regions and between rural and urban areas. Recent regional productivity studies of China (e.g., Zheng and Hu, 2006; Yang and Lahr, 2010; Jiang, 2011) often fail to explore the pattern of spatial interdependence of China's regions. Such studies tend to treat each region as an isolated and independent entity and overlook spatial effects and interregional dynamics.[2] Ignoring spatial interdependence in regional studies could generate serious misspecification problems and lead to questionable parameter estimates and statistical inferences (Abreu et al., 2005; Fingleton and López-Bazo, 2006; Özyurt and Mitze, 2012). Spatial interdependence implies interactions between China's different regions. In this chapter we are interested in examining how interregional market integration (interregional trade) between coastal and inland regions in China affects TFP growth in inland regions. Intuitively, coastal–inland market integration in China implies that inland regions can realize growth in TFP by taking advantage of technology spillovers from higher TFP coastal regions or of gains from regional production specialization facilitated by interregional trade.

Human capital in inland regions is yet another factor that can be crucial in promoting local TFP growth. Human capital may exert a dual effect on income growth. First, human capital has a direct static impact on income growth as an accumulable factor of production. Second, human capital may have an indirect dynamic impact on income growth via its contribution to TFP growth. The key point is, as Benhabib and Spiegel (1994) have pointed out, the most important contribution of human capital to income growth may lie not in its static effect as a direct production input, but in its dynamic role in promoting TFP growth.

The remainder of this chapter is organized as follows. In the second section 'The model' we present the theoretical framework and empirical model on which our later regression analysis will be based. In the third section 'The variables and data', following the empirical model presented in the preceding section, we discuss various issues concerning the sample, data, and variables. In the fourth section 'Regressions and results' we discuss our regression methods, run the regressions, and present the results.

The model

Before we set up the theoretical framework and empirical model in this section, we need to state our key hypothesis first. This hypothesis is that the ability of an inland (i.e., economically backward) region in China to achieve regional growth in TFP depends on three basic factors: (i) the level of direct openness of this inland region to international economic activities such as foreign trade and FDI, (ii) the degree of domestic coastal–inland market integration between this inland region and coastal regions in China, and (iii) the level of per-worker human capital in this inland region. The first factor, international openness (to foreign trade and FDI) of an inland Chinese region, implies that the region can achieve TFP growth, say, by reaping the rewards of production specialization facilitated by foreign trade and/or by taking advantage of technology spillovers from foreign countries via regional inflows of FDI. The second factor, domestic coastal–inland market integration, likewise, implies that an inland Chinese region can achieve growth in TFP by reaping the rewards of regional production specialization facilitated by this coastal–inland market integration (i.e., interregional trade) and/or by taking advantage of technology spillovers from higher TFP coastal regions. The third factor, the level of per-worker human capital in this inland region, can also be important in facilitating local TFP growth as better educated or better trained workers generally have a comparative advantage in absorbing technology spillovers from foreign countries or from higher TFP coastal regions.

Before we provide our theoretical framework, we first assume a Cobb–Douglas aggregate production function with Hicks-neutral technology (or TFP) for an inland Chinese region (province).[3] That is, for any inland Chinese region i at time t we assume

$$Y_{it} = A_{it}K_{it}^{\alpha}H_{it}^{1-\alpha} = A_{it}K_{it}^{\alpha}(h_{it}L_{it})^{1-\alpha} \tag{6.1}$$

where Y is the total output, A is the Hicks-neutral technology (TFP), K is the stock of physical capital, H is our measure of human capital stock, L is the number of workers, and h ($\equiv H/L$) is per-worker human capital stock otherwise called 'human capital intensity'.[4] The production function in Eq. 6.1 can be written in per-worker intensive form as

$$y_{it} = A_{it}k_{it}^{\alpha}h_{it}^{1-\alpha} \tag{6.2}$$

where we define $y \equiv Y/L$ and $k \equiv K/L$ (similar to $h \equiv H/L$) as output per worker and physical capital stock per worker, respectively. Taking logs on both sides of Eq. 6.2 yields

$$\ln y_{it} = \ln A_{it} + \alpha \ln k_{it} + (1 - \alpha) \ln h_{it} \tag{6.3}$$

By employing Eq. 6.3, we can calculate the values of $\ln A_{it}$ as a residual.

In line with the ideas of Nelson and Phelps (1966), Aiyar and Feyrer (2002), Lucas (2009), and Jiang (2011, 2012b), we build a theoretical framework capturing the hypothesis that the TFP growth rate in an inland Chinese region is positively related to the size of the gap between its actual TFP level at a point in time and its potential (target) TFP level at the same point in time. Furthermore, international openness, coastal–inland market integration, and human capital accumulation of the region all positively affect TFP growth in this region. Formally, we hypothesize that TFP growth in an inland region is governed by

$$\frac{A_{i,t+1}}{A_{it}} = \left(\frac{A_{it}^{*}}{A_{it}}\right)^{\lambda} \tag{6.4}$$

where $\lambda > 0$, and A_{it}^{*} denotes the potential (target) TFP level of region i at time t. This equation captures our earlier hypothesis that the TFP growth of an inland Chinese region at a certain point in time is positively affected by the size of the gap between actual and target TFP levels of the region at the same point in time. In order to model the expected positive effects of international openness, coastal–inland market integration, and human capital accumulation on TFP growth, we further assume that A_{it}^{*} is determined by

$$A_{it}^* = C_i O_{it}^\pi M_{it}^\mu h_{it}^\omega W_t \qquad (6.5)$$

where $\pi > 0$, $\mu > 0$, and $\omega > 0$. C_i captures a set of time-constant region-specific factors that influence TFP growth in region i. O_{it} represents the level of direct openness of the inland region to international economic activities. M_{it} represents the degree of coastal–inland market integration between this inland region and coastal regions in China.[5] h_{it}, as defined earlier, is the level of per-worker human capital stock. Finally, W_t denotes the world frontier TFP, which is assumed to grow exogenously over time.

Taking logs on both sides of Eqs. 6.4 and 6.5 yields, respectively

$$\ln A_{i,t+1} - \ln A_{it} = \lambda(\ln A_{it}^* - \ln A_{it}) \qquad (6.6)$$

$$\ln A_{it}^* = \ln C_i + \pi \ln O_{it} + \mu \ln M_{it} + \omega \ln h_{it} + \ln W_t \quad (6.7)$$

Inserting Eqs. 6.7 into 6.6 gives

$$\ln A_{i,t+1} - \ln A_{it} = \lambda(\ln W_t - \ln A_{it}) + \lambda\pi \ln O_{it} + \lambda\mu \ln M_{it}$$
$$+ \lambda\omega \ln h_{it} + \lambda \ln C_i \qquad (6.8)$$

Eq. 6.8 shows that the rate of TFP growth of inland region i at time t is dependent on (at least) five factors. First, the wider the gap between local TFP and world frontier TFP, the faster local TFP tends to grow, probably through a process of technology diffusion from the world frontier to the local Chinese region. A higher level of frontier technology (relative to the level of local technology) leads to faster technology diffusion so that local TFP grows faster. Second, the local TFP growth rate is positively related to the level of direct openness of the local region to international economic activities (such as foreign trade and FDI). As mentioned earlier, international openness implies that the local region can achieve growth in TFP via specialization gains due to foreign trade or via technology diffusion from foreign countries due to inflows of FDI. Third, the local TFP growth rate is positively related to the degree of coastal–inland market integration (between the local inland region and coastal regions in China). This coastal–inland market integration implies that an inland region can achieve TFP growth by taking advantage of specialization gains due to coastal–inland interregional trade or of technology diffusion from higher TFP coastal regions. Fourth, local TFP growth is also positively related to the level of per-worker human capital stock in the region, which is thought to be a crucial determinant of the ability of the local region to adopt technologies, say, from the world technology frontier, as better educated workers have a comparative advantage in implementing new technologies (Benhabib and Spiegel, 1994; Prescott, 1998). Fifth, regional TFP growth may also depend on a set of time-constant region-specific factors that are usually hard to observe.

To take account of potential interactions between international openness, coastal–inland market integration, and human capital accumulation, we allow parameters π, μ, and ω to be variables in themselves. That is, we assume

$$\pi = \pi_0 + \pi_1 \ln M_{it} + \pi_2 \ln h_{it} \tag{6.9}$$

$$\mu = \mu_0 + \mu_1 \ln O_{it} + \mu_2 \ln h_{it} \tag{6.10}$$

$$\omega = \omega_0 + \omega_1 \ln O_{it} + \omega_2 \ln M_{it} \tag{6.11}$$

Inserting Eqs. 6.9, 6.10, and 6.11 into Eq. 6.8 yields

$$\ln A_{i,t+1} = \lambda \ln W_t + (1 - \lambda) \ln A_{it} + \beta_1 \ln O_{it} + \beta_2 \ln M_{it} + \beta_3 \ln h_{it}$$
$$+ \delta_1 \ln O_{it} \ln M_{it} + \delta_2 \ln O_{it} \ln h_{it} + \delta_3 \ln M_{it} \ln h_{it}$$
$$+ \lambda \ln C_i \tag{6.12}$$

where we define $\beta_1 \equiv \lambda \pi_0$, $\beta_2 \equiv \lambda \mu_0$, $\beta_3 \equiv \lambda \omega_0$, $\delta_1 \equiv \lambda(\pi_1 + \mu_1)$, $\delta_2 \equiv \lambda(\pi_2 + \omega_1)$, and $\delta_3 \equiv \lambda(\mu_2 + \omega_2)$. Eq. 6.12 allows us to formulate our baseline empirical model as follows

$$\ln A_{i,t+1} = \eta_t + \gamma \ln A_{it} + \beta_1 \ln O_{it} + \beta_2 \ln M_{it} + \beta_3 \ln h_{it}$$
$$+ \delta_1 \ln O_{it} \ln M_{it} + \delta_2 \ln O_{it} \ln h_{it} + \delta_3 \ln M_{it} \ln h_{it}$$
$$+ \nu_i + \varepsilon_{it} \tag{6.13}$$

where $\gamma \equiv 1 - \lambda$, η_t is the time intercept, ν_t is time-constant region heterogeneity, and ε_{it} is idiosyncratic error. Coefficients on the explanatory variables in Eq. 6.13 have the following partial effect interpretations

$$\partial \ln A_{i,t+1} / \partial \ln A_{it} = \gamma \tag{6.14}$$

$$\partial \ln A_{i,t+1} / \partial \ln O_{it} = \beta_1 + \delta_1 \ln M_{it} + \delta_2 \ln h_{it} \tag{6.15}$$

$$\partial \ln A_{i,t+1} / \partial \ln M_{it} = \beta_2 + \delta_1 \ln O_{it} + \delta_3 \ln h_{it} \tag{6.16}$$

$$\partial \ln A_{i,t+1} / \partial \ln h_{it} = \beta_3 + \delta_2 \ln O_{it} + \delta_3 \ln M_{it} \tag{6.17}$$

Eq. 6.14 shows that an estimated value of γ that is lower than unity (remembering $\gamma \equiv 1 - \lambda$) implies there is a tendency for low-TFP regions to catch up, where the parameter λ measures the speed of (conditional) convergence of TFP among inland regions. Eqs. 6.15, 6.16, and 6.17 show, in a symmetrical way, that the partial effect of each of the three variables, $\ln O_{it}$, $\ln M_{it}$, and $\ln h_{it}$, depends on the levels of the other two variables.

The variables and data

Our sample comprises 18 provincial-level inland divisions in China over the period 1996–2011. As mentioned in Note 3 on p. 94, these inland regions are Shanxi, Inner Mongolia, Jilin, Heilongjiang, Anhui, Jiangxi, Henan, Hubei, Hunan, Guangxi, Sichuan, Guizhou, Yunnan, Shaanxi, Gansu, Qinghai, Ningxia, and Xinjiang. Two inland regions, Tibet and Chongqing, are not included in our sample owing to missing data. The coastal regions involved in this study comprise ten provincial-level coastal divisions: Beijing, Tianjin, Hebei, Liaoning, Shanghai, Jiangsu, Zhejiang, Fujian, Shandong, and Guangdong. One coastal province, Hainan, is not included owing to missing data.

We need to obtain data on the variables in Eq. 6.13, especially the TFP variable A, the international openness variable O, the domestic coastal–inland market integration variable M, and the (per-worker) human capital variable h. We discuss the construction of each of these variables one by one in the following subsections.

Regional human capital intensity

As can be seen from our specification of the production function in Eq. 6.1, our measure of human capital stock H augments raw labor L by h, where the level of regional human capital intensity h is usually assumed to be a function of the distribution of educational attainment of the labor force in the region. Therefore, the method we use here for calculating regional human capital intensity h essentially follows Hall and Jones (1999), Aiyar and Feyrer (2002), and Jiang (2012b), who assume that h is related to educational attainment by $\ln h = \rho(E)$, where E denotes the average number of years of schooling attained by a worker in the labor force. The function $\rho(E)$ indicates the relative efficiency of one worker with E years of schooling compared with one with zero schooling (where $\rho(0) = 0$). The derivative $d\rho(E)/dE$ is the return to schooling estimated in a Mincerian wage regression (Mincer, 1974). In Hall and Jones (1999), Aiyar and Feyrer (2002), and Jiang (2012b), $\rho(E)$ is assumed to be piecewise linear, with the rates of return being 13.4, 10.1, and 6.8 percent, respectively, for the first four years of schooling, the second four years, and that beyond the eighth year. These rates of return are all based on Psacharopoulos (1994)'s survey of evidence from many countries on return-to-schooling estimates.[6]

In this study, our measure of per-worker human capital in inland region i at time t (i.e., h_{it}), is constructed as

$$h_{it} = (1/L_{it}^{6+}) \sum_j h^j L_{it}^j \qquad (6.18)$$

where $\sum_j L_{it}^j = L_{it}^{6+}$ ($j = a, b, c, d, e$). L_{it}^{6+} denotes the population aged 6 and over in inland region i at time t, which is divided into five groups by educational attainment, group a through group e. L_{it}^a is the total number of people aged 6 and over who have received zero schooling while L_{it}^b through L_{it}^e are, respectively, the total number of people aged 6 and over who have received schooling up to primary school level, junior secondary school level, senior secondary school level, and university level.[7] h^a through h^e are per-worker human capital in each of the five groups, respectively. Therefore, regional per-worker human capital h_{it} is a weighted average of the h^j ($j = a, b, c, d, e$), with the respective weight being L_{it}^j/L_{it}^{6+}.

Data on L_{it}^j/L_{it}^{6+} ($j = a, b, c, d, e$) for the 18 inland Chinese regions for each year in the period 1996–2011 can be found in the corresponding issues of the *China Statistical Yearbook*.[8] Constructing h_{it} thus boils down to determining the values of the h^j ($j = a, b, c, d, e$). Obviously, $h^a = 1$ must hold by construction. We further set $h^b = 2.01$, $h^c = 2.60$, $h^d = 3.16$, and $h^e = 4.39$ (for all the inland regions in each year of our sample period). These values are calculated according to the aforementioned piecewise linear rates of return to schooling based on the survey of Psacharopoulos (1994).[9] In passing, it should be noted that there is no need to worry about nationwide change in the quality of education (in terms of its ability to enhance human capital) over time. Instead, all we need to focus on here is cross-sectional (cross-region) comparison of the levels of regional human capital intensity at any given t. This is because the variable h_{it} enters the regression equation (Eq. 6.13) in log form so that any nationwide time trend in h_{it} will be directly captured by the time intercept term in the regression equation (i.e., the η_t term in Eq. 6.13).

Calculated levels of regional human capital intensity for the 18 inland provinces in selected years (1996, 2002, and 2008) during the 1996–2011 period are graphically shown and compared in Figure 6.1.

The level of regional TFP

The level of TFP for region i at time t (i.e., A_{it}) can be obtained by applying Eq. 6.3, where $\ln A_{it}$ can be calculated as a residual. In order to do so, we need to first obtain the level of physical stock K_{it} and the corresponding

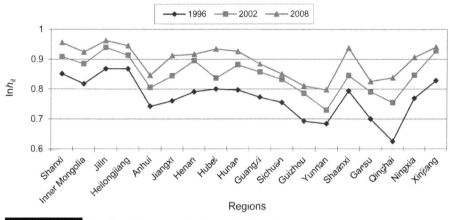

| Figure 6.1 | Levels of human capital intensity in selected years |

Note: Calculated levels of regional human capital intensity for the 18 inland provinces in selected years (i.e., 1996, 2002, and 2008) during 1996–2011 are shown and compared.

level of per-worker physical stock k_{it}. However, the *China Statistical Yearbook* does not provide direct data on regional physical capital stock for China's regions. Therefore, to calculate K_{it}, we follow the basic procedure of Zhang (2008), who uses a perpetual inventory method (PIM) to construct physical capital stock data for China's regions, taking special care of issues related to the initial levels of physical capital stock, capital deflators, depreciation rates, and missing data. By following Zhang (2008) we specifically assume that the annual depreciation rates of physical capital are uniformly 9.6 percent for all inland regions throughout our sample period.

Having calculated the panel of regional physical capital stock K_{it}, it then becomes straightforward to obtain the corresponding levels of regional per-worker physical capital stock k_{it} by applying the definition $k_{it} \equiv K_{it}/L_{it}$, where the total number of employed persons (i.e., workers, L_{it}) for the 18 inland regions in 1996–2011 are directly available from the corresponding issues of the *China Statistical Yearbook*. Series of nominal gross regional product (GRP) and GRP indexes for each region i are also available from the *Yearbooks*, so that the values of real GRP can be calculated. Real per-worker output y_{it} in Eq. 6.3 is then calculated as real GRP divided by the total number of employed persons.

We need to assume an appropriate value of the structural parameter α in Eq. 6.3 to calculate the panel of regional TFP levels. Alternatively, the value of α can be estimated by using a regression approach based on Eq. 6.3. However, we are deeply uncomfortable with this approach because the endogeneity problem of $\ln k_{it}$ is difficult to address. Therefore, our preference here is to use independent evidence to determine the appropriate value of α and then use this value of α to construct the levels of $\ln A_{it}$ according to Eq. 6.3. There is some evidence showing that α is close to 0.5 in the case of China (Chow and Li, 2002; Chow, 2008; Zheng et al., 2009; Brandt and Zhu, 2010; Jiang, 2012a). For example, Brandt and Zhu (2010) point out that the factor share of capital α is roughly 0.5 in non-agricultural sectors and about 0.3 in the agricultural sector according to the national income accounts and the national input–output tables constructed by the National Bureau of Statistics of China (NBS). However, they argue that the high-factor share of labor in agriculture is inconsistent with estimates obtained based on household data, which suggest a labor share in the vicinity of 0.5. As a result, Brandt and Zhu (2010) assume that α is 0.5 for all the sectors in their study throughout their sample period. In our present study, we follow prior research and assume $\alpha = 0.5$ when calculating the panel of regional TFP levels for China's inland regions.[10]

Calculated levels of regional TFP for the 18 inland provinces in selected years (1996, 2005, and 2011) during the overall 1996–2011 period are graphically shown and compared in Figure 6.2. To take a closer look at the calculated levels of provincial TFP, we compare the TFP levels of the 18 inland provinces in 2011 with those of coastal provinces in China in Table 6.1. The first column lists our calculated levels of regional TFP for western inland provinces (those located in the west of China) while the middle

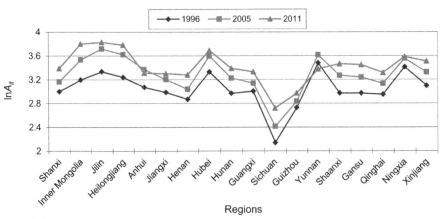

Figure 6.2 **Levels of TFP in selected years**

Note: Calculated levels of regional TFP for the 18 inland provinces in selected years (i.e., 1996, 2005, and 2011) during 1996–2011 are shown and compared.

Table 6.1 Calculated levels of regional TFP in 2011

Inland–western		Inland–central		Coastal	
Province	**TFP**	**Province**	**TFP**	**Province**	**TFP**
Guangxi	0.923	Shanxi	1.000	Beijing	1.400
Sichuan	0.586	Inner Mongolia	1.536	Tianjin	2.750
Guizhou	0.672	Jilin	1.422	Hebei	1.376
Yunnan	0.870	Heilongjiang	1.406	Liaoning	1.977
Shaanxi	1.108	Anhui	0.812	Shanghai	3.664
Gansu	1.029	Jiangxi	0.879	Jiangsu	1.651
Qinghai	0.950	Henan	0.876	Zhejiang	1.419
Ningxia	1.156	Hubei	1.302	Fujian	1.670
Xinjiang	1.087	Hunan	0.997	Shandong	1.470
				Guangdong	1.430
Average	**0.931**	**Average**	**1.137**	**Average**	**1.881**

The calculated level of TFP for Shanxi (in 2011) is normalized to unity.

column lists those levels for central inland provinces (inland provinces not located in the west of China). For comparison purposes, the last column lists the corresponding levels of regional TFP for the 10 coastal provinces in China.[11] Unlike Figure 6.2, the TFP levels given in Table 6.1 are calculated levels of A_{it}, rather than its log form $\ln A_{it}$. To ease comparison between provinces, the level of A_{it} for the province Shanxi (in 2011) is normalized to unity in Table 6.1.

International openness

We need to construct the openness variable O that appears (in log form) on the right-hand side of Eq. 6.13. One basic openness indicator commonly used in the literature is the ratio of foreign trade to output. That is

$$f_{it} \equiv \frac{F_{it}}{GRP_{it}} \tag{6.19}$$

where F_{it} and GRP_{it} are, respectively, the total real value of foreign trade (exports plus imports) and the total value of real GRP in region i at time t. f_{it} is therefore an indicator of the degree of openness to foreign trade of region i at time t. The panel of f_{it} can be easily calculated, as relevant data on F_{it} are directly available from the annual issues of the *China Statistical Yearbook*.

In our current study, however, we adjust the openness indicator in Eq. 6.19 to take account of differences in region size and the level of development. It has often been argued that a large country (or region) in terms of output or population tends to have (relatively) less foreign trade, as there is larger scope for trade within the country (or region). It has also been argued that a country (or region) with a high level of per-capita output may be biased toward having a lower trade–output ratio, because the share of the service sector tends to increase while the service sector is largely non-tradable as the country (or region) develops (Low et al., 1998). To correct for the differences in region size and the level of development, we follow the method of Low et al. (1998) and consider this regression

$$\ln f_{it} = \vartheta_0 + \vartheta_1 GRP_{it} + \vartheta_2 GRP_{it}^2 + \vartheta_3 pop_{it} + \vartheta_4 pop_{it}^2$$
$$+ \vartheta_5(GRP_{it}/pop_{it}) + \vartheta_6(GRP_{it}/pop_{it})^2 + u_{it}^f \qquad (6.20)$$

where u_{it}^f is the error term, and pop_{it} stands for regional population, data on which can also be obtained from the *China Statistical Yearbook*. We run a pooled OLS regression based on the specification in Eq. 6.20 and construct the corresponding fitted value, denoted $\hat{f}_{it}$, such that

$$\ln \hat{f}_{it} = \hat{\vartheta}_0 + \hat{\vartheta}_1 GRP_{it} + \hat{\vartheta}_2 GRP_{it}^2 + \hat{\vartheta}_3 pop_{it} + \hat{\vartheta}_4 pop_{it}^2$$
$$+ \hat{\vartheta}_5(GRP_{it}/pop_{it}) + \hat{\partial}_6(GRP_{it}/pop_{it})^2 \qquad (6.21)$$

where the $\hat{\vartheta}$'s are the values of intercepts and slopes in Eq. 6.20 estimated from the pooled OLS regression. This is an appropriate moment to point out that the regression equation (Eq. 6.20) does not contain a time-variant intercept on its right-hand side. Nor have we opted for other regression methods, such as the within estimator, to obtain the $\hat{\vartheta}$'s in Eq. 6.21. This is because the plain (pooled) OLS regression we use here, which considers neither a time-variant intercept nor region heterogeneity, leaves exactly what we want to keep in the error term. This point will become clearer in Eq. 6.23.

$\hat{f}_{it}$, calculated according to Eq. 6.21, indicates what the 'normal' or average degree of openness an inland Chinese region would have, given the level of regional GRP and the size of regional population. Following this idea, our adjusted openness variable to be used in the regression model in Eq. 6.13 is then constructed as

$$O_{it} \equiv \frac{f_{it}}{\hat{f}_{it}} \tag{6.22}$$

This adjusted openness variable, which will be our measure of the degree of international openness of an inland Chinese region, indicates what the openness deviation of region i is with respect to the 'normal' level of openness of inland regions that have output and population of the same size. Taking logs on both sides of Eq. 6.22 yields

$$\ln O_{it} = \ln f_{it} - \ln \hat{f}_{it} - \hat{u}_{it}^f \tag{6.23}$$

where $\hat{u}_{it}^f$ is obviously the residual (for each region i at each time t) obtained from our pooled OLS regression.

Domestic coastal–inland market integration

In this subsection we construct the variable for domestic coastal–inland market integration, M, in Eq. 6.13. We basically follow the price-based approach used by Parsley and Wei (2001) and Sheng and Mao (2011) to do this. The central idea behind this price-based approach is that the dispersion (across goods) of common currency price differentials of identical goods between two countries (or regions) can serve as an inverse indicator of the degree of market integration between the two countries (or regions).

Let $p(i, t, k)$ be the price of good k in inland region i at time t and $p(j, t, k)$ the price of good k in coastal region j at time t. We define

$$D(ij, t, k) \equiv \ln \left[\frac{p(i, t, k)}{p(i, t - 1, k)} \right] - \ln \left[\frac{p(j, t, k)}{p(j, t - 1, k)} \right] \tag{6.24}$$

which measures the difference between inland region i and coastal region j in the percentage change of the price of good k during the interval $(t - 1, t)$. A useful way to study inland–coastal goods market integration is to study the cross-sectional dispersion (across goods) of $D(ij, t, k)$ for each inland–coastal region pair and time period. Any particular realization of $D(ij, t, k)$ can be positive or negative without triggering arbitrage as long as the absolute value of $D(ij, t, k)$ is lower than the cost of arbitrage. The existence of the arbitrage cost implies that $D(ij, t, k)$ must fall within a range – not that it must equal or trend toward zero (Parsley and Wei, 2001). Any reduction in the barriers to trade should thus reduce the no-arbitrage range. Therefore, the dispersion of $D(ij, t, k)$ across goods can be an inverse indicator of the degree of market integration between inland region i and coastal region j at time t.

We can take another step before we calculate dispersion. We remove the time t mean of $D(ij, t, k)$ (across region pairs) for each good k separately, in order to filter goods-specific effects from our dispersion calculation. Mathematically, we define

$$\ddot{D}(ij, t, k) \equiv D(ij, t, k) - \bar{D}(t, k) \qquad (6.25)$$

where $\bar{D}(t, k)$ denotes the mean of $D(ij, t, k)$ across ij region pairs. Having constructed $\ddot{D}(ij, t, k)$ in this way by de-meaning $D(ij, t, k)$, we then calculate the variance (as our measure of dispersion) of $\ddot{D}(ij, t, k)$, rather than that of $D(ij, t, k)$, across all goods for each inland–coastal region pair ij and time period t, and denote this variance as $\text{var}[\ddot{D}(ij, t)]$. In order to construct the coastal–inland market integration variable M_{it} (for inland region i at time t) in Eq. 6.13, we need to sum all such variances $\text{var}[\ddot{D}(ij, t)]$ for any given i (i.e., inland region) at time t over all the j's (i.e., all coastal regions). To do this, we define

$$V(i, t) \equiv \sum_{j} \text{var}[\ddot{D}(ij, t)] \qquad (6.26)$$

Finally, we construct our coastal–inland market integration variable M_{it} as follows

$$M_{it} \equiv \frac{1}{\sqrt{V(i, t)}} \qquad (6.27)$$

Because the variable M_{it} enters our regression specification equation (Eq. 6.13) in log form, it makes sense to write Eq. 6.27 in log form as well

$$\ln M_{it} = -(1/2) \ln V(i, t) \qquad (6.28)$$

We need to select a specific set of k (types of) goods to construct Eqs. 6.24–6.28. Based on the data availability of the *Yearbooks*, the k types of goods we select in this study are (a) grain, (b) oil and fat, (c) meat, poultry, and related processed products, (d) eggs, (e) fish and shellfish, (f) vegetables, (g) fresh and dried fruit, (h) tobacco, (i) liquor, (j) garments, (k) clothing fabric, (l) footwear and hats, (m) durable consumer goods, (n) daily use household articles, and (o) cosmetics.

Regressions and results

In this section we carry out our regression analysis and present the results. Subsection 4.1 introduces the regression methods used in this analysis. In Subsection 4.2 we present and discuss our regression results.

Regression methods

The very fact of our baseline empirical model (Eq. 6.13) being dynamic in nature renders the pooled OLS estimator and the random effects (RE) estimator inconsistent. In such a dynamic structure, however, the fixed effects (FE) estimator is still valid in a sense: though in this case the FE estimator is inconsistent when asymptotic properties are viewed from the $N \to \infty$ direction, but proves to be consistent (and asymptotically equivalent to the maximum likelihood estimator) when they are viewed from the $T \to \infty$ direction (Amemiya, 1967; Islam, 1995). Therefore, FE estimation is one of the regression methods we opt for in this chapter. Besides this FE method, we use a variety of other panel data regression methods including the FD (first-differencing) and FD 2SLS (first-differenced two-stage least squares) estimators. We also use a dynamic GMM method to generate and compare our regression results.

The FD 2SLS and GMM methods used in this chapter are based on the 'sequential exogeneity' assumption (see, for example, Wooldridge, 2001), which implies that the error term is taken to be uncorrelated with current and past (and in certain cases only the past) values of explanatory variables. Our regression specification in Eq. 6.13 necessarily violates the 'strict exogeneity' assumption owing to its dynamic nature. However, the sequential exogeneity assumption can be applied in such a case. Under this assumption, a general approach to estimating Eq. 6.13 is to first use a transformation to remove unobserved effects and then search for instrumental variables. As strictly exogenous instruments are difficult to come by, we cannot in the present analysis use the FE transformation to remove the unobserved effect. Therefore, we use a 2SLS method based on FD transformation. We can write out a dynamic panel data model like this

$$y_{it} = \gamma y_{i,t-1} + \sum_{j=1}^{k} \beta_j x_{it}^j + \eta_t + \nu_i + \varepsilon_{it} \tag{6.29}$$

the FD transformation yields

$$\Delta y_{it} = \gamma \Delta y_{i,t-1} + \sum_{j=1}^{k} \beta_j \Delta x_{it}^j + \Delta \eta_t + \Delta \varepsilon_{it} \qquad (6.30)$$

where $\Delta y_{it} \equiv y_{it} - y_{i,t+1}$ and so forth. Under the sequential exogeneity assumption, we have

$$E(\mathbf{w}_{ijis}' \varepsilon_{it}) = \mathbf{0}, \quad s = 1, 2, \ldots, t \qquad (6.31)$$

where $\mathbf{w}_{is} \equiv (y_{i,s-1}, x_{is}^j), j = 1, 2, \ldots, k$. Eq. 6.31 implies the orthogonality conditions

$$E(\mathbf{w}_{is}' \Delta \varepsilon_{it}) = \mathbf{0}, \quad s = 1, 2, \ldots, t - 1 \qquad (6.32)$$

Therefore, at time t we can use $\mathbf{w}_{i,t-1}^0$ as potential instruments for $\Delta \mathbf{w}_{it}$, where $\mathbf{w}_{it}^0 \equiv (\mathbf{w}_{i1}, \mathbf{w}_{i2}, \ldots, \mathbf{w}_{it})$. This forms the basis of this chapter's dynamic panel data approach. In the FD 2SLS and GMM estimations we present below, we employ subsets of $\mathbf{w}_{i,t-1}^0$ as instrumental variables for (a subset of) $\Delta \mathbf{w}_{it}$ with respect to FD transformation of our regression specification in Eq. 6.13.

In passing, we should point out that the extended GMM method proposed by Blundell and Bond (2000), in which lagged first differences are also used as instruments for levels equations, is generally considered to work better than the standard first-differenced GMM method when variables are so highly persistent that lagged values are only weakly correlated with subsequent first differences. However, in the present analysis we do not choose to use this extended GMM method – owing to the fact that the series of variables in our regressions turn out later not to be highly persistent.

In practice, however, we use a variant of Eq. 6.13 as our regression equation in all our regressions, which goes as

$$\ln A_{i,t+1} = \eta_0 + \varphi_1 d99 + \varphi_2 d02 + \varphi_3 d05 + \varphi_4 d08 + \gamma \ln A_{it} + \beta_1 \ln \bar{O}_{it}$$

$$+ \beta_2 \ln \bar{M}_{it} + \beta_3 \ln \bar{h}_{it} + \delta_1 \ln \bar{O}_{it} \ln \bar{M}_{it} + \delta_2 \ln \bar{O}_{it} \ln \bar{h}_{it}$$

$$+ \delta_3 \ln \bar{M}_{it} \ln \bar{h}_{it} + v_i + \varepsilon_{it} \qquad (6.33)$$

The total sample period of 1996–2011 is partitioned into five 3-year spans: 1996–1999, 1999–2002, 2002–2005, 2005–2008, and 2008–2011. That is to say, the variables $\ln A_{i,t+1}$ and $\ln A_{it}$ in Eq. 6.33 are three calendar years apart (i.e., when A_{it} pertains to 1996, $A_{i,t+1}$ would pertain to 1999, and so forth). The values of variables with bars, $\bar{O}_{it}$, $\bar{M}_{it}$, and $\bar{h}_{it}$, are calculated as averages over the corresponding 3-year spans (i.e., when t pertains to 1996, $\bar{O}_{it}$ is then calculated as the arithmetic average of its three yearly values in

1996, 1997, and 1998, and so forth). Using such a setup, transitory error terms are three calendar years apart and hence may be less likely to be serially correlated than is the case in a yearly data setup (Islam, 1995). In addition, to account for the time-variant intercept η_t in Eq. 6.13, we design and include four period dummy variables (denoted by $d99$, $d02$, $d05$, and $d08$, along with a common intercept η_0) in Eq. 6.33 to take care of secular changes associated with the four time spans other than just the first span 1996–1999.

Regression results

Table 6.2 summarizes the major regression results of our estimation methods. For brevity's sake, we do not report estimated intercepts (i.e., the estimated common intercept and estimated coefficients on the four period dummy variables in this table). The first two regressions are regular FE and FD estimations. The third regression is a 2SLS estimation based on FD transformation. In this regression, we use the lags of explanatory variables in periods $(t-1)$ and $(t-2)$ as instrumental variables for the first-differenced form of Eq. 6.33 at period t. The latter three regressions employ a panel data GMM method, the Arellano–Bond dynamic estimation (Arellano and Bond, 1991), in which all possible lags of dependent and independent variables are used as instrumental variables for the first-differenced form of Eq. 6.33 at period t. The first GMM regression in Table 6.2, denoted GMM(1), takes explanatory variables other than $\ln A_{it}$ as exogenous and uses all lags of $\ln A_{it}$ up to the period $(t-2)$ as instruments for the first-differenced form of Eq. 6.33 at period t. The second GMM regression, GMM(2), takes explanatory variables other than $\ln A_{it}$ as 'predetermined' and uses their lags up to period $(t-1)$ and all lags of $\ln A_{it}$ up to period $(t-2)$ as instruments for the first-differenced form of Eq. 6.33 at period t. The third GMM regression, GMM(3), takes all explanatory variables (besides $\ln A_{it}$) as endogenous and uses their lags up to period $(t-2)$ for the first-differenced form of Eq. 6.33 at period t.

Throughout the six regressions contained in Table 6.2, the estimated values of γ (the coefficient on $\ln A_{it}$) are all significantly greater than zero (which is no surprise) and significantly lower than unity at the usual 5 percent level.[12] Therefore, ceteris paribus, a higher initial level of TFP is associated with slower subsequent growth in TFP, and vice versa. This result basically shows that the 18 inland provinces in China have exhibited (conditional) convergence in TFP growth over the sample

Table 6.2	Summary of the major regression results of our estimation methods (dependent variable, $\ln A_{l,t+1}$; sample, 18 Chinese inland provinces, 1996–2011)

	Regressions					
Variables	FE	FD	FD 2SLS	GMM (1)	GMM (2)	GMM (3)
$\ln A_{it}$	0.812* [0.000]	0.631* [0.000]	0.604* [0.000]	0.686* [0.000]	0.717* [0.000]	0.841* [0.000]
$\ln \bar{O}_{it}$	−0.682 [0.663]	0.193 [0.502]	0.371 [0.660]	0.201 [0.403]	−0.135 [0.355]	0.293 [0.187]
$\ln \bar{M}_{it}$	0.508 [0.054]	0.825 [0.010]	0.668 [0.086]	0.545 [0.079]	0.648* [0.048]	0.820* [0.039]
$\ln \bar{h}_{it}$	1.040* [0.019]	0.714* [0.046]	1.163* [0.026]	1.249* [0.040]	1.178* [0.021]	1.485* [0.034]
$\ln \bar{O}_{it} \ln \bar{M}_{it}$	0.052 [0.843]	0.097 [0.612]	0.227 [0.653]	−0.004 [0.787]	0.083 [0.798]	0.148 [0.663]
$\ln \bar{O}_{it} \ln \bar{h}_{it}$	−0.344 [0.702]	0.146 [0.454]	−0.115 [0.801]	0.272 [0.444]	0.228 [0.423]	0.108 [0.241]
$\ln \bar{M}_{it} \ln \bar{h}_{it}$	0.419 [0.257]	0.850 [0.274]	0.528 [0.423]	0.395 [0.599]	0.632 [0.274]	0.761 [0.203]
No. observations	90	72	54	54	54	54

The asterisk * denotes significance at the 5 percent level. Related p-values are in brackets. The results of GMM regressions in this table are one-step results. For the sake of brevity, we do not report estimated intercepts (common intercepts and estimated coefficients on period dummy variables) in the table.

period. In all the six regressions, the estimated values of β_1 (the coefficient on $\ln \bar{O}_{it}$) are not significant at the 5 and 10 percent levels. For β_2 (the coefficient on $\ln \bar{M}_{it}$), all the six regressions produce significantly positive estimates at the 10 percent level while two of the six produce significantly positive estimates at the usual 5 percent level. In contrast, the estimated values of β_3 (the coefficient on $\ln \bar{h}_{it}$) generated by the six regressions are all significantly positive at the usual 5 percent level. The magnitudes of these estimates of β_3 are in the vicinity of unity. The estimated values of δ_1, δ_2, and δ_3 (the coefficients on the three interaction terms) are all very insignificant. In fact, for all the six regressions in Table 6.2, it can be shown that dropping the three interaction terms from the regression Eq. 6.33 does not change our estimated values of the three β's in any important way.

The significantly positive partial effect of $\ln \bar{h}_{it}$ on $\ln A_{i,t+1}$ can be understood as showing that human capital exerts a dual effect on the economic growth of China's inland provinces. On the one hand, human capital has a direct static impact on regional economic growth as an accumulable factor of production, while, on the other hand, human capital has an indirect dynamic impact on regional economic growth by promoting local TFP growth. Therefore, in this sense, when dealing with human capital, the dichotomy of factor accumulation and TFP growth provided by the traditional growth accounting approach can be misleading. This is because the traditional approach ignores the possibility of spillovers between factor accumulation and TFP growth. An important idea behind our empirical result of statistically significant (and in practice large) estimates of β_3 (the coefficient on $\ln \bar{h}_{it}$) may be that human capital is a crucial determinant of the ability of a backward economy (an inland province in China in the current case) to adopt new technologies and hence promote TFP growth in the production process. The key point is, as Benhabib and Spiegel (1994) have argued, the most important contribution of human capital to income growth may lie not in its direct effect as an accumulable factor in the production function, but in its salutary effect on TFP growth.

To gain further insights, we can measure and compare the relative magnitudes of the static and dynamic impacts of human capital. For simplicity, suppose there is a one-time permanent increase in a representative province's human capital intensity of 1 percent. From Eq. 6.2, we can easily see that this 1 percent increase in h_{it} immediately raises the province's output per capita by 0.5 percent, other relevant factors remaining constant.[13] However, this 0.5 percent instantaneous increase in per-capita output is only the direct static effect of human capital. According to Eq. 6.5 and our regression results in Table 6.2, this one-time shock in human capital intensity will lead to a long-run increase in TFP of about 5 percent.[14] That is to say, in the long run, after the indirect dynamic effect of the one-time shock in provincial human capital intensity has fully shown itself, output per capita will increase by a total of 3 percent.[15] Thus in our example the full indirect dynamic effect of this one-time increase in human capital intensity is roughly five times as large as its direct static effect on per-capita output. Neglecting the dynamic role of human capital as a TFP enhancer therefore overlooks the crucial link between human capital and output.

The role of human capital as a TFP enhancer is shown in an informal way in Figure 6.3, which is a scatterplot of the levels of provincial TFP against the levels of provincial human capital intensity, using pooled data of 1996–

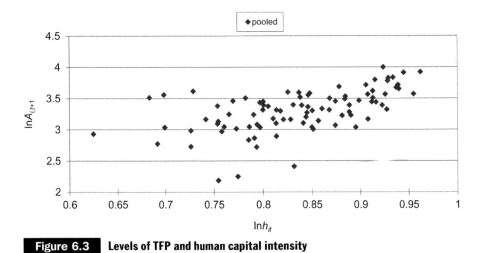

Figure 6.3   **Levels of TFP and human capital intensity**

Note: This scatterplot uses pooled data of 1996–2011 (90 observations). Levels (in logs) of provincial human capital intensity are measured on the horizontal axis and levels (in logs) of subsequent provincial TFP (three calendar years apart) are measured on the vertical axis.

2011 (90 observations altogether). Levels (in logs) of provincial human capital intensity are measured on the horizontal axis and levels (in logs) of subsequent provincial TFP (three calendar years apart) are measured on the vertical axis. Figure 6.3 shows the positive relationship between the levels of regional TFP and the corresponding levels of regional human capital intensity.

Concluding remarks

In this chapter we focus on TFP growth in China's inland provinces. We empirically investigate the potential effects of three factors – international openness, domestic coastal–inland market integration, and human capital accumulation – on TFP growth in these inland provinces. Our key hypothesis is that TFP growth of an inland region in China is shaped by three factors: the level of direct openness of the region to international economic activities, the degree of domestic coastal–inland market integration between the region and coastal parts of China, and the level of per-worker human capital in this inland region. By using a variety of panel data regression techniques, we show that human capital accumulation does indeed play an important role in promoting local TFP growth in inland provinces. Our empirical results support

Benhabib and Spiegel (1994)'s argument that the most important contribution of human capital to income growth lies not in its static direct effect as an accumulable factor in the production function, but rather in its dynamic role in promoting TFP growth. To a lesser degree, our empirical results in this chapter are further evidence of the positive role coastal–inland market integration plays in promoting TFP growth in China's inland regions.

Notes

1. Works on economics are often classified according to JEL classification codes, a system set up by the *Journal of Economic Literature*.
2. A few exceptions include Madariaga and Poncet (2007), Ouyang and Fu (2012), and Özyurt and Mitze (2012).
3. In the empirical part of this chapter, the inland regions under study are 18 Chinese provincial-level divisions: Shanxi, Inner Mongolia, Jilin, Heilongjiang, Anhui, Jiangxi, Henan, Hubei, Hunan, Guangxi, Sichuan, Guizhou, Yunnan, Shaanxi, Gansu, Qinghai, Ningxia, and Xinjiang. Two inland regions, Tibet and Chongqing, are excluded owing to missing data.
4. See, for example, Hall and Jones (1999) for a justification of this functional form.
5. In the empirical part of this chapter, the coastal regions in China are 10 provincial-level divisions: Beijing, Tianjin, Hebei, Liaoning, Shanghai, Jiangsu, Zhejiang, Fujian, Shandong, and Guangdong. One coastal province, Hainan, is excluded owing to missing data.
6. The rate for the first four years, 13.4 percent, corresponds to the average return to an additional year of schooling in sub-Saharan Africa. The rate for the second four years, 10.1 percent, is the average return to an additional year of schooling worldwide, while that for schooling above the eighth year, 6.8 percent, is taken from the average return to an additional year in member countries of the OECD.
7. We undertake this five-group division on the regional population aged 6 and over only because data on the distribution of educational attainment of the regional employed population or working age population are not available.

8. The reported data are based on the *National Sample Survey on Population Changes* which is published annually.
9. To calculate h^e, we assume that a worker who has completed university has 17 years of schooling on average.
10. Cross-country studies such as those of Hall and Jones (1999) and Aiyar and Feyrer (2002) assume a value of 1/3 for α, because this value is broadly consistent with national income accounts data for developed countries. However, considering the evidence in the literature, we think that 1/3 is too low for China's regions.
11. Data on coastal provinces are obtained from the same data sources given earlier.
12. The 5 percent significance level is always applied, unless otherwise stated, when we discuss statistical significance in the present analysis.
13. We assume, as before, the output elasticity of capital is 0.5.
14. Based on the regression results in Table 6.1, we take λ to be about 0.2, and $\lambda\omega$ to be about 1.0 in Eq. 6.8. Therefore, we take ω to be about 5 in Eq. 6.5.
15. This is clearly seen when Eqs. 6.2 and 6.5 are combined. To keep the matter as simple as possible, we assume that all other relevant factors, including the technology frontier, remain unchanged throughout this exercise.

References

Abreu, M.; de Groot, H.L.F.; and Florax, R.J.G.M. (2005) 'Space and growth: a survey of empirical evidence and methods,' *Région et Développement*, **21**, 13–44.

Aiyar, S.; and Feyrer, J. (2002) *A Contribution to the Empirics of Total Factor Productivity* (Dartmouth College Working Paper No. 02-09), Hanover, NH: Dartmouth College.

Amemiya, T. (1967) *A Note on the Estimation of Balestra–Nerlove Models* (Technical Report No. 4), Stanford, CA: Institute for Mathematical Studies in Social Sciences, Stanford University.

Arellano, M.; and Bond, S.R. (1991) 'Some specification tests for panel data: Monte Carlo evidence and an application to employment equations,' *Review of Economic Studies*, **58**, 277–98.

Benhabib, J.; and Spiegel, M.M. (1994) 'The role of human capital in economic development: evidence from aggregate cross-country data,' *Journal of Monetary Economics*, **34**(2), 143–73.

Blundell, R.; and Bond, S. (2000) 'GMM estimation with persistent panel data: an application to production functions,' *Econometric Reviews*, **19**(3), 321–40.

Brandt, L.; and Zhu, Xiaodong (2010) *Accounting for China's Growth* (Working Paper tecipa-394), Toronto, Canada: Department of Economics, University of Toronto.

Chow, G.C. (2008) 'Another look at the rate of increase in TFP in China,' *Journal of Chinese Economic and Business Studies*, 6(2), 219–24.

Chow, G.C.; and Li, Kui-Wai (2002) 'China's economic growth: 1952–2010,' *Economic Development and Cultural Change*, 51(1), 247–56.

Fan, C.C.; and Sun, Mingjie (2008) 'Regional inequality in China, 1978–2006,' *Eurasian Geography and Economics*, 49(1): 1–20.

Fan, Shenggen; Kanbur, R.; and Zhang, Xiaobo (2009) 'Regional inequality in China: an overview,' in Shenggen Fan, R. Kanbur, and Xiaobo Zhang (Eds.) *Regional Inequality in China: Trends, Explanations and Policy Responses*, London: Routledge.

Fingleton, B; and López-Bazo, E. (2006) 'Empirical growth models with spatial effects,' *Papers in Regional Science*, 85(2), 177–98.

Hall, R.E.; and Jones, C.I. (1999), 'Why do some countries produce so much more output per worker than others?' *Quarterly Journal of Economics*, 114, 83–116.

Harrison, A.E. (1996) 'Openness and growth: a time series, cross-country analysis for developing countries,' *Journal of Development Economics*, 48(2), 419–47.

Islam, N. (1995) 'Growth empirics: a panel data approach,' *Quarterly Journal of Economics*, 110, 1127–70.

Jiang, Yanqing (2011) 'Understanding openness and productivity growth in China: an empirical study of the Chinese provinces,' *China Economic Review*, 22(3), 290–8.

Jiang, Yanqing (2012a) 'Openness, the spatial spillover effect of productivity, and regional growth of inland provinces in China,' *Review of Urban and Regional Development Studies*, 24(1/2), 1–16.

Jiang, Yanqing (2012b) 'Technology diffusion, spatial effects and productivity growth in the Chinese provinces,' *International Review of Applied Economics*, 26(5), 643–56.

Low, P.; Olarreaga, M.; and Suarez, J. (1998) *Does Globalization Cause a Higher Concentration of International Trade and Investment Flow?* (WTO Staff Working Paper ERAD-98-08), Geneva, Switzerland: Economic Research and Analysis Division, World Trade Organization.

Lucas, R.E. (2009) 'Trade and the diffusion of the Industrial Revolution,' *American Economic Journal: Macroeconomics*, 1(1), 1–25.

Madariaga, N.; and Poncet, S. (2007) 'FDI in Chinese cities: spillovers and impact on growth,' *The World Economy*, 30(5), 837–62.

Mincer, J. (1974) *Schooling, Experience, and Earnings*, New York: Columbia University Press.

Nelson, R.; and Phelps, E. (1966) 'Investment in humans, technological diffusion, and economic growth,' *American Economics Review*, 56, 69–75.

Ouyang, P.; and Fu, Shihe (2012) 'Economic growth, local industrial development and inter-regional spillovers from foreign direct investment: evidence from China,' *China Economic Review*, 23(2), 445–60.

Özyurt, S.; and Mitze, T. (2012) *The Spatial Dimension of Trade- and FDI-driven Productivity Growth in Chinese Provinces: A Global Cointegration Approach* (Ruhr Economic Paper No. 308), Dortmund, Germany: Westfälisches Institut für Wirtschaftsforschung, Ruhr-Universität Bochum, Universität Dortmund, Universität Duisberg-Essen..

Parsley, D.C.; and Wei, Shang-Jin (2001) *Limiting Currency Volatility to Stimulate Goods Markets Integration: A Price Based Approach* (NBER Working Paper No. 8468), Cambridge, MA: National Bureau of Economic Research.

Prescott, E.C. (1998) 'Needed: a theory of total factor productivity,' *International Economic Review*, 39(3), 525–51.

Psacharopoulos, G. (1994) 'Returns to investment in education: a global update,' *World Development*, 22, 1325–43.

Sheng, Bin; and Mao, Qilin (2011) 'Trade openness, domestic market integration, and provincial economic growth in China: 1985–2008,' *Journal of World Economy*, November, 44–66 [in Chinese].

Sisci, F. (2005) 'Is China headed for a social red alert?' *Asia Times Online*, 20 October 2005. Available from: *http://www.atimes.com/atimes/China_Business/GJ20Cb01.html*

WB (2005) *World Development Report 2006: Equity and Development*, New York: Oxford University Press [World Bank].

Wooldridge, J.M. (2001) *Econometric Analysis of Cross Section and Panel Data*, Cambridge, MA, MIT Press.

Yang, Ling; and Lahr, M.L. (2010) 'Sources of Chinese labor productivity growth: a structural decomposition analysis, 1987–2005,' *China Economic Review*, 21(4), 557–70.

Yin, Heng (2011) 'Characteristics of inter-regional income disparities in China,' *Social Sciences in China*, 32(3), 123–44.

Zhang, Jun (2008) 'Estimation of China's provincial capital stock (1952–2004) with applications,' *Journal of Chinese Economic and Business Studies*, 6(2), 177–96.

Zheng, Jinghai; and Hu, Angang (2006) 'An empirical analysis of provincial productivity in China (1979–2001),' *Journal of Chinese Economic and Business Studies*, 4(3), 221–39.

Zheng, Jinghai; Hu, Angang; and Bigsten, A. (2009) 'Measuring potential output in a rapidly developing economy: the case of China in comparison with the US and EU', *Federal Reserve Bank of St. Louis Review*, July/August, 317–42.

7

Economic change and restructuring, dual economy, and development strategies

Abstract: Openness to foreign trade and FDI increases the efficiency in which production factors are allocated by lifting barriers to the mobility of resources across different sectors. In this chapter we empirically examine the relationship between openness to foreign trade and FDI and China's structural change. Our regression results support the usefulness of the Lewis model for analyzing China's process of industrialization. Our empirical analyses also show that openness to foreign trade and FDI plays an important role in the process of China's structural transformation. The results suggest that regional openness promotes regional structural transformation in terms of labor share shifts from the agricultural to the manufacturing sector, and that structural transformation in poorer regions tends to be faster, as a result of which convergence in per-worker income can be seen across China's different regions.

Key words: economic change and restructuring, dual economy, industry mix, openness, productivity, the Lewis Model.

JEL classification codes: F41; O11; O57.[1]

Introduction

Openness to foreign trade and FDI affects the level of efficiency in which production factors are allocated. Various studies have revealed that barriers to the efficient allocation of labor and other production resources are key to explaining why some regions in China are less developed than others (Lee and Malin, 2009). The barriers are usually associated with the mobility of labor and human capital (Hayashi and Prescott, 2008; Vollrath, 2009), or with the capacity of technology innovation or adoption (Parente and Prescott, 1994). As labor and other production factors overcome the barriers and flow from low-productivity sectors into relatively higher productivity sectors, less developed regions will experience an overall growth in income because of the structural transformation in its industrial mix. Openness to foreign trade and FDI helps lift the barriers.

Indeed, as evidenced by its persistently high rate of growth over the past 35 years, China has experienced a dramatic transition involving substantial economic change and restructuring. For example, as millions of workers moved from the agricultural sector into the manufacturing and service sectors, the share of workers in agriculture declined from over 70 percent of all workers in 1978 to below 50 percent in 2003 (Dekle and Vandenbroucke, 2006). Meanwhile, overall labor productivity has been increasing at a very fast pace (Brandt et al., 2008). What is the relationship between the rapid growth of labor productivity and structural change in terms of labor shares in the industrial mix? More importantly, what roles do openness to foreign trade and inflows of FDI play in promoting economic change and restructuring in China's regions? This chapter strives to answer these and related questions.[2]

The rest of this chapter is structured as follows. In the second section 'A theoretical model', we present a basic model to illustrate structural change in terms of labor shares and technological progress. In the third section 'Decomposition of productivity growth', we break down labor productivity growth from the perspective of regional industry mix. In the fourth section 'Dual economy', we look at China's dual economy from the perspective of the Lewis growth model, focusing on the model's implications for China. In the fifth section 'Some empirical evidence', we complete our empirical analysis and report our major results.

A theoretical model

Before presenting the statistics and empirical analyses, it is helpful to take a look at a simple theoretical model, the model of Lucas (2009), for us to get a feel for the potential relationship between openness to trade and FDI, structural change in terms of sectoral labor shares, and overall output growth. To keep the model as simple as possible, we consider a world of one-sector economies, where in any single economy, output per capita is proportional to its stock of technology. There are two types of economies: the leading economies (the leaders) and the follower economies (the followers). In the leading economies, the stock of technology is assumed to grow exogenously at a constant rate:

$$A(t) = A_0 e^{gt} \qquad (7.1)$$

where A denotes the level of technology and g is the exogenous growth rate of technology. By contrast, accumulation of technology in a follower economy is determined by

$$\frac{da}{dt} = ga^{1-\theta}A^{\theta} \qquad (7.2)$$

where the level of technology in a follower economy is denoted by a. Eq. 7.2 implies that while output per capita of a leading economy grows at the constant exogenous rate g, output per capita of a follower economy grows at the rate

$$\omega = g\left(\frac{A}{a}\right)^{\sigma} \qquad (7.3)$$

where ω is greater than g because $A > a$. Therefore, a follower grows faster than a leader, at a rate that increases according to the size of the output gap, A/a, and the size of the spillover parameter, σ. We can reasonably assume that the magnitude of the spillover parameter σ is positively related to the degree of openness to foreign trade and FDI of the follower economy (e.g., a Chinese region) with respect to the rest of the world (the leading economies).

It can be shown that the solution to the differential equation for $a(t)$ with the initial value a_0 is

$$a(t, a_0) = A_0 e^{gt} \{1 - [1 - (a_0/A_0)^{\sigma}]e^{-g\sigma t}\}^{1/\sigma} \qquad (7.4)$$

Now this model can be extended to accommodate multiple sectors of an economy so as to study economic change and restructuring. Assume a dual economy where there are two sectors called 'farm' and 'city', respectively. A fraction $(1 - \lambda)$ of each unit of labor in the economy is allocated to the city sector, where it produces

$$y_c = a(1 - \lambda) \qquad (7.5)$$

The remaining fraction λ is allocated to the farm sector, where it produces y_f units of the same single-output good:

$$y_f = \Lambda a^{\xi} \lambda^{\eta} \qquad (7.6)$$

In Eq. 7.6 land per capita is taken to be fixed and is captured in the coefficient Λ. The parameter ξ is interpreted as reflecting a spillover effect of city technology on agricultural productivity. Labor is assumed to be mobile so that the equilibrium output is then given by

$$y(a) = \max_{\lambda}[\Lambda a^\xi \lambda^\eta + a(1 - \lambda)] \tag{7.7}$$

If an only if $\eta \Lambda a^\xi \lambda^{\eta-1} > a$, then $\lambda = 1$, otherwise λ is determined by the following

$$\lambda(a) = \left(\frac{\eta\Lambda}{a^{1-\xi}}\right)^{1/(1-\eta)} \tag{7.8}$$

Eqs. 7.7 and 7.8 imply the way in which the employment share in agriculture varies with output per capita. That is, when $a \to \infty$, $\lambda(a) \to 0$, which means the traditional agricultural sector eventually empties as the level of technology increases. Eq. 7.2 is now extended to the following form

$$\frac{da}{dt} = g[1 - \lambda(a)]^\varsigma a^{1-\sigma} A^\sigma \tag{7.9}$$

In Eq. 7.9 another parameter ς has been included. The new term $[1 - \lambda(a)]^\varsigma$ is seen as capturing an agglomeration effect, whereby the rate of technology inflow to any individual is an increasing function of the fraction of city labor.

Eqs. 7.8 and 7.9 jointly lead to

$$\frac{da}{dt} = g[1 - (\eta\Lambda/a^{1-\xi})^{1/(1-\eta)}]^\varsigma a^{1-\sigma} A^\sigma \tag{7.10}$$

Eq. 7.10 implies that the level of technology a will grow indefinitely if a is high enough. The agglomeration term will tend to unity and the follower economy will eventually behave exactly the same as in the previous one-sector model, with both the level and growth rate of its output approaching the values of the leading economy.

Decomposition of productivity growth

Following the idea of the model presented in the preceding section, we can now present some descriptive statistics on regional sectoral productivities for China's regions. Regional overall labor productivity can be broken down as $y = y_1 l_1 + y_2 l_2$, where y_1 and y_2 are the levels of productivity in the agricultural and non-agricultural sectors, respectively, while l_1 and l_2 are the corresponding sectoral labor shares, respectively (with $l_1 + l_2 = 1$ by construction). It is quite straightforward to obtain the following growth decomposition:

$$d \ln y = \frac{y_1 l_1}{y} d \ln y_1 + \frac{y_2 l_2}{y} d \ln y_2 + \frac{y_2 - y_1}{y} dl_2 \tag{7.11}$$

which shows there are three contributors to the growth of overall labor productivity: growth of agricultural labor productivity, growth of non-agricultural labor productivity, and an increase in the non-agricultural labor share.

Substantial disparities in labor productivity (and per-capita income) exist across China's different regions. Our own calculations show that, when China initiated its various economic reforms in 1978, the coefficient of variation (CV) of regional productivity across China's provinces was about 0.70.[3] In 2009, however, the corresponding CV dropped to 0.63. It declined gradually over the 1978–1989 period, rose steadily thereafter until it reached its peak of 0.76 in 2001, and then fell steadily to 0.63 by 2009.

To facilitate looking in greater detail at the characteristics of labor productivity growth across China's provinces, Table 7.1 shows the CV values of the various components in Eq. 7.11. Infinitesimal changes $d \ln y$, $d \ln y_1$, $d \ln y_2$, and dl_2 are calculated as corresponding annual changes from the previous year to the current year, and levels y, y_1, y_2, l_1, and l_2 are values of the current year. To avoid cluttering the notation, we drop province and year subscripts from the variables in Table 7.1. The values of y_1, y_2, l_1, and l_2 at the provincial level over 1981–2005 can be calculated using relevant data from the *China Statistical Yearbook* in its various annual issues. The agricultural sector includes farming, forestry, animal husbandry, fishery, and services in support of these industries. Table 7.1 shows the high CV of $d \ln y$ in 1981 results from the very high CV of $d \ln y_2$. Therefore, to a large degree, cross-province variation in productivity growth in 1981 can be explained by variation in non-agricultural productivity growth across China's provinces. Another high CV of $d \ln y$ (in 1990), however, appears to result from the joint high CV values of $d \ln y_2$ and dl_2, which suggests that growth in both non-agricultural productivity and non-agricultural labor share in this year contribute to overall provincial productivity growth in China's provinces.

To facilitate subsequent analysis, we rewrite Eq. 7.11 as

$$\delta_y = \delta_1 + \delta_2 + \delta_3 \tag{7.12}$$

where we define $\delta_y \equiv d \ln y$, $\delta_1 \equiv (y_1 l_1/y) \, d \ln y_1$, $\delta_2 \equiv (y_2 l_2/y) \, d \ln y_2$, and $\delta_3 \equiv [(y_2 - y_1)/y] \, dl_2$. The decomposition in Eq. 7.12 implies that the cross-sectional variance of provincial labor productivity growth δ_y can be broken down according to

$$1 = \frac{\text{Var}(\delta_{yi})}{\text{Var}(\delta_{yi})} = \frac{\text{Cov}(\delta_{yi}, \delta_{1i})}{\text{Var}(\delta_{yi})} + \frac{\text{Cov}(\delta_{yi}, \delta_{2i})}{\text{Var}(\delta_{yi})} + \frac{\text{Cov}(\delta_{yi}, \delta_{3i})}{\text{Var}(\delta_{yi})} \tag{7.13}$$

Table 7.1 CV values of the components of provincial productivity growth

Year	$d\ln y$	$d\ln y_1$	$d\ln y_2$	dl_2	$y_1 l_1/y$	$y_2 l_2/y$	$(y_2 - y_1)/y$
1981	0.99	0.77	3.36	2.50	0.38	0.21	0.34
1982	0.73	0.91	1.76	1.58	0.36	0.21	0.35
1983	0.61	1.20	0.68	1.73	0.34	0.19	0.40
1984	0.35	0.59	0.90	0.87	0.33	0.17	0.40
1985	0.28	0.85	0.75	0.48	0.37	0.17	0.35
1986	0.44	0.89	0.61	0.57	0.37	0.16	0.36
1987	0.31	0.52	0.61	1.28	0.37	0.16	0.37
1988	0.19	0.47	0.22	1.49	0.37	0.15	0.40
1989	0.33	1.36	0.25	1.35	0.38	0.14	0.38
1990	0.92	1.11	0.96	3.87	0.36	0.15	0.38
1991	0.38	4.15	0.33	1.83	0.38	0.14	0.36
1992	0.35	0.57	0.47	0.62	0.39	0.13	0.35
1993	0.26	0.46	0.31	0.84	0.41	0.12	0.38
1994	0.19	0.31	0.30	0.73	0.40	0.12	0.38
1995	0.25	0.40	0.38	0.98	0.40	0.12	0.38
1996	0.24	0.70	0.32	1.52	0.40	0.12	0.33
1997	0.30	0.88	0.38	2.29	0.42	0.12	0.33
1998	0.48	4.17	0.53	7.74	0.41	0.11	0.32
1999	0.47	3.58	0.44	13.10	0.44	0.10	0.33
2000	0.34	3.60	0.66	4.76	0.46	0.10	0.30
2001	0.35	1.33	0.63	11.64	0.45	0.09	0.39
2002	0.25	0.48	0.39	0.81	0.46	0.09	0.38
2003	0.30	0.66	0.59	1.19	0.47	0.08	0.34
2004	0.29	0.35	0.39	0.56	0.47	0.08	0.34
2005	0.29	0.52	0.53	1.18	0.48	0.08	0.34

The sample includes 31 province-level divisions in China. There are missing data for a few regions during the study period (1981–1985). Infinitesimal changes $d\ln y$, $d\ln y_1$, $d\ln y_2$, and dl_2 are calculated as annual changes from the previous year to the current year, and levels y, y_1, y_2, l_1 and l_2 are values of the current year.

We perform the decomposition in Eq. 7.13 on a yearly basis across China's 31 provinces. Our results show that during 1979–1991, cross-province variation in the agricultural component δ_1 explains on average over 50 percent of total cross-province variation in provincial productivity growth δ_y. By contrast, during 1992–2011 the agricultural component δ_1 contributes little to provincial productivity growth δ_y. Moreover, during most years between 1979 and 1991, cross-province variation in the non-agricultural component δ_2 explains on average about 50 percent of total cross-province variation in provincial productivity growth δ_y, while, during most years of 1992–2011, cross-province variation in δ_2 accounts for, on average, over 88 percent of total cross-province variation in δ_y. Overall, the non-agricultural component δ_2 takes the lion's share when accounting for disparities in provincial labor productivity growth across China's provinces over the period 1979–2011. We can perform a further decomposition with respect to δ_2 as

$$1 = \frac{\text{Var}(\ln \delta_2)}{\text{Var}(\ln \delta_2)} = \frac{\text{Cov}[\ln \delta_2, \ln(y_2 l_2 / y)]}{\text{Var}(\ln \delta_2)} + \frac{\text{Cov}[\ln \delta_2, \ln(d \ln y_2)]}{\text{Var}(\ln \delta_2)} \quad (7.14)$$

where we have dropped the subscript i for brevity's sake. Our results show that, compared with the non-agricultural sector's share in output (i.e., $y_2 l_2 / y$), non-agricultural productivity growth $d \ln y_2$ contributes overwhelmingly more to the non-agricultural component δ_2. In sum, we see that labor productivity growth in the non-agricultural sector plays the most important role when accounting for aggregate labor productivity growth in China's provinces throughout the period 1979–2011.

Dual economy: Lewis growth model and China

Even a cursory observation suggests the Chinese economy has many of the features that the Lewis growth model tries to capture (Islam and Yokota, 2008). This section discusses China's economic change and development in light of the Lewis growth model (Lewis, 1954), the hallmark of which is the assumption that an economy has a dual structure. We will use 'modern–traditional' terminology to describe the Lewis dualism. The first difference between the two sectors is that essentially the same type of labor has higher productivity in the modern sector than in the traditional sector. That is to say, the marginal product of labor in the modern sector MPM^M is greater than that in the traditional sector MPL^T (i.e., $MPM^M > MPL^T$). This inequality is a departure from the neoclassical assumption of perfect factor mobility and equalization of factor returns, and thus implies that total output may increase by moving labor from the traditional to the modern sector. The second difference between the two sectors is concerned with income distribution. In the modern sector, income distribution follows the rule $w^M = MPL^M$, where w^M is the wage rate in the modern sector. By contrast, in the traditional sector it is assumed that $w^T > MPL^T$, where w^T is the wage rate in the traditional sector, in which income distribution follows what is called a 'kinship/community rule'. This represents a second departure from the neoclassical economy. In general, two conditions are needed for these differences to emerge. One is that there should exist an abundance of labor in the traditional sector, relative to other production resources such as land. The second is that there should exist some restrictions on the free movement of labor from the traditional sector to the modern sector.

As Islam and Yokota (2008) point out, demographic disequilibrium – in which there is overpopulation or surplus labor in the traditional sector – often occurs in developing countries. Restrictions on labor mobility may be either formal or informal, and may come from either the traditional or modern sector side. In the traditional sector, various informal customs may discourage migration of labor to the modern sector, which is usually located in urban areas. In the case of China, the *Hukou* (household registration) system is a formal barrier to rural–urban labor movement. Higher living costs, loss of familial, social and environmental benefits, and entry restrictions by the modern sector and by the authorities of urban areas where the modern sector resides are all barriers to rural–urban migration. Given this, the assumption that $MPL^M > MPL^T$ is not difficult to justify. As for the other assumption, $w^T > MPL^T$, it should be noted that various institutional settings can accommodate the 'kinship/community' rule. Family farms, for example, may engage in output maximization instead of profit maximization, and push the employment of labor to very low marginal product levels. In the case of China, the Communes allow 'wages' to have a 'sharing' feature and be higher than the marginal product, so that the condition $w^T > MPL^T$ is met. Given all this, a dual economy such as China's is therefore characterized by the condition $MPL^M = w^M > w^T > MPL^T$.

The dualism of the economy enables the modern sector to grow by drawing labor from the traditional sector without having to raise its wage level. The relocation of labor from the traditional to the modern sector increases MPL^T without increasing w^T and w^M as long as $w^M > w^T > MPL^T$ holds. Only when the flow of labor pushes MPL^T up so high that it approaches w^T will a further flow of labor lead to increases in w^T, which in turn create pressure for w^M to rise. Ranis and Fei (1961), in their extension of the Lewis model, suggest that the marginal product curve of the traditional sector is characterized by three phases. In the first phase MPL^T is zero so that the movement of labor from the traditional to the modern sector does not result in any reduction in total output of the traditional sector. The second phase begins when MPL^T becomes positive. The second phase ends and the third phase begins when the marginal product of labor in the traditional sector catches up with the wage level, and any further flow of labor now pushes both the marginal product and wage level up in the traditional sector by more or less the same degree.

When applying the Lewis model to China, as Islam and Yokota (2008) point out, one faces several complications because of the country's specific institutional characteristics. First, the theoretical 'traditional–modern' dichotomy does not coincide with the empirical 'rural–urban' or 'agriculture–industry' dichotomy. On the one hand, there are many informal enterprises in China using pre-industrial technologies in the urban sector, while, on the other hand, the rural sector is also heterogeneous owing to the continuous emergence of township and village enterprises that use industrial technologies inside rural areas. Second, the Lewis model assumes that the labor flow proceeds ideally in an unrestricted fashion as industrialization deepens. This assumption does not hold true for China because of its *Hukou* system. Although *Hukou* restrictions have gradually been lifted, the system remains and the situation is still not one of free mobility of labor from the traditional to the modern sector. The situation is further complicated by the fact that China is currently neither under central planning or under a completely market system. The complicated institutional context in China, despite making empirical analysis more subtle and challenging, also provides more opportunities for revealing the impacts of institutional factors on the process of industrialization and expansion of the modern sector.

Some empirical evidence

We follow the procedure of Islam and Yokota (2008) to carry out our empirical analysis. The analysis requires comparison between the marginal product of labor and the wage level in the traditional sector. To obtain an estimation of the marginal product, we first estimate the production function of the agricultural sector, using province-level data. In this current analysis, we equate the theoretical traditional sector with China's 'agricultural' sector, rather than the 'rural' sector as a whole for reasons mentioned earlier. The basic specification for regression is given as

$$\ln Y_i = \beta_0 + \beta_L \ln L_i + \beta_R \ln R_i + \beta_K \ln K_i + \delta_E DE_i + \delta_W DW_i + u_i \quad (7.15)$$

where Y_i is the value added for the agricultural sector, and L_i, R_i, and K_i are labor, land, and capital, respectively, with i indexing the province. Using the value added, instead of gross output, as the dependent variable enables us to obviate the necessity of including 'materials' as an additional explanatory variable. Mainland China is divided into three big zones: the eastern (coastal) zone, the central zone, and the western zone. It is well known that as far as resource endowment, geographic and climatic conditions, market opportunities and institutions are concerned China differs more sharply interzonally than across provinces within the same zone. DE_i and DW_i are two zone dummy variables that take care of the eastern zone and western zone, respectively, while the central zone is arbitrarily taken as the base group. We assume that systematic differences in agricultural TFP across the different zones can be captured by individual zone intercepts (the coefficients on zone dummies) while random differences in TFP are subsumed in the error term u_i.

Owing to a shortage of data, we restrict the agricultural sector to the farming sub-sector, leaving out the sub-sectors of fishery, forestry, and animal husbandry. The labor variable can be calculated as the product of the total number of agricultural employees and the share of the farming sub-sector in the total value added of the agricultural sector. The land variable is taken as total sown area for farming. The capital variable is not directly available, so we use total power of agricultural machinery to proxy for agricultural capital stock. Cross-sectional data are applied to estimate Eq. 7.15 for each individual year in the sample period. In general, regression results are unsatisfactory in that the partial effects of both the labor variable and the capital variable turn out to be insignificant. For the capital variable, the problem probably lies in using total power of agricultural machinery to proxy for agricultural capital stock. The insignificant effect of the labor variable may be due to its high correlation with the land variable. Despite these disappointments, the results show that the assumption of constant returns to scale cannot be rejected for most years in the sample period.

To improve the results of our regression analysis, we need to modify our regression specification. We make two changes: we omit the capital variable and we rewrite the regression specification in per unit of labor terms. Therefore, we have the following new specification

$$\ln(Y_i/L_i) = \beta_0 + \beta_R \ln(R_i/L_i) + \delta_E DE_i + \delta_W DW_i + u_i \quad (7.16)$$

where the main explanatory variable is now land per unit of labor and the explained variable is output per unit of labor. Based on earlier support for the assumption of constant returns to scale, the coefficient on labor can be obtained by subtracting the estimate of β_R from unity. Results show that the estimates of β_R are (unsurprisingly) significant. Other variants of regression methods, such as pooled OLS, are also tried. Based on our regressions, our major conclusion is that land is still the overwhelming determinant for the value added in the agricultural sector, while labor makes a relatively minor contribution.

Given the Cobb–Douglas form of the production function, the marginal product of labor at time t can be computed as $MPL(t) = \beta_L \cdot APL(t)$, where $APL(t)$ stands for the average product of labor at time t, which is given by Y/L in the current case. Our purpose is to compare estimated values of the marginal product of labor with corresponding wage levels. Data on real wages in the agricultural sector are not easy to come by. We follow Islam and Yokota (2008) and use average net income per unit of labor in the farming sector to proxy for the real wage in agriculture. Our computations show that both the marginal product of labor and the wage level increase over time. This should not be taken as conflicting with the hypothesis of the Lewis model, as the model does not rule out increases in wage even before the turning point is reached. In fact, as Ranis and Fei (1961) point out, some improvement in productivity in the traditional sector is actually needed so that progress toward the turning point does not get aborted (Islam and Yokota, 2008). Although the marginal product and wage level both increase over time, we find that the former increases at a much faster pace than the latter. Therefore, our brief analysis here supports Islam and Yokota (2008) in vindicating the validity of using the Lewis model to analyze China's process of industrialization.

In what way are openness to foreign trade and FDI involved in the process of China's industrialization? We are now in a position to examine the effect of openness to foreign trade and FDI on shifts in regional sectoral labor shares across China's regions. The dependent variables are the changes in sectoral labor shares for each of the three broad sectors Δl^j_{it} in China, which is defined as $\Delta l^j_{it} = l^j_{it} - l^j_{i,t-1}$ for $j = a, b, c$ where $j = a, b, c$ stand for the agricultural, manufacturing, and service sector in China, respectively. The two explanatory variables are (the log of) the initial level of regional per-worker GDP and the regional openness variable, which is constructed as the ratio of total value of foreign trade to regional GDP of the same year averaged over the corresponding time span (see also Jiang, 2011).

For both the agricultural sector and the manufacturing sector, estimated coefficients on the openness variable take the expected negative and positive signs. Estimated coefficients on the openness variable for the agricultural sector are all negative, while for the manufacturing sector they are all positive. However, single-span regressions do not generate precise estimates probably because sample sizes are too small. Many of the estimates are found to be insignificant. Estimated coefficients on lagged per-worker income also take the expected signs. Estimated coefficients on lagged per-worker income for the manufacturing sector are negative, while for the agricultural sector they are positive. The signs of these coefficients show that, at least during 1994–2005, poorer regions tend to experience faster structural transformation (in terms of shifts in the labor share). This result implies that structural transformation had a convergence effect, through which it contributed to narrowing the income gap between rich and poor regions in China. The last regression in Table 7.2 pools the five time spans together. The results of this regression suggest that regional openness promotes regional structural transformation in terms of shifts in the share of labor from the agricultural to the manufacturing sector, and that structural transformation in poorer regions tends to be faster, as a result of which per-worker income across China's different regions can clearly be seen.

Concluding remarks

Openness to foreign trade and FDI improves the way production factors are allocated by lifting barriers to the mobility of resources across different sectors. Even a cursory observation shows China's economy has many of the features that the Lewis growth model tries to capture. In this chapter we empirically examine the relationship between openness to foreign trade and FDI and China's structural change. Our regression results support the usefulness of the Lewis model for analyzing the process of industrialization in China. Our empirical analyses also show that openness to foreign trade and FDI has played an important role in the structural transformation of China. The results suggest that regional openness promotes regional structural transformation in terms of shifts in the share of labor from the agricultural sector to the manufacturing sector, and that structural transformation in poorer regions tends to be faster, as a result of which

Table 7.2 The effect of openness on sectoral labor shares: regressions

Explained variable	Explanatory variables	Period					
		1982–1987 Obs: 26	1988–1993 Obs: 31	1994–1999 Obs: 31	2000–2005 Obs: 31	2006–2011 Obs: 31	Pooled Obs: 150
Δl_{it}^{a}	$\ln(y_{i,t+1})$	0.008 (0.018)	0.002 (0.010)	0.036* (0.010)	0.040* (0.014)	0.005 (0.018)	0.012** (0.006)
	F_{it}	-0.108 (0.131)	-0.085** (0.045)	-0.061* (0.015)	-0.036 (0.028)	-0.006 (0.027)	-0.025* (0.013)
	R-squared	0.142	0.142	0.422	0.236	0.003	0.249
Δl_{it}^{b}	$\ln(y_{i,t+1})$	-0.014 (0.015)	-0.006 (0.007)	-0.040* (0.009)	-0.046* (0.011)	-0.032** (0.018)	-0.021* (0.006)
	F_{it}	0.083 (0.112)	0.085* (0.030)	0.063* (0.014)	0.044* (0.021)	0.048 (0.030)	0.039* (0.012)
	R-squared	0.090	0.233	0.491	0.402	0.101	0.310
Δl_{it}^{c}	$\ln(y_{i,t+1})$	0.006 (0.006)	0.004 (0.006)	0.004 (0.009)	0.006 (0.008)	0.027** (0.014)	0.009* (0.004)
	F_{it}	0.024 (0.048)	0.000 (0.028)	-0.002 (0.015)	-0.009 (0.015)	-0.042** (0.023)	-0.014** (0.008)
	R-squared	0.106	0.026	0.005	0.019	0.123	0.168

Standard errors are in parentheses. * denotes significance at the 5 percent level while ** denotes significance at the 10 percent level. For brevity, we do not report estimated intercepts in this table. The pooled regression in the last column includes period dummy variables (four of them altogether) besides the common intercept.

convergence in per-worker income across China's different regions can clearly be seen.

Notes

1. Works on economics are often classified according to JEL classification codes, a system set up by the *Journal of Economic Literature*.
2. Some related recent studies include Laitner (2000), Gollin et al. (2002), Hansen and Prescott (2002), O'Leary (2003a, b, 2006), Dekle and Vandenbroucke (2006), Ngai and Pissarides (2007), Brandt et al. (2008), Lee and Malin (2009), Vollrath (2009), Dessy et al. (2010), and Jiang (2010, 2011).
3. The coefficient of variation, by definition, is calculated as the ratio between standard deviation and the absolute value of the mean.

References

Brandt, L.; Hsieh, C.; and Zhu, X. (2008) 'Growth and structural transformation in China,' in L. Brandt and T. Rawski (Eds.), *China's Great Economic Transformation*, New York: Cambridge University Press, pp. 683–728.

Dekle, R.; and Vandenbroucke, G. (2006) *A Quantitative Analysis of China's Structural Transformation* (Working Paper 2006-37), San Francisco, CA: Federal Reserve Bank of San Francisco.

Dessy, S.; Mbiekop, F.; and Pallage, S. (2010) 'On the mechanics of trade-induced structural transformation,' *Journal of Macroeconomics*, **32**(1), 251–64.

Gollin, D.; Parente, S.; and Rogerson, R. (2002) 'The role of agriculture in development,' *American Economic Review*, **92**(2), 160–4.

Hansen, G.D.; and Prescott, E. (2002) 'Malthus to Solow,' *American Economic Review*, **92**(4), 1205–17.

Hayashi, F.; and Prescott, E.C. (2008) 'The depressing effect of agricultural institutions on the prewar Japanese economy,' *Journal of Political Economy*, **116**(4), 573–632.

Islam, N.; and Yokota, K. (2008) *Lewis Growth Model and China's Industrialization* (Working Paper 2008-17), Kitakyushu, Japan: International Centre for the Study of East Asian Development.

Jiang, Yanqing (2010) 'An empirical study of structural factors and regional growth in China,' *Journal of Chinese Economic and Business Studies*, **8**(4), 335–52.

Jiang, Yanqing (2011) 'Structural change and growth in China under economic reforms: patterns, causes and implications,' *Review of Urban and Regional Development Studies*, **23**(1), 48–65.

Laitner, J. (2000) 'Structural change and economic growth,' *Review of Economic Studies*, **67**(3), 545–61.

Lee, Soohyung; and Malin, B.A. (2009) *Education's Role in China's Structural Transformation* (Finance and Economics Discussion Series No. 2009-41), Washington, D.C.: Board of Governors of the Federal Reserve System.

Lewis, A.W. (1954) 'Economic development with unlimited supplies of labor,' *The Manchester School*, 22, 139–91.

Lucas, R.E. (2009) 'Trade and the diffusion of the Industrial Revolution,' *American Economic Journal: Macroeconomics*, 1(1), 1–25.

Ngai, L.R.; and Pissarides, C.A. (2007) 'Structural change in a multi-sector model of growth,' *American Economic Review*, 97, 429–43.

O'Leary, E. (2003a) 'Aggregate and sectoral convergence among Irish regions: the role of structural change: 1960–96,' *International Regional Science Review*, 26(4), 483–501.

O'Leary, E. (2003b) 'Sources of regional divergence in the Celtic Tiger: policy responses,' *Journal of the Statistical and Social Inquiry Society of Ireland*, 32, 1–32.

O'Leary, E. (2006) *The Role of Structural Change in Productivity Convergence among EU Regions*, Angra do Heroísmo, Azores, Portugal: Regional Science Association International (British and Irish Section).

Parente, S.L.; and Prescott, E.C. (1994) 'Barriers to technology adoption and development,' *Journal of Political Economy*, 102(2), 298–321.

Ranis, G.; and Fei, J.C.H. (1961) 'A theory of economic development,' *American Economic Review*, 51, 533–65.

Vollrath, D. (2009) 'How important are dual economy effects for aggregate productivity?' *Journal of Development Economics*, 88, 325–34.

8

Static and dynamic comparative advantages

Abstract: This chapter focuses on the linkage between change in the pattern of China's comparative advantage and in the economic structure of the country's ongoing transformation. After formalizing the processes of structural transformation and the shift of comparative advantage across sectors, we use specialization indexes to proxy for the intensity of comparative advantage in our empirical analysis. Results show that the specialization index of primary goods has been declining while that of manufactured goods has been climbing over time. Results further show that of the various subdivisions of primary goods, the specialization index of mineral fuels and non-edible raw materials has been falling, while of the various subdivisions of manufactured goods, the specialization index of machinery and transport equipment has been rising. To a large degree, empirical results support the hypothesis of the theoretical model presented in this chapter.

Key words: specialization, comparative advantage, structural transformation, opening up, the Ricardian Model, labor-intensive manufacturing.

JEL classification codes: F41; O11; O57.[1]

Introduction

Over the past 35 years China's economy has undergone a rapid transformation. This had important impacts on other economies in the rest of the world as China opened up to more foreign trade and FDI. Little research has been conducted on the economic forces underpinning this transformation. One important issue is the relationship between China's foreign trade, the pattern and structure of its comparative advantage, and the way in which the country's economic structure has been transformed. There is a concern that when developing countries engage in international trade they often face a tradeoff between specializing in low-tech goods where they currently enjoy comparative advantage and entering the high-tech market where they currently lack comparative advantage but may foster such a comparative advantage in the future as a result of the potential for productivity growth or of positive intersectoral interactions. If this is the case, then it is possible that specialization according to current static comparative advantage is welfare reducing, while protectionist measures can be welfare enhancing. Moreover, for any open developing economy, continually updating knowledge of overseas markets and anticipating global market changes are crucial elements in trade success. The more a developing country adopts a static view of comparative advantage, the greater the risk of failure in international trade as global markets change and develop.

China can act as a timely and important illustration of dynamic comparative advantage (Lim and Feng, 2005). Overall, labor-intensive economic activity dominates China's production, as demonstrated by its rapid growth since the early and mid 1980s. Because of its labor abundance, China's labor-intensive industries enjoy comparative advantage. However, using specialization indexes to proxy for comparative advantage, studies have shown that China's early post-reform growth in labor-intensive manufacturing occurred despite the sector having a negative specialization index (Kwan, 2001; Lim and Feng, 2005). Moreover, as labor-intensive manufacturing increased its share of total GDP so agriculture's share decreased, even though agriculture could be shown to enjoy much stronger comparative advantage than labor-intensive manufacturing at that time. Could the same economic forces that fueled the growth of labor-intensive manufacturing have also played a part in the shift of comparative advantage from agriculture to labor-intensive manufacturing? Moreover, if China's comparative advantage is shaped by its labor abundance, what was it that caused the rapid expansion of manufacturing over agriculture, when both are labor intensive?

This chapter reviews the literature and investigates theoretically and empirically the linkage between observed patterns of economic development, especially the way in which China's economic structure developed and its comparative advantage evolved. The rest of this chapter is organized as follows. In the second section 'A dynamic Ricardian model', we present a dynamic model to formally illustrate a situation in which specialization according to existing comparative advantage under free trade may be welfare reducing while protectionist measures may be welfare increasing. In the third section 'Implications for

China', we discuss the policy implications of dynamic comparative advantage for China. In the fourth section 'Structural transformation and comparative advantage in China', we discuss the relationship between China's structural transformation and the evolution of comparative advantage. We present both a theoretical foundation and empirical evidence in this section.

A dynamic Ricardian model

For specialization according to the current comparative advantage under free trade to be welfare reducing and protectionist measures to be welfare increasing, we formally illustrate the situation by presenting the dynamic Ricardian model of Redding (1999), developed from a standard Ricardian model with a specification for productivity dynamics, where productivity is assumed to evolve endogenously over time. For simplicity, we consider trade between two countries, named 'Home' and 'Foreign', where all Foreign's variables are denoted by asterisks. We assume that each country has a single production factor (i.e., labor) and can produce two goods: good 1, a low-tech good (wheat), and good 2, a high-tech good (machinery). According to Cobb–Douglas instantaneous utility, consumer preferences are identical in the two countries.

$$u(c_1, c_2) = c_1^\alpha \cdot c_2^{1-\alpha} \tag{8.1}$$

Each worker–consumer is endowed with one unit of labor and the total labor supplies in Home and Foreign are L and L^*, respectively. Time is continuous and the representative consumer spends at each point in time all her instantaneous income on instantaneous consumption. The unit labor requirements for goods 1 and 2 are denoted a_1 and a_2 for Home, and correspondingly, a_1^* and a_2^* for Foreign, respectively.

We assume that the unit labor requirement in each sector of Home at time t is a function of the stock of production experience as

$$a_i(t) = F_i[e_i(t)] \tag{8.2}$$

with $\partial F_i(e_i)/\partial e_i < 0$ and $i = 1, 2$ for the two goods, where $e_i(t)$ is used to denote the stock of production experience at time t.[2] To fix ideas, we specify $e_i(t)$ such that $1/a_i(t) = \xi_i \cdot e_i(t)$, with $\xi_i > 0$ for $i = 1, 2$. We further assume that

$$de_i(t)/dt \equiv \dot{e}_i(t) = \eta_i \cdot e_i(t) \cdot L_i(t) \tag{8.3}$$

where $L_i(t)$ is labor input in sector i at time t, and η_i captures the speed at which experience can be accumulated in sector i.[3]

Under autarky, in accordance with Eq. 8.1, the consumer's utility maximization problem is written as

$$\text{Max}_{c_1, c_2} (c_1^{\alpha} \cdot c_2^{1-\alpha})$$
$$\text{subject to } p_1 c_1 + p_2 c_2 = w, p_1/p_2 = a_1/a_2 \tag{8.4}$$

Note that w is both the wage rate of a representative consumer and the total income of the consumer, as each worker–consumer has one unit of labor. Moreover, if both goods are produced in the country, under autarky $p_1/p_2 = w_1 a_1/w_2 a_2 = a_1/a_2$ must hold because the wage rate in the two sectors must be the same (i.e., $w_1 = w_2$). The problem posed by Eq. 8.4 requires that the optimal consumption levels of goods 1 and 2 are such that

$$\frac{c_2}{c_1} = \frac{1-\alpha}{\alpha} \cdot \frac{p_1}{p_2} = \frac{1-\alpha}{\alpha} \cdot \frac{a_1}{a_2} \tag{8.5}$$

Under autarky, the production levels of goods 1 and 2 in the country (i.e., y_1 and y_2) must equal the consumption levels of the two goods so that Eq. 8.5 implies $y_2/y_1 = [(1-\alpha)/\alpha](a_1/a_2)$. Let L_1 and L_2 be the labor supplies in sectors 1 and 2 (where $L_1 + L_2 = L$). By using $y_1 = L_1/a_1$ and $y_2 = L_2/a_2$ we see that the optimal consumption levels of goods 1 and 2 require

$$L_1 = \alpha L, \quad L_2 = (1-\alpha)L \tag{8.6}$$

Now suppose that Home and Foreign begin to trade from some arbitrary point in time t_s onward and that there are zero transport costs. Suppose at time t_s Home enjoys comparative advantage in producing good 1 (i.e., $a_1(t_s)/a_2(t_s) < a_1^*(t_s)/a_2^*(t_s)$). Analysis can now be carried out within a general equilibrium framework. Relative free trade price and relative quantity can be simultaneously determined by the intersection of the world relative supply (RS) curve and the world relative demand (RD) curve. According to Cobb–Douglas instantaneous utility, the world RD curve can be shown to be $\bar{Q} \equiv (Q_1 + Q_1^*)/(Q_2 + Q_2^*) = [\alpha/(1-\alpha)](p_2/p_1)$. In the case of complete specialization for both countries, each country specializes in the production of the good in which it has comparative advantage. The equilibrium world relative price is then $\bar{p} \equiv p_1/p_2 = [\alpha/(1-\alpha)](L^*/a_2^*)/(L/a_1)$. Before time t_s we can see that Home acquires production experience at rates $\eta_1 \alpha L$ and $\eta_2(1-\alpha)L$ in sectors 1 and 2, respectively, while Foreign acquires production experience in the two sectors at rates $\eta_1^* \alpha L^*$ and $\eta_2^*(1-\alpha)L^*$, respectively. However, from time t_s onward the two countries are engaged in free trade, which induces Home's specialization in the production of good 1, where Home is assumed to have comparative advantage at time t_s, and Foreign's specialization in the production of good 2, where Foreign is assumed to have comparative advantage at time t_s.[4] In this case, Home acquires production experience only in the low-tech sector, where the relative rate of experience accumulation is $\eta_1 L$, while Foreign acquires production experience only in the high-tech sector, where the relative rate of experience acquisition is $\eta_2^* L^*$.

We need to compare intertemporal welfare under autarky and under free trade. If Home still remains autarkic from time t_s onward, then the intertemporal welfare of a representative Home consumer from time t_s onward is

$$U^A(t_s) = \int_{t_s}^{\infty} e^{-\rho(t-t_s)} \cdot [\alpha/a_1^A(t)]^\alpha \cdot [(1-\alpha)/a_2^A(t)]^{1-\alpha}\, dt \qquad (8.7)$$

where ρ is the subjective discount rate.[5] Suppose, instead, the two countries begin to trade freely from time t_s onward. Then the intertemporal welfare of the representative Home consumer from time t_s onward is given by[6]

$$U^T(t_s) = \int_{t_s}^{\infty} e^{-\rho(t-t_s)} \cdot [\alpha/a_1^T(t)]^\alpha \cdot \{(1-\alpha) \cdot p_1^T(t)/[a_1^T(t) \cdot p_2^T(t)]\}^{1-\alpha}\, dt$$

$$(8.8)$$

It can straightforwardly be demonstrated that $a_1^A(t) = a_1(t_s) \cdot e^{-\eta_1 \alpha L(t-t_s)}$, $a_2^A(t) = a_2(t_s) \cdot e^{-\eta_2(1-\alpha)L(t-t_s)}$, and $a_1^T(t) = a_1(t_s) \cdot e^{-\eta_1 L(t-t_s)}$, respectively, for all $t \geq t_s$. Using the first two equations, we can write the expression for intertemporal welfare under autarky as

$$U^A(t_s) = \frac{\alpha^\alpha \cdot (1-\alpha)^{1-\alpha} \cdot [a_1(t_s)]^{-\alpha} \cdot [a_2(t_s)]^{\alpha-1}}{\rho - \alpha^2 \eta_1 L - (1-\alpha)^2 \eta_2 L} \qquad (8.9)$$

In contrast, the intertemporal welfare under free trade can be shown to be

$$U^T(t_s) = \frac{\alpha[a_1(t_s)]^{-\alpha} \cdot [a_2^*(t_s)]^{\alpha-1} \cdot (L^*/L)^{1-\alpha}}{\rho - \alpha \eta_1 L - (1-\alpha)\eta_2^* L^*} \qquad (8.10)$$

where we insert $p_1^T(t)/p_2^T(t) = [\alpha/(1-\alpha)](L^*/a_2^{*T}(t))/(L/a_1^T(t))$ (the world relative demand function), $a_1^T(t) = a_1(t_s) \cdot e^{-\eta_1 L(t-t_s)}$, and $a_2^{*T}(t) = a_2^*(t_s) \cdot e^{-\eta_2^* L^*(t-t_s)}$ into Eq. 8.8.

Intertemporal welfare under free trade will be lower than that under autarky if and only if

$$\frac{\alpha[a_1(t_s)]^{-\alpha} \cdot [a_2^*(t_s)]^{\alpha-1} \cdot (L^*/L)^{1-\alpha}}{\rho - \alpha \eta_1 L - (1-\alpha)\eta_2^* L^*} < \frac{\alpha^\alpha \cdot (1-\alpha)^{1-\alpha} \cdot [a_1(t_s)]^{-\alpha} \cdot [a_2(t_s)]^{\alpha-1}}{\rho - \alpha^2 \eta_1 L - (1-\alpha)^2 \eta_2 L}$$

The numerator on the left-hand side of the inequality must exceed that on the right-hand side owing to the static gain that free trade brings at t_s, because the numerators represent instantaneous utility under free trade and under autarky, respectively, at time t_s. Then it follows that intertemporal welfare under free trade may be lower than that under autarky if and only if $\rho - \alpha\eta_1 L - (1-\alpha)\eta_2^* L^* > \rho - \alpha^2\eta_1 L - (1-\alpha)^2\eta_2 L$ holds, which implies

$$\alpha\eta_1 L + [\eta_2^* L^* - (1-\alpha)\eta_2 L] < 0 \qquad (8.11)$$

Inequality 8.11 is a necessary condition for intertemporal welfare under free trade to be lower than that under autarky. The first term on the left-hand side $\alpha\eta_1 L$ is unambiguously positive. However, Home's relative rate of experience acquisition in the high-tech sector under autarky $(1-\alpha)\eta_2 L$ may or may not exceed Foreign's relative rate of experience acquisition in the high-tech sector under free trade $\eta_2^* L^*$. If $(1-\alpha)\eta_2 L$ exceeds $\eta_2^* L^*$ by a certain degree, intertemporal welfare under free trade will be lower than that under autarky. A large L relative to L^*, or a high η_2 relative to η_2^*, tend to widen the difference between $(1-\alpha)\eta_2 L$ and $\eta_2^* L^*$.

This model indicates that international trade affects economic welfare dynamically (due to the change in productivity growth rates induced by specialization based on comparative advantage), which means that free trade is no longer necessarily welfare increasing. A necessary condition for free trade to be welfare reducing is that the rate of experience acquisition in the high-tech sector is lower under free trade than under autarky, and that the effect of this on the growth rate of instantaneous utility outweighs that of the increase in the rate of experience acquisition in the low-tech sector. For a large developing country such as China, this necessary condition for free trade to be welfare reducing is more likely to be satisfied. The larger Home's potential for experience accumulation in the high-tech sector relative to that of Foreign's in this sector, and the smaller Foreign's economy (as measured by its labor force) relative to that of Home's, the more likely the necessary condition implied by Inequality 8.11 is satisfied.

Implications for China

The theoretical model presented in the preceding section shows that developing countries may face a tradeoff between specializing according to existing comparative advantage (in low-tech goods) and moving into industries where they currently lack comparative advantage but may acquire it in the future as a result of potential productivity growth (in high-tech goods). In other words, it is possible that specialization according to current comparative advantage under free trade is welfare reducing while protectionist measures that induce specialization in industries where the country does not currently have comparative advantage may be welfare increasing. The model focuses on the relationship between endogenous comparative advantage, economic growth, and economic welfare. Analysis suggests that specialization according to initial comparative advantage may exert negative effects on productivity growth rates and economic welfare. By contrast, selective industrial and trade policies that induce specialization in industries where the economy lacks initial comparative advantage may be welfare improving. The endogenous dynamic nature of comparative advantage explains the evolution of international trade over time and sheds light on related policy implications.[8]

From World War II until the 1970s many developing countries set about fostering a manufacturing industry serving the domestic market to bring about economic takeoff,. They did this by limiting imports of foreign-manufactured goods. According to arguments for import substitution, developing countries have potential (but not current) comparative advantage in manufacturing. To allow manufacturing to get a toehold in developing countries, governments should support new industries until they have grown strong enough to stand international competition. Hence the need for a developing country to use tariffs or other instruments as temporary measures to get industrialization started.[9]

The model leads to the inevitable question: Is it possible for policy-makers to lead the economy to specialize in the sector where it currently lacks comparative advantage but is expected to acquire it over time? Comparing welfare under free trade and welfare under a trade policy that imposes tariffs on imports should be insightful. The central point here is whether a developing country might lose or reduce its potential future comparative advantage in another industry by specializing according to its existing comparative advantage when free trade is allowed. Therefore, policy intervention can be effective in the way comparative advantage develops and can thus be used to optimize a country's welfare within a certain time horizon.

Given its abundance of labor, China enjoys comparative advantage in labor-intensive industries (Adams and Shachmurove, 1997; Kwan, 2002a). However, using specialization indexes to proxy for comparative advantage, Kwan (2001) shows that the early post-reform growth in labor-intensive manufacturing industries in China took place when industries had a negative specialization index. The increase in labor-intensive manufacturing was accompanied by a fall in the contribution of agriculture to overall GDP, even though agriculture had a much stronger comparative advantage than manufacturing during that period (Lim and Feng, 2005). Lim and Feng (2005) show, by means of specialization indexes, that China's comparative advantage had shifted from agriculture in favor of labor-intensive manufacturing by the 1990s. This finding is echoed by examining China's export success at that time, which was primarily grounded in labor-intensive industries (Rowen, 2001; Kwan 2002b; Lai, 2004). Lim and Feng (2005) also predict that China's comparative advantage is likely to shift to capital-intensive industries in the decade to come. This inevitably leads to the question: Why might market forces drive an industry to grow even if the industry lacks comparative advantage to begin with? More specifically, if labor abundance currently underlies China's comparative advantage, then how do we explain the rapid growth of manufacturing over agriculture when both are labor-intensive? Moreover, could the economic forces that have driven the growth of labor-intensive manufacturing eventually succeed in fostering a shift of comparative advantage to this sector? To answer these and other questions, we turn to the next section for a more detailed discussion.

Structural transformation and comparative advantage in China

No better example of dynamic comparative advantage can be found than China because of its astonishing trade performance since the initiation of the economic reform, the impacts of its exports and imports on the rest of the world, and the prospect of it transiting from export growth based on labor intensity to capital and technology intensity (Lai, 2004). In the early reform period, especially the early 1980s, agriculture in China was abundant in labor but had relatively little capital. The agricultural sector was the first major sector to be liberalized under the various reforms, with land leased to individual households and prices increasingly freed up. The state planning system continued to suppress development of a labor-intensive rural industrial sector for fear that non-farm rural enterprises would draw labor away from farming, compromising the country's objective of being self-sufficient in food. However, the impacts of agricultural reform were so strong that they afforded greater leeway for the government to relax its controls over the non-farm rural sector (Lin, 1992). By 1985 the Chinese government liberalized rural industries by allowing labor to move from farming to non-farm township and village enterprises (Lim and Feng, 2005).

According to Lim and Feng (2005), a mutualistic relationship began to emerge between traditional agriculture and newly formed township and village enterprises. The decollectivization of farming brought with it formation of a virtuous circle of higher farm incomes, more farm investment, higher incomes, and so forth. Labor-saving farm investments freed up labor from agriculture facilitating the mobility of labor from traditional farming to rural manufacturing industries. The savings accrued by farmers as a result of their rising incomes were further channeled by banks into manufacturing startups. The newly developed rural manufacturing sectors also used agriculture as demand linkages. The former supplied the farmers with farm implements, basic consumer goods, and construction and transport services. As rural manufacturing grew, it opened up more opportunities for employment, which were filled by surplus labor from agriculture (Findlay et al., 1994). The growth of rural manufacturing also raised off-farm incomes, part of which was spent on or remitted to the agricultural sector. Farm income rose enabling farmers to increase their expenditure on inputs (machinery) provided by manufacturing. A further virtuous circle emerged where 'agriculture and manufacturing expanded in tandem' (Byrd and Lin, 1990; Findlay and Watson, 1992; Sicular, 1992; Islam and Jin, 1994; Ratha et al., 1994; Lin, 1995). This eventually led to the labor-intensive manufacturing sector gaining comparative advantage (Kwan, 2001).

The processes of structural transformation and the shift of comparative advantage across sectors can be formalized using the model of Lim and Feng (2005). Let $A(t)$ be the number of farms in the agricultural sector at time t, where all farms are assumed to be identical and produce the same quantity of output. The level of $A(t)$ is thus closely related to sectoral output or income. Let sector growth accord with an intrinsic per-unit rate r_A, the rate at which the sector would grow in isolation, without receiving positive or negative impacts from other sectors. The rate r_A, however, may depend on factors like the economic environment and social infrastructure. We use $\bar{A}$ (where $\bar{A} > 0$) to denote the physical upper limit to the number of farms that can exist in the agricultural sector, owing to resource constraints. $\bar{A}$ can thus be called the carrying capacity or potential sectoral size of the agricultural sector. The logistic growth of the agricultural sector is given by

$$\dot{A} = r_A(1 - A/\bar{A})A = (r_A - a_A A)A \qquad (8.12)$$

where we define $a_A = r_A/\bar{A}$. The term $(1 - A/\bar{A})$ reflects intrasectoral competition according to which the actual per-unit growth rate $r_A(1 - A/\bar{A})$ tends to zero as the number of farms approaches potential $\bar{A}$. Now we incorporate the manufacturing sector into the model. Suppose two sectors, agriculture and manufacturing, are mutually supportive or complementary such that

$$\left.\begin{array}{l} \dot{A} = (r_A - a_A A + a_M M)A \\ \dot{M} = (r_M - m_M M + m_A A)M \end{array}\right\} \tag{8.13}$$

where $M(t)$ represents the number of manufacturing firms, and $m_M = r_M/\bar{M}$ by definition, in which r_M is the intrinsic growth rate of the manufacturing sector and $\bar{M}$ is its carrying capacity. The parameters a_M and m_A each capture the respective intersectoral interactions, both of which are assumed to be strictly positive. Non-trivial equilibrium for the system in Eq. 8.13 is given by

$$\left.\begin{array}{l} A^* = \dfrac{\bar{A} + \alpha\bar{M}}{1 - \alpha\beta} \\[2ex] M^* = \dfrac{\bar{M} + \beta\bar{A}}{1 - \alpha\beta} \end{array}\right\} \tag{8.14}$$

where $\alpha = a_M/a_A$, and $\beta = m_A/m_M$. Provided the equilibrium in Eq. 8.14 is stable with mutually beneficial intersectoral spillovers, it can be proven that $A^* > \bar{A}$ and $M^* > \bar{M}$, where again $\bar{A}$ and $\bar{M}$ are the maximum sizes of agriculture and manufacturing when the sectors are each left to grow independently.

Therefore, the model of Lim and Feng (2005) reinforces Akamatsu (1962)'s view of intersectoral complementarities. A positive stimulus from agriculture enhances the growth of manufacturing. As discussed earlier, the agricultural reforms made by China in the early 1980s brought with them massive output and productivity growth. Rising farm incomes enabled farmers not only to channel greater savings to the emerging non-farm sector via the banks, but also invest in labor-saving farm technologies thus facilitating the release of labor to rural manufacturing. The complementarities between sectors led to structural transformation of the economy – defined as the shift from one stage of the development process to a higher stage. If we measure structural transformation by an increase in X^*, the ratio between the equilibrium level of manufacturing M^* and that of agriculture A^*, then it can be proven that X^* rises if there is an increase in the positive intersectoral coefficient from agriculture to manufacturing m_A and at the same time a reduction in the positive intersectoral coefficient from manufacturing to agriculture a_M. If output by the manufacturing sector supplied as input to agriculture changes, then the positive intersectoral coefficient from manufacturing to agriculture a_M falls. Agriculture now tends to require more of other inputs, such as labor, to support its expansion. As this labor is no longer available for release to manufacturing, the expansion of agriculture thus brings about a higher opportunity cost in terms of manufactured goods forgone. On the other hand, an increase in the positive intersectoral coefficient from agriculture to manufacturing m_A arises from resource transfers from agriculture. Rising farm incomes brought about by China's agricultural reforms enhanced investment in labor-saving technologies, so that underemployed farm labor was released to manufacturing at a low opportunity cost in terms of farm output forgone (Shi et al., 1993). The implication here is that if comparative advantage initially lies in the agricultural sector, then structural transformation (an increase in the ratio between the equilibrium level of manufacturing M^* and that of agriculture A^*) means a relative shift in comparative advantage from agriculture to manufacturing. This is because an increase in m_A expands the manufacturing sector at a low opportunity cost in terms of agricultural output forgone while a fall in a_M forces the agricultural sector to expand at a higher opportunity cost. As manufacturing expands at a lower opportunity cost compared with agriculture, comparative advantage shifts from agriculture to manufacturing (Lim and Feng, 2005).

If we can find some observable variable to proxy for comparative advantage, we can then empirically examine the issue of structural transformation and dynamic comparative advantage as it relates to China. Like Kwan (2001) and Lim and Feng (2005) we make use of specialization indexes to provide a rough guide to changing comparative advantage. A specialization index for a given industry can be constructed – defined as the country's trade balance (exports minus imports) divided by the volume of total trade (exports plus imports). Strong comparative advantage in an industry predicts a high ratio of exports to imports. Relevant data needed for calculating the values of a specialization index are available from the *China Statistical Yearbook* (in this case the 2012 edition) compiled by the National Bureau of Statistics of China. We consider two broad categories of commodities. The first is primary goods, which are broken down into (a) food and live animals mainly used for food; (b) beverages and tobacco; (c) non-edible raw materials; (d) mineral fuels, lubricants and related materials; and (e) animal and vegetable oils, fats, and waxes. The second category is manufactured goods, which include (f) chemicals and related products; (g) light textile industry products,

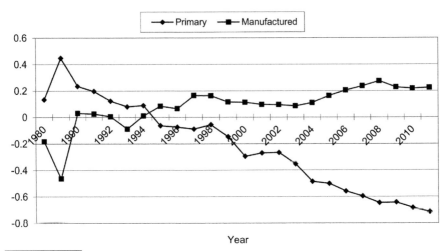

Figure 8.1 **Specialization indexes in China: two broad categories of goods**

Specialization indexes of two broad categories of goods, primary goods and manufactured goods, in 1980, 1985, and in each year of the period 1990–2011.

rubber products, minerals, and metallurgical products; (h) machinery and transport equipment; and (i) miscellaneous products. Specialization indexes calculated for the two broad categories of commodities, primary and manufactured, are depicted in Figure 8.1 whereas those for the five subdivisions of primary goods and the four subdivisions of manufactured goods are depicted in Figures 8.2 and 8.3, respectively.

Figure 8.1 shows the specialization index of primary goods steadily declining since the 1990s while that of manufactured goods has been climbing over time since then. Figures 8.2 and 8.3 further show that of the various subdivisions of primary goods the specialization index of mineral fuels, lubricants, non-edible raw materials, and related products steadily fell, while that of the various subdivisions of manufactured goods (i.e., machinery and transport equipment) steadily rose over time since the 1990s. What stands out from the trends (as shown in Figure 8.3) is the specialization index of miscellaneous (manufactured) products, which has remained high, even higher that that of general primary goods since the 1990s. Lim and Feng (2005) point out that until China embarked on rural industrial reforms, the Chinese economy suffered from major sectoral imbalances. In rural areas the focus was mainly on grain production while in urban areas heavy industry was the emphasis. This structural imbalance has changed dramatically since the mid 1980s with the liberalization of rural manufacturing. Light industry expanded as

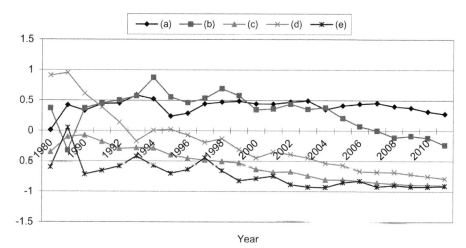

Figure 8.2   Specialization indexes in China: various kinds of primary goods

Specialization indexes of various kinds of primary goods, denoted (a), (b), (c), (d), and (e), in 1980, 1985, and in each year of the period 1990–2011.

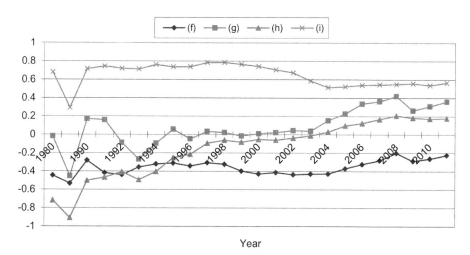

Figure 8.3   Specialization indexes in China: various kinds of manufactured goods

Specialization indexes of various kinds of manufactured goods, denoted (f), (g), (h), and (i), in 1980, 1985, and in each year of the period 1990–2011.

agricultural and other resources switched to more profitable rural enterprises. This is captured by the rapid rise of the specialization index of miscellaneous (manufactured) products in the late 1980s.

Concluding remarks

As stated earlier, no better example of dynamic comparative advantage can be found than China. Over the past 35 years, China's economy has undergone rapid transformation. However, little research has been done into the underlying economic forces facilitating this economic transformation. In this chapter we focus on the linkages between the way in which China's foreign trade has evolved, change in the pattern and structure of the country's comparative advantage, and the way in which China's economic structure has continually transformed. The processes involved in structural transformation and the shift of comparative advantage across sectors have been formalized using the theoretical model of Lim and Feng (2005). Based on this model, we use specialization indexes to proxy for the intensity of comparative advantage. Empirical analysis shows that since the 1990s the specialization index of primary goods has been steadily declining while that of manufactured goods has been climbing. Moreover, of the various subdivisions of primary goods, the specialization index of mineral fuels, lubricants, non-edible raw materials and related products has been steadily falling while, of the various subdivisions of manufactured goods, the specialization index of machinery and transport equipment has been steadily rising since the 1990s. Empirical results largely support the hypothesis of the theoretical model presented in this chapter.

Notes

1. Works on economics are often classified according to JEL classification codes, a system set up by the *Journal of Economic Literature*.
2. For Foreign we have $a_i^*(t) = F_i^*[e_i^*(t)]$ with $\partial F_i^*(e_i^*)/\partial e_i^* < 0$, $i = 1, 2$.
3. For Foreign the rate at which the production experience accumulates at time t is determined by $de_i^*(t)/dt \equiv \dot{e}_i^*(t) = \eta_i^* \cdot e_i^*(t) \cdot L_i^*(t)$.
4. For simplicity, we assume complete specialization in both countries (i.e., from t_s onward Home will only produce good 1 and Foreign will only produce good 2).

5. The superscript A denotes 'autarky'. According to Cobb–Douglas instantaneous utility, the consumer divides constant proportions of her income between the consumption of the two goods. Note that the Home consumer's income is given by the wage rate $w(t) = p_1^A(t)/a_1^A(t) = p_2^A(t)/a_2^A(t)$.

6. The superscript T denotes 'free trade'. Note that under free trade the income of a representative Home consumer is given by the wage rate in the low-tech sector $w(t) = p_1^T(t)/a_1^T(t)$.

7. The numerator of the right-hand side of Eq. 8.9 is instantaneous utility at time t_s under autarky, while the numerator of the right-hand side of Eq. 8.10 is instantaneous utility at t_s under free trade.

8. The relationship between foreign trade and economic growth as well as issues related to endogenous dynamic comparative advantage can be found, for example, in Krugman (1987), Grossman and Helpman (1990, 1991), and Young (1991).

9. See Krugman and Obstfeld (2003).

References

Adams, G.; and Shachmurove, Y. (1997) 'Trade and development patterns in the East Asian economies,' *Asian Economic Journal*, **4**, 345–60.

Akamatsu, K. (1962) 'A historical pattern of economic growth in developing countries,' *The Developing Economies*, **1**, 1–23.

Byrd, W.; and Lin, Q. (1990) *China's Rural Industry: Structure, Development and Reform*, New York: Oxford University Press.

Findlay, C.; and Watson, A. (1992) 'Surrounding the cities from the countryside,' in R. Garnaut and G. Liu (Eds.), *Economic Reform and Internationalisation: China and the Pacific Region*, St. Leonard's, Australia: Allen & Unwin.

Findlay, C.; Watson, A.; and Wu, H. (1994) 'Rural enterprises in China: overview, issues and prospects,' in C. Findlay, A. Watson, and H. Wu (Eds.), *Rural Enterprises in China*, London: Macmillan.

Grossman, G.; and Helpman, E. (1990) 'Comparative advantage and long-run growth,' *American Economic Review*, **80**, 796–815.

Grossman, G.; and Helpman, E. (1991) *Innovation and Growth in the Global Economy*, Cambridge, MA: MIT Press.

Islam, R.; and Jin, H. (1994) 'Rural industrialization: an engine of prosperity in postreform rural China,' *World Development*, **11**, 1643–62.

Krugman, P. (1987) 'The narrow moving band, the Dutch disease, and the competitive consequences of Mrs Thatcher: notes on trade in the presence of dynamic scale economies,' *Journal of Development Economics*, **27**, 41–55.

Krugman, P.; and Obstfeld, M. (2003) *International Economics*, Sixth Edition, Hong Kong/Beijing, China: Pearson Education Asia/Tsinghua University Press.

Kwan, C.H. (2001) 'The rise of China as an economic power,' *Journal of Japanese Trade and Industry*, November/December.

Kwan, C.H. (2002a) *The Rise of China's Flying-Geese Pattern of Economic Development: An Empirical Analysis Based on US Import Statistics* (NRI Paper 52), Chiyoda, Tokyo: Nomura Research Institute, pp. 1–11.

Kwan, C.H. (2002b) *Overcoming Japan's 'China Syndrome'*, New York: KWR International.

Lai, P. (2004) 'China's foreign trade: achievements, determinants and future policy challenges,' *China and World Economy*, 6, 38–50.

Lim, S.; and Feng, G. (2005) 'Dynamic comparative advantage: implications for China,' *Review of Applied Economics*, 1(2), 207–22.

Lin, B. (1995) 'The rapid expansion of township and village enterprises and its impacts on agricultural production in China' (mimeo), Manila, Philippines: Asian Development Bank.

Lin, J. (1992) 'Rural reforms and agricultural growth in China,' *American Economic Review*, 1, 34–51.

Ratha, D.; Singh, I.; and Xiao, G. (1994) 'Non-state enterprises as an engine of growth: analysis of provincial industrial growth in post-reform China' (mimeo), New York: Transition Economics Division, World Bank.

Redding, S. (1999) 'Dynamic comparative advantage and the welfare effects of trade,' *Oxford Economic Papers*, 51(1), 15–39.

Rowen, H. (2001) 'US–China economic and security relations,' in S. Chen and C. Wolfs (Eds.), *China, the United States, and the Global Economy*, Santa Monica, CA: RAND Research.

Shi, R.; Yao, C.; Zhang, Y.; Hsueh, T.; and Woo, T. (1993) 'A quantitative analysis of rural non-agricultural development and migration of agricultural labor force in China,' in T. Hsueh, Y. Sung, and J. Yu (Eds.), *Studies on Economic Reforms and Development in the People's Republic of China*, Hong Kong, China: The Chinese University Press.

Sicular, T. (1992) 'China's agricultural policy during the reform period,' in Joint Economic Committee, Congress of the United States (Eds.), *China's Economic Dilemmas in the 1990s: The Problems of Reforms, Modernization and Interdependence*, New York: M.E. Sharpe.

Young, A. (1991) 'Learning by doing and the dynamic effects of international trade,' *Quarterly Journal of Economics*, 106, 369–405.

9

Transaction efficiency and patterns of specialization

Abstract: This chapter deals theoretically with transaction efficiency and patterns of specialization. It has important implications for empirical analysis and policy evaluation with respect to a large developing country like China. In this theoretical study, we revisit the old Ricardian model of comparative advantage. Following an inframarginal methodology, we build an extended theoretical model based on the concepts of comparative advantage and transaction efficiency to explain development and inequality in developing economies. According to our model, an increase in domestic transaction efficiency reduces inequality within a developing economy while an increase in international transaction efficiency enhances the overall welfare level in a developing economy. The results of our model have important policy implications for China in its policy-making.

Key words: transaction efficiency, comparative advantage, inframarginal analysis, specialization, corner solution, general equilibrium.

JEL classification codes: F41; O10; O40.[1]

Introduction

This chapter looks at transaction efficiency and patterns of specialization from a theoretical perspective. It has important implications for empirical analysis and policy evaluation in large developing countries.

Inframarginal analysis is a method that combines marginal and total cost–benefit analysis. Up to the moment it has been used by a number of researchers to study the division of labor. For example, Cheng et al. (1999) use it to incorporate technological comparative advantage and transaction costs into the Heckscher–Olin (HO) model and thereby refine the HO theorem, the Stolper–Samuelson theorem, the Rybczynski theorem, and the factor equalization theorem. Having refined these core theorems they can be further used to justify empirical evidence that may be at odds with traditional core theorems. By applying the method of inframarginal analysis to the Ricardian model, Cheng et al. (2000) show that in a two-country two-good Ricardian model there exists a unique general equilibrium given a certain level of transaction efficiency. They further show that the comparative statics of the equilibrium involve discontinuous jumps; that is, as transaction efficiency increases, the general equilibrium structure jumps from autarky to partial division of labor and then to complete division of labor. Zhang and Shi (2006) point out the existence of a dual structure in the division of labor and trade that is missed by Cheng et al. (2000) and investigate an interesting way of using a general equilibrium model within the framework of inframarginal analysis to describe the dual structure of underemployment in a transitional period of economic development.

Other theoretical works involving inframarginal analysis of the division of labor include Yang (1991), Wen (1998), Sun et al. (1999, 2003), Yang and Zhang (1999), Yao (2002a, b), Sun (2003). By means of inframarginal analysis, this chapter aims to fill a lacuna in the theoretical literature by proposing a coherent framework to investigate underlying forces shaping development and inequality in developing economies. We build a theoretical model that is diametrically different from the neoclassical growth framework to explain development and inequality in developing economies. In this model we deliberately avoid modeling technological progress and capital accumulation and concentrate instead on looking at the alternative mechanisms through which a developing economy can achieve development. We revisit the old Ricardian model of comparative advantage. Following Cheng et al. (2000)'s inframarginal analysis of the Ricardian model, we build an extended theoretical model based on comparative advantage and transaction efficiency to explain development and inequality in developing economies.

The rest of this chapter is organized as follows. In the second section 'Inframarginal analysis of the Ricardian model', we briefly review Cheng et al. (2000)'s analysis of the Ricardian model and focus on the model's finding of the welfare-changing effect of transaction efficiency. In the third section 'Transaction efficiency and inequality', we build our extended theoretical model and incorporate features of regional development and inequality into the general inframarginal analysis framework.

Inframarginal analysis of the Ricardian model: a brief recap

In this section we recap Cheng et al. (2000)'s inframarginal analysis of the Ricardian model. The methodology of inframarginal analysis will form the basis of our theoretical model in the next section.

There are two countries in the world, Home (H) and Foreign (F). Each country has only one factor of production (i.e., labor) and each country is able to produce two goods (i.e., x and y). Every individual in both countries is endowed with one unit of labor, and the total number of individuals is L in Home and L^* in Foreign. Individuals within a country are assumed to be identical. The utility function for the representative consumer producer in Home is assumed to take the Cobb–Douglas form

$$U = (x + k\hat{x})^\alpha (y + k\hat{y})^{1-\alpha} \tag{9.1}$$

where x and y are quantities of good x and good y that are produced *and* consumed by the representative Home consumer–producer, while $\hat{x}$ and $\hat{y}$ are quantities of good x and good y that are produced in Foreign but consumed by the representative Home consumer (i.e., imported goods the Home consumer consumes). k is the transaction efficiency coefficient, $0 < k < 1$. The transaction cost is assumed to take the iceberg form: for each unit of a good bought the buyer only receives k units of the good (i.e., when the buyer pays one dollar, he gets only k dollars' worth of the good, $0 < k < 1$); the rest is lost in transit. Transaction cost may result from different sources: costs of storage, costs of transportation, and costs of finding a transaction partner, to name a few. Analogous to Eq. 9.1, the utility function of the representative consumer in Foreign is

$$U^* = (x^* + k\hat{x}^*)^\alpha (y^* + k\hat{y}^*)^{1-\alpha} \tag{9.2}$$

where x^* and y^* are quantities of good x and good y that are produced and consumed by the representative Foreign consumer–producer, while $\hat{x}^*$ and $\hat{y}^*$ are quantities of good x and good y that are produced in Home but consumed by the Foreign consumer (i.e., imports the Foreign consumer consumes).

The unit labor requirements for good x and good y are a_x and a_y, respectively, in Home and a_x^* and a_y^*, respectively, in Foreign. Therefore, the production function for each consumer–producer in Home is

$$x + \check{x} = l_x/a_x, \quad y + \check{y} = l_y/a_y, \quad l_x + l_y = 1 \tag{9.3}$$

where $\check{x}$ and $\check{y}$ are quantities of good x and good y produced by the representative Home consumer–producer but exported to Foreign. l_x and l_y are the fraction of labor of the consumer–producer engaged in the production of good x and good y, respectively. Analogous to Eqs. 9.3, the production function for the representative Foreign consumer–producer is

$$x^* + \check{x}^* = l_x^*/a_x^*, \quad y^* + \check{y}^* = l_y^*/a_y^*, \quad l_x^* + l_y^* = 1 \qquad (9.4)$$

For simplicity we arbitrarily assume that Home enjoys comparative advantage in producing good x (i.e., $a_x/a_y < a_x^*/a_y^*$). When there is a sufficiently high k (close to unity), trade is intuitively possible and desirable between the two countries. If k is sufficiently low, the two countries may instead find themselves better off remaining in autarky. Generally, there are three possible modes of division of labor between the two countries: (i) each country is completely specialized in the production of the good in which it enjoys comparative advantage (i.e., Home only produces good x and Foreign only produces good y); (ii) one country is completely specialized in the production of the good in which it has comparative advantage, while the other country produces both goods; (iii) each country remains in autarky and produces both goods.

To ascertain the general equilibrium we first find the corner equilibrium for each mode. Then we identify the range of the transaction efficiency k within which each corner equilibrium is the general equilibrium.

Corner equilibrium in Mode (1)

In this mode of the division of labor, Home will exclusively produce and export good x, and Foreign will exclusively produce and export good y. Therefore, for Home $x, \check{x}, \hat{y} > 0$ and $\hat{x}, y, \check{y} = 0$; for Foreign $y^*, \check{y}^*, \hat{x}^* > 0$ and $\hat{y}^*, x^*, \check{x}^* = 0$. The decision-making of the representative consumer in Home is described by

$$\text{Max } U = x^\alpha (k\hat{y})^{1-\alpha}$$
$$\text{subject to } x + \check{x} = 1/a_x, \hat{y} = p\check{x}, \text{ where } p \equiv p_x/p_y \qquad (9.5)$$

The maximization of U in Eq. 9.5 leads to

$$\check{x} = \frac{1-\alpha}{a_x}, \quad x = \frac{\alpha}{a_x}, \quad \hat{y} = p \cdot \frac{1-\alpha}{a_x} \qquad (9.6)$$

Analogous to Eq. 9.5, the decision-making of the representative foreign consumer is described by

$$\text{Max } U^* = (k\hat{x}^*)^\alpha y^{*1-\alpha}$$
$$\text{subject to } y^* + \check{y}^* = 1/a_y^*, \check{y}^* = p\hat{x}^* \qquad (9.7)$$

The maximization problem in Eq. 9.7 leads to

$$\check{y}^* = \frac{\alpha}{a_y^*}, \quad y^* = \frac{1-\alpha}{a_y^*}, \quad \hat{x}^* = \frac{1}{p}\cdot\frac{\alpha}{a_y^*} \tag{9.8}$$

In equilibrium, $\check{x}L = \hat{x}^*L^*$ (and also $\hat{y}L = \check{y}^*L^*$), from which we can solve for the equilibrium relative price p as

$$p = \frac{\alpha}{1-\alpha}\cdot\frac{L^*/a_y^*}{L/a_x} \tag{9.9}$$

In equilibrium, the individual utility levels in Home and Foreign are therefore, respectively

$$U = \alpha\cdot\left(\frac{1}{a_x}\right)^{\alpha}\cdot\left(\frac{kL^*}{a_y^*L}\right)^{1-\alpha}, \quad U^* = (1-\alpha)\cdot\left(\frac{kL}{a_xL^*}\right)^{\alpha}\left(\frac{1}{a_y^*}\right)^{1-\alpha} \tag{9.10}$$

Corner equilibrium in Mode (2)

In this mode of the division of labor, one country will specialize in producing the one good in which it enjoys comparative advantage while the other country will produce both goods. This is further divided into two sub-modes: Mode (2a) and Mode (2b).

Mode (2a)

In this mode we assume Home produces both good x and good y while Foreign completely specializes in the production of good y (where it has been assumed to have comparative advantage). In Mode (2a) it can be seen that $x, \check{x}, y, \hat{y} > 0$, $\hat{x}, \check{y} = 0$ for Home, and $y^*, \check{y}^*, \hat{x}^* > 0$, $\hat{y}^*, x^*, \check{x}^* = 0$ for Foreign. The maximization problem for the Home consumer is now

$$\text{Max } U = x^{\alpha}(y + k\hat{y})^{1-\alpha}$$
$$\text{subject to } x + \check{x} = l_x/a_x, y = l_y/a_y, l_x + l_y = 1, \hat{y} = p\check{x} \tag{9.11}$$

In order for Home to produce both goods, p must be such that $p = a_x/(ka_y)$. The maximization of U in Eq. 9.11 requires

$$\frac{-\alpha}{l_x/a_x - \check{x}} + \frac{(1-\alpha)kp}{(1-l_x)/a_y + kp\check{x}} = 0 \tag{9.12}$$

Solving for $\check{x}$ and inserting the result back into the constraints, we obtain

$$\left.\begin{array}{l}p = a_x/(ka_y), \quad \check{x} = (l_x - \alpha)/a_x, \quad x = \alpha/a_x, \\ y = (1-l_x)/a_y, \quad \hat{y} = (l_x - \alpha)/(ka_y)\end{array}\right\} \tag{9.13}$$

The utility maximization problem for a representative Foreign consumer is

$$\text{Max } U^* = (k\hat{x}^*)^\alpha y^{*1-\alpha}$$
$$\text{subject to } y^* + \check{y}^* = 1/a_y^*, \check{y}^* = p\hat{x}^* \tag{9.14}$$

The first-order condition in Eq. 9.14 requires $\dfrac{\alpha k}{k\hat{x}^*} = \dfrac{(1-\alpha)p}{1/a_y^* - p\hat{x}^*}$, which in turn implies

$$\hat{x}^* = \frac{\alpha k a_y}{a_x a_y^*}, \quad \check{y}^* = \frac{\alpha}{a_y^*}, \quad y^* = \frac{1-\alpha}{a_y^*} \tag{9.15}$$

In equilibrium, $\check{x}L = \hat{x}^* L^*$. Therefore, we have

$$\check{x}L = \hat{x}^* L^* \Leftrightarrow \frac{l_x}{a_x} \cdot \frac{\alpha}{\cdot} \cdot L = \frac{\alpha k a_y}{a_x a_y^*} \cdot L^* \Rightarrow l_x = \frac{\alpha k a_y L^*}{a_y^* L} + \alpha \tag{9.16}$$

As $l_x = \dfrac{\alpha k a_y L^*}{a_y^* L} + \alpha < 1$ if and only if $k < \dfrac{1-\alpha}{\alpha} \cdot \dfrac{L/a_y}{L^*/a_y^*}$, we have to require that $k < \dfrac{1-\alpha}{\alpha} \cdot \dfrac{L/a_y}{L^*/a_y^*}$ in order for l_x to be less than one. In equilibrium, it is straightforward to see that the individual utility levels in Home and Foreign are, respectively

$$U = \left(\frac{\alpha}{a_x}\right)^\alpha \cdot \left(\frac{1-\alpha}{a_y}\right)^{1-\alpha}, \quad U^* = \left(\frac{\alpha k^2 a_y}{a_x a_y^*}\right)^\alpha \left(\frac{1-\alpha}{a_y^*}\right)^{1-\alpha} \tag{9.17}$$

Mode (2b)

In this mode of the division of labor, Home only produces and exports good x, where it enjoys comparative advantage, while Foreign produces both good x and good y. In Mode (2b) $x, \check{x}, \hat{y} > 0$, $\hat{x}, y, \check{y} = 0$ for Home, and $x^*, \hat{x}^*, y^*, \check{y}^* > 0$, $\check{x}^*, \hat{y}^* = 0$ for Foreign. The utility maximization problem for a representative Home consumer is $\text{Max } U = x^\alpha (k\hat{y})^{1-\alpha}$, subject to $x + \check{x} = 1/a_x$ and $\hat{y} = p\check{x}$, while that for a representative Foreign consumer is $\text{Max } U^* = (x^* + k\hat{x}^*)^\alpha y^{*1-\alpha}$, subject to $x^* = l_x^*/a_x^*$, $y^* + \check{y}^* = l_y^*/a_y^*$, $l_x^* + l_y^* = 1$, and $\check{y}^* = p\hat{x}^*$. Following the same procedure as in Mode (2a), we can obtain

$$\left. \begin{array}{c} p = \dfrac{k a_x^*}{a_y^*}, \quad \check{y}^* = \dfrac{\alpha - l_x^*}{a_y^*}, \quad y^* = \dfrac{1-\alpha}{a_y^*}, \quad \hat{x}^* = \dfrac{\alpha - l_x^*}{k a_x^*} \\[2mm] \check{x} = \dfrac{1-\alpha}{a_x}, \quad x = \dfrac{\alpha}{a_x}, \quad \hat{y} = \dfrac{k(1-\alpha)a_x^*}{a_x a_y^*}, \quad l_x^* = \alpha - \dfrac{k(1-\alpha)a_x^* L}{a_x L^*} \end{array} \right\} \tag{9.18}$$

For $0 < l_x^* < 1$ to hold, we have to require that

$$k < \frac{\alpha}{1-\alpha} \cdot \frac{L^*/a_x^*}{L/a_x}$$

In equilibrium, the individual utility levels in Home and Foreign are, respectively

$$U = \left(\frac{\alpha}{a_x}\right)^\alpha \left(\frac{k^2(1-\alpha)a_x^*}{a_x a_y^*}\right)^{1-\alpha}, \quad U^* = \left(\frac{\alpha}{a_x^*}\right)^\alpha \left(\frac{1-\alpha}{a_y^*}\right)^{1-\alpha} \quad (9.19)$$

Corner equilibrium in Mode (3)

It is possible that both countries choose to remain in autarky. In this case both countries obviously produce both goods. The utility maximization problem for the Home consumer is then Max U, subject to $x = l_x/a_x$, $y = l_y/a_y$, and $l_x + l_y = 1$. It is easy to see that, in equilibrium, $x = \alpha/a_x$ and $y = (1-\alpha)/a_y$ for Home. Analogously, in equilibrium, we have $x^* = \alpha/a_x^*$, $y^* = (1-\alpha)/a_y^*$ for Foreign. In equilibrium, the individual utility levels in Home and Foreign are therefore:

$$U = (\alpha/a_x)^\alpha [(1-\alpha)/a_y]^{1-\alpha}, \quad U^* = (\alpha/a_x^*)^\alpha [(1-\alpha)/a_y^*]^{1-\alpha} \quad (9.20)$$

The general equilibrium

To ease the exposition, we define

$$\left. \begin{array}{c} k_a \equiv \left(\dfrac{a_x a_y}{a_x^* a_y^*}\right)^{1/2}, \quad k_b \equiv \dfrac{1-\alpha}{\alpha} \cdot \dfrac{L}{L^*}, \quad k_0 \equiv \left(\dfrac{a_x/a_y}{a_x^*/a_y^*}\right)^{1/2} \\[3mm] k_1 \equiv \dfrac{1-\alpha}{\alpha} \cdot \dfrac{L/a_y}{L^*/a_y^*}, \quad k_2 \equiv \dfrac{\alpha}{1-\alpha} \cdot \dfrac{L^*/a_x^*}{L/a_x} \end{array} \right\} \quad (9.21)$$

General equilibrium modes can be summarized as follows.[2] If $0 < k \leq k_0$, the general equilibrium structure is Mode (3), with both countries remaining in autarky. If $k_a < k_b$, and $k_0 \leq k < k_1$, then the general equilibrium structure is Mode (2a), with Home producing both good x and good y while Foreign completely specializes in the production of good y. If $k_a < k_b$, and $k_1 \leq k < 1$, then the general equilibrium structure is Mode (1), with the two countries engaging in complete specialization according to their respective comparative advantages. If $k_a > k_b$, and $k_0 \leq k < k_2$, then the general equilibrium structure is Mode (2b), where Foreign produces both good x and good y while Home completely specializes in the production of good x. If $k_a > k_b$, and $k_2 \leq k < 1$, then the general equilibrium structure is Mode (1) with the two countries engaging in complete specialization according to their respective comparative advantages.[3]

These results show that when k increases from a low value to k_0 and further to k_1 or k_2, the general equilibrium will then jump from complete autarky (Mode (3)) to incomplete division of labor (Mode (2a) or (2b)) and finally to complete specialization (Mode (1)). Whether the transitional structure is Mode (2a) or Mode (2b) depends on the relative size (as indicated by L/L^*) and the relative productivity (as indicated by a_x^*/a_x, a_y^*/a_y) of the two countries, as well as individuals' relative preference for the two goods (as indicated by $\alpha/(1-\alpha)$). The major point of all this analysis is that the level of transaction efficiency k really *does* matter in determining the pattern of the division of labor and hence the pattern of trade between two countries. As a general result, the economy develops as transaction efficiency k increases from a sufficiently low level to a sufficiently high level. In this simple model, transaction efficiency is the final determinant of the level of development of the economy. Unlike neoclassical growth models, our model does not need technological progress or capital accumulation to explain changes in the economy.

Transaction efficiency and inequality: a theoretical model

In this section we develop a theoretical model to illustrate the impact of transaction efficiency on inequality in the level of welfare (utility). Again, there are two countries, Home (H) and Foreign (F). The general specification is the same as that of the Ricardian model in the preceding section. The difference is that in this model, Home is divided into two regions (i.e., a developed region versus a backward region) denoted H_1 and H_2, respectively. Individuals in the two regions are otherwise the same, except for their transaction efficiency with Foreign (F).

Individuals in H_1 are assumed to have a sufficiently high transaction efficiency coefficient k such that the general equilibrium structure of the division of labor between H_1 and F is Mode (1) (complete specialization with H_1 exclusively producing good x and F exclusively producing good y). Based on the results in the previous section, for Mode (1) to be the general equilibrium structure between H_1 and F, we have to assume

that $\quad 1 > k > k_1 \equiv \dfrac{1-\alpha}{\alpha} \cdot \dfrac{L_1/a_y}{L^*/a_y^*}$ if $\left(\dfrac{a_x a_y}{a_x^* a_y^*}\right)^{1/2} < \dfrac{1-\alpha}{\alpha} \cdot \dfrac{L_1}{L^*}$ and

$1 > k > k_2 \equiv \dfrac{\alpha}{1-\alpha} \cdot \dfrac{L^*/a_x^*}{L_1/a_x}$ if $\left(\dfrac{a_x a_y}{a_x^* a_y^*}\right)^{1/2} > \dfrac{1-\alpha}{\alpha} \cdot \dfrac{L_1}{L^*}.$

In contrast, individuals in H_2 are assumed to have a low transaction efficiency coefficient k' such that no *direct* trade is possible between H_2 and F. However, (domestic) trade is possible between H_1 and H_2, and the transaction efficiency coefficient between H_1 and H_2 is assumed to be τ, where $0 < \tau < 1$. Therefore, *indirect* trade between H_2 and F is possible via H_1 if τ is not too low. It is easy to see that there are three possible modes of trade between H_1 and H_2: Mode (1^d),[4] in which H_2 exclusively produces good x and sells good x to H_1 in exchange for good y (originally produced in F) from H1; Mode $(2a^d)$, in which H_2 produces both goods and sells good x to H_1 in exchange for good y (originally produced in F) from H_1; Mode (3^d), in which H_2 is completely self-sufficient, producing both goods for itself and has no trade with H_1 at all.

We now turn to ascertaining the corner equilibrium for each trade mode between H_1 and H_2, given that the general equilibrium trade mode between H_1 and F has been assumed to be Mode (1).

Corner equilibrium in Mode (1^d)

In Mode (1^d), H_2 exclusively produces good x and sells it to H_1 in exchange for good y (originally produced in F) from H_1.

The utility maximization problems facing a representative individual in H_1, H_2, and F are respectively:[5]

$$\text{Max } U_1 = (1/a_x + \tau \hat{x}_{1d} - \check{x}_1)^\alpha (k\hat{y}_1 - \check{y}_{1d})^{1-\alpha}$$
$$\text{subject to } \hat{y}_1 = p\check{x}_1, \check{y}_{1d} = p_d \hat{x}_{1d} \tag{9.22}$$

$$\text{Max } U_2 = (1/a_x - \check{x}_{2d})^\alpha (\tau \hat{y}_{2d})^{1-\alpha}$$
$$\text{subject to } \hat{y}_{2d} = p_d \check{x}_{2d} \tag{9.23}$$

$$\text{Max } U^* = (k\hat{x}^*)^\alpha (1/a_y^* - \check{y}^*)^{1-\alpha}$$
$$\text{subject to } \check{y}^* = p\hat{x}^* \tag{9.24}$$

For a representative individual in H_1, the first-order condition requires

$$\frac{-\alpha}{1/a_x + \tau \hat{x}_{1d} - \check{x}_1} + \frac{(1-\alpha)kp}{kp\check{x}_1 - p_d \hat{x}_{1d}} = 0 \tag{9.25}$$

which leads to

$$
\left.\begin{aligned}
\check{x}_1 &= \frac{1-\alpha}{a_x} + \left((1-\alpha)\tau + \frac{\alpha p_d}{kp} \right)\hat{x}_{1d}, \\
\hat{y}_1 &= \left[\frac{1-\alpha}{a_x} + \left((1-\alpha)\tau + \frac{\alpha p_d}{kp} \right)\hat{x}_{1d} \right] p
\end{aligned}\right\}
\tag{9.26}
$$

Similarly, for a representative individual in H_2, the first-order condition leads to

$$
\check{x}_{2d} = \frac{1-\alpha}{a_x}, \quad \hat{y}_{2d} = \frac{(1-\alpha)p_d}{a_x}
\tag{9.27}
$$

For a representative individual in F, the first-order condition leads to

$$
\hat{x}^* = \frac{1}{p} \cdot \frac{\alpha}{a_y^*}, \quad \hat{y}^* = \frac{\alpha}{a_y^*}
\tag{9.28}
$$

In equilibrium, we must have $\check{x}_1 L_1 = \hat{x}^* L^*$ and $\check{x}_{2d} L_2 = \hat{x}_{1d} L_1$. These two equations combined imply

$$
\left.\begin{aligned}
\hat{x}_{1d} &= \frac{(1-\alpha)L_2}{a_x L_1}, \\
\check{x}_1 &= \frac{1}{p} \cdot \frac{\alpha L^*}{a_y^* L_1} = \frac{1-\alpha}{a_x} + \left((1-\alpha)\tau + \frac{\alpha p_d}{kp} \right)\frac{(1-\alpha)L_2}{a_x L_1}
\end{aligned}\right\}
\tag{9.29}
$$

In equilibrium, it is easy to show that if an H_1 individual is willing to buy good y from F at the (relative) price p and resell it to H_2 at the (relative) price p_d, the domestic relative price p_d must be such that $p_d = \tau kp$. Inserting this back into Eqs. 9.29 (second equation) and rearranging, we end up with

$$
\left.\begin{aligned}
p &= \frac{\alpha a_x L^*}{(1-\alpha)a_y^*(L_1+\tau L_2)}, \quad p_d = \frac{\tau k\alpha a_x L^*}{(1-\alpha)a_y^*(L_1+\tau L_2)}, \\
\check{x}_1 &= \frac{(1-\alpha)(L_1+\tau L_2)}{a_x L_1}, \quad \hat{y}_1 = \frac{\alpha L^*}{a_y^* L_1}
\end{aligned}\right\}
\tag{9.30}
$$

The utility levels of individuals in H_1, H_2, and F can now be calculated as

$$
\left.\begin{aligned}
U_1 &= \alpha \left(\frac{1}{a_x} \right)^\alpha \left(\frac{kL^*}{a_y^*(L_1+\tau L_2)} \right)^{1-\alpha}, \\
U_2 &= \alpha \left(\frac{1}{a_x} \right)^\alpha \left(\frac{k\tau^2 L^*}{a_y^*(L_1+\tau L_2)} \right)^{1-\alpha}, \\
U^* &= (1-\alpha) \left(\frac{k(L_1+\tau L_2)}{a_x L^*} \right)^\alpha \left(\frac{1}{a_y^*} \right)^{1-\alpha}
\end{aligned}\right\}
\tag{9.31}
$$

Corner equilibrium in Mode (2a^d)

In Mode (2a^d), H_2 produces both goods and sells good x to H_1 in exchange for good y (originally produced in F) from H_1. The utility maximization problems facing a representative individual in H_1, H_2, and F are, respectively

$$\text{Max } U_1 = (1/a_x + \tau\hat{x}_{1d} - \check{x}_1)^\alpha (k\hat{y}_1 - \check{y}_{1d})^{1-\alpha}$$
$$\text{subject to } \hat{y}_1 = p\check{x}_1, \check{y}_{1d} = p_d\hat{x}_{1d} \tag{9.32}$$

$$\text{Max } U_2 = \left(\frac{l_{2x}}{a_x} - \check{x}_{2d}\right)^\alpha \left(\frac{1 - l_{2x}}{a_y} + \tau\hat{y}_{2d}\right)^{1-\alpha}$$
$$\text{subject to } \hat{y}_{2d} - p_d\check{x}_{2d} \tag{9.33}$$

$$\text{Max } U^* = (k\hat{x}^*)^\alpha (1/a_y^* - \check{y}^*)^{1-\alpha}$$
$$\text{subject to } \check{y}^* = p\hat{x}^* \tag{9.34}$$

Since H_2 produces both goods, in equilibrium, we must have $p_d = \dfrac{a_x}{\tau a_y}$. Following the same procedure as above, we get

$$\left.\begin{aligned}
\check{x}_1 &= \frac{1-\alpha}{a_x} + \left((1-\alpha)\tau + \frac{\alpha p_d}{kp}\right)\hat{x}_{1d}, \\[2mm]
\hat{y}_1 &= \left[\frac{1-\alpha}{a_x} + \left((1-\alpha)\tau + \frac{\alpha p_d}{kp}\right)\hat{x}_{1d}\right]p, \\[2mm]
\check{x}_{2d} &= \frac{l_{2x} - \alpha}{a_x}, \quad \hat{y}_{2d} = \frac{l_{2x} - \alpha}{\tau a_y}, \quad \hat{x}^* = \frac{1}{p}\cdot\frac{\alpha}{a_y^*}, \quad \check{y}^* = \frac{\alpha}{a_y^*}
\end{aligned}\right\} \tag{9.35}$$

In equilibrium, we must have $\check{x}_1 L_1 = \hat{x}^* L^*$ and $\check{x}_{2d}L_2 = \hat{x}_{1d}L_1$. These two equations combined imply that

$$\left.\begin{aligned}
\hat{x}_{1d} &= \frac{(l_{2x} - \alpha)L_2}{a_x L_1} \\[2mm]
\check{x}_1 &= \frac{1}{p}\cdot\frac{\alpha L^*}{a_y^* L_1} = \frac{1-\alpha}{a_x} + \left((1-\alpha)\tau + \frac{\alpha p_d}{kp}\right)\frac{(l_{2x} - \alpha)L_2}{a_x L_1}
\end{aligned}\right\} \tag{9.36}$$

Again, in equilibrium, we must have $p_d = \tau kp$. Using this and inserting $p_d = \dfrac{a_x}{\tau a_y}$ back into Eq. 9.36 (second equation), we end up with

$$p = \frac{a_x}{k\tau^2 a_y}, \quad l_{2x} = \frac{\alpha k\tau a_y L^*}{a_y^* L_2} - \frac{(1-\alpha)L_1}{\tau L_2} + \alpha \tag{9.37}$$

Since H_2 produces both goods, we must have $l_{2x} < 1$. Therefore, we must have

$$\tau < \frac{L_2 + \sqrt{L_2^2 + 4\alpha k a_y L^* L_1/[(1-\alpha)a_y^*]}}{2\alpha k a_y L^*/[(1-\alpha)a_y^*]} \tag{9.38}$$

Further, $l_{2x} \geq \alpha$ must hold (since α is the equilibrium labor input in the production of good x under autarky), which implies that $\tau \geq \left(\frac{(1-\alpha)a_y^* L_1}{k\alpha a_y L^*}\right)^{1/2}$. With our earlier assumptions concerning k, it can easily be seen that $\left(\frac{(1-\alpha)a_y^* L_1}{k\alpha a_y L^*}\right)^{1/2} < 1$.

It is now easy to obtain the utility levels of individuals in H_1, H_2, and F as

$$\left.\begin{array}{l} U_1 = \left(\dfrac{\alpha}{a_x}\right)^\alpha \left(\dfrac{1-\alpha}{\tau^2 a_y}\right)^{1-\alpha}, \quad U_2 = \left(\dfrac{\alpha}{a_x}\right)^\alpha \left(\dfrac{1-\alpha}{a_y}\right)^{1-\alpha} \\[2ex] U^* = \left(\dfrac{k^2\tau^2\alpha a_y}{a_x a_y^*}\right)^\alpha \left(\dfrac{1-\alpha}{a_y^*}\right)^{1-\alpha} \end{array}\right\} \tag{9.39}$$

Corner equilibrium in Mode (3^d)

In Mode (3^d), H_2 is completely self-sufficient, producing both goods for itself, and has no trade with H_1 at all. Based on the relevant analysis in the previous section, it is now easy to ascertain that

$$\left.\begin{array}{l} \check{x}_1 = \dfrac{1-\alpha}{a_x}, \quad \hat{y}_1 = p \cdot \dfrac{1-\alpha}{a_x}, \quad \hat{x}^* = \dfrac{1}{p} \cdot \dfrac{\alpha}{a_y^*}, \\[2ex] \check{y}^* = \dfrac{\alpha}{a_y^*}, \quad p = \dfrac{\alpha}{1-\alpha} \cdot \dfrac{L^*/a_y^*}{L_1/a_x} \end{array}\right\} \tag{9.40}$$

In equilibrium, the individual utility levels in H_1, H_2, and F are, respectively

$$\left.\begin{array}{l} U_1 = \alpha \cdot \left(\dfrac{1}{a_x}\right)^\alpha \left(\dfrac{kL^*}{a_y^* L_1}\right)^{1-\alpha}, \quad U_2 = \left(\dfrac{\alpha}{a_x}\right)^\alpha \left(\dfrac{1-\alpha}{a_y}\right)^{1-\alpha}, \\[2ex] U^* = (1-\alpha)\left(\dfrac{kL_1}{a_x L^*}\right)^\alpha \left(\dfrac{1}{a_y^*}\right)^{1-\alpha} \end{array}\right\} \tag{9.41}$$

The general equilibrium

We ar now in a position to turn to a discussion of resultant general equilibrium structures based on interactions between individuals in H_1,

H_2, and F. First, consider the equilibrium in Mode ($2a^d$). In order for the equilibrium in Mode ($2a^d$) to take the structure of the general equilibrium, then at the equilibrium relative price $p = (a_x/k\tau^2 a_y)$, individuals in F must prefer complete specialization in good y to autarky. Thus, the condition $\left(\dfrac{k^2\tau^2\alpha a_y}{a_x a_y^*}\right)^\alpha \left(\dfrac{1-\alpha}{a_y^*}\right)^{1-\alpha} \geq \left(\dfrac{\alpha}{a_y^*}\right)^\alpha \left(\dfrac{1-\alpha}{a_y^*}\right)^{1-\alpha}$ must hold,

which implies $\tau \geq \left(\dfrac{a_x a_y^*}{k^2 a_x^* a_y}\right)^{1/2}$. Comparing this result with our earlier

requirement that $\tau \geq \left(\dfrac{(1-\alpha)a_y^* L_1}{k\alpha a_y L^*}\right)^{1/2}$, under the assumptions we

have made concerning the value of k, it is easy to see that $\left(\dfrac{(1-\alpha)a_y^* L_1}{k\alpha a_y L^*}\right)^{1/2} > \left(\dfrac{a_x a_y^*}{k^2 a_x^* a_y}\right)^{1/2}$. Also, at $p_d = a_x/\tau a_y$, individuals in H_2

must prefer Mode ($2a^d$) to complete specialization in good x *and* to autarky. That is

$$\left(\frac{\alpha}{a_x}\right)^\alpha \left(\frac{1-\alpha}{a_y}\right)^{1-\alpha} \geq \left(\frac{\alpha}{a_x}\right)^\alpha \left(\frac{\tau(1-\alpha)p_d}{a_x}\right)^{1-\alpha} \Leftrightarrow \frac{a_x}{a_y} \geq \tau p_d = \frac{a_x}{a_y}$$

which holds automatically, as well as $\left(\dfrac{\alpha}{a_x}\right)^\alpha \left(\dfrac{1-\alpha}{a_y}\right)^{1-\alpha} \geq \left(\dfrac{\alpha}{a_x}\right)^\alpha \left(\dfrac{1-\alpha}{a_y}\right)^{1-\alpha}$

which holds trivially. Still, at $p = \dfrac{a_x}{k\tau^2 a_y}$ and $p_d = \dfrac{a_x}{\tau a_y}$, individuals in H_1 will

still prefer Mode ($2a^d$) to Mode (3^d) concerning trade with H_2. Therefore, we should have

$$\left(\frac{\alpha}{a_x}\right)^\alpha \left(\frac{1-\alpha}{\tau^2 a_y}\right)^{1-\alpha} \geq \left(\frac{\alpha}{a_x}\right)^\alpha \left(k \cdot \frac{a_x}{k\tau^2 a_y} \cdot \frac{1-\alpha}{a_x}\right)^{1-\alpha}$$

which holds automatically.

Therefore, in order for the (corner) equilibrium in Mode ($2a^d$) to take the structure of the general equilibrium, we have to require that

$$\tau_0 \equiv \left(\frac{(1-\alpha)a_y^* L_1}{k\alpha a_y L^*}\right)^{1/2} \leq \tau < \frac{L_2 + \sqrt{L_2^2 + 4\alpha k a_y L^* L_1/[(1-\alpha)a_y^*]}}{2\alpha k a_y L^*/[(1-\alpha)a_y^*]} \equiv \tau_1$$

$$(9.42)$$

Obviously, a prerequisite for Inequality 9.42 to hold is

$$\left(\frac{(1-\alpha)a_y^* L_1}{k\alpha a_y L^*}\right)^{1/2} < \frac{L_2 + \sqrt{L_2^2 + 4\alpha k a_y L^* L_1/[(1-\alpha)a_y^*]}}{2\alpha k a_y L^*/[(1-\alpha)a_y^*]}$$

which can be shown to hold automatically.

In addition, for $\tau_1 \equiv \dfrac{L_2 + \sqrt{L_2^2 + 4\alpha k a_y L^* L_1 / [(1-\alpha)a_y^*]}}{2\alpha k a_y L^* / [(1-\alpha)a_y^*]} < 1$ to hold, it
can easily be shown that we have to further assume

$$k > \frac{1-\alpha}{\alpha} \cdot \frac{L/a_y}{L^*/a_y^*} \tag{9.43}$$

where $L \equiv L_1 + L_2$.

Now, in order for the (corner) equilibrium in Mode (1^d) to take the structure of the general equilibrium, then at the corner equilibrium relative

price $p = \dfrac{\alpha a_x L^*}{(1-\alpha)a_y^*(L_1 + \tau L_2)}$, individuals in F must prefer complete
specialization in good y to autarky. Thus, we must have

$$\tau \geq \frac{\alpha a_x L^*}{k(1-\alpha)a_x^* L_2} - \frac{L_1}{L_2} \tag{9.44}$$

With our earlier assumptions concerning k, it can easily be shown that
$\dfrac{\alpha a_x L^*}{k(1-\alpha)a_x^* L_2} - \dfrac{L_1}{L_2} < 0$. Therefore, the condition in Eq. 9.44 holds
automatically.

Moreover, for the equilibrium in Mode (1^d) to take the structure of the

general equilibrium, at $p_d = \dfrac{\tau k \alpha a_x L^*}{(1-\alpha)a_y^*(L_1 + \tau L_2)}$, individuals in H_2 must
prefer Mode (1^d) to autarky, which requires

$$\tau \geq \frac{L_2 + \sqrt{L_2^2 + 4\alpha k a_y L^* L_1 / [(1-\alpha)a_y^*]}}{2\alpha k a_y L^* / [(1-\alpha)a_y^*]} \tag{9.45}$$

Nevertheless, at $p = \dfrac{\alpha a_x L^*}{(1-\alpha)a_y^*(L_1 + \tau L_2)}$ and $p_d = \dfrac{\tau k \alpha a_x L^*}{(1-\alpha)a_y^*(L_1 + \tau L_2)}$,
individuals in H_1 will still prefer Mode (1^d) to Mode (3^d) concerning
trade with H_2. Therefore, we should have

$$\alpha \left(\frac{1}{a_x}\right)^\alpha \left(\frac{kL^*}{a_y^*(L_1 + \tau L_2)}\right)^{1-\alpha} \geq \left(\frac{\alpha}{a_x}\right)^\alpha \left(k \cdot \frac{\alpha a_x L^*}{(1-\alpha)a_y^*(L_1 + \tau L_2)} \cdot \frac{1-\alpha}{a_x}\right)^{1-\alpha}$$

which holds automatically. Therefore, in order for the equilibrium in
Mode (1^d) to take the structure of the general equilibrium, we have to
require that

$$\tau \geq \frac{L_2 + \sqrt{L_2^2 + 4\alpha k a_y L^* L_1 / [(1-\alpha)a_y^*]}}{2\alpha k a_y L^* / [(1-\alpha)a_y^*]} \equiv \tau_1 \tag{9.46}$$

Let us now consider the (corner) equilibrium in Mode (3^d). In order for this to take the structure of the general equilibrium, we have to make a series of comparisons. First, taking relative prices at the corner equilibrium

$$p = \frac{\alpha a_x L^*}{(1-\alpha)a_y^* L_1} \quad \text{and} \quad p_d = \frac{\tau k \alpha a_x L^*}{(1-\alpha)a_y^* L_1},$$ we compare the utility levels of H_1, H_2, and F in Mode (3^d) against the corresponding utility levels of H_1, H_2, and F in Mode (1^d). In order for Mode (3^d) to take the structure of the general equilibrium, the following must be required:

$$\alpha \cdot \left(\frac{1}{a_x}\right)^\alpha \left(\frac{kL^*}{a_y^* L_1}\right)^{1-\alpha} \geq \left(\frac{\alpha}{a_x}\right)^\alpha \left(\frac{k\alpha L^*}{a_y^* L_1} - \frac{\tau k \alpha a_x L^*}{(1-\alpha)a_y^* L_1} \cdot \frac{(1-\alpha)L_2}{a_x L_1}\right)^{1-\alpha}$$

which holds automatically, and

$$\left(\frac{\alpha}{a_x}\right)^\alpha \left(\frac{1-\alpha}{a_y}\right)^{1-\alpha} \geq \left(\frac{1}{a_x} - \frac{1-\alpha}{a_x}\right)^\alpha \left(\tau \cdot \frac{(1-\alpha)}{a_x} \cdot \frac{\tau k \alpha a_x L^*}{(1-\alpha)a_y^* L_1}\right)^{1-\alpha}$$

which in turn implies

$$\tau \leq \left(\frac{(1-\alpha)a_y^* L_1}{k \alpha a_y L^*}\right)^{1/2} \tag{9.47}$$

and

$$(1-\alpha)\left(\frac{kL_1}{a_x L^*}\right)^\alpha \left(\frac{1}{a_y^*}\right)^{1-\alpha} \geq \left(k \cdot \frac{(1-\alpha)a_y^* L_1}{\alpha a_x L^*} \cdot \frac{\alpha}{a_y^*}\right)^\alpha \left(\frac{1}{a_y^*} - \frac{\alpha}{a_y^*}\right)^{1-\alpha}$$

which holds automatically. Therefore, in order for Mode (3^d) to take the structure of the general equilibrium, we have to require that

$$\tau \leq \left(\frac{(1-\alpha)a_y^* L_1}{k \alpha a_y L^*}\right)^{1/2} \equiv \tau_0 \tag{9.48}$$

To sum up, so far we have managed to get the following results. If $0 < \tau \leq \left(\frac{(1-\alpha)a_y^* L_1}{k \alpha a_y L^*}\right)^{1/2} \equiv \tau_0$, the general equilibrium trade structure between H_1 and H_2 is Mode (3^d), in which H_2 is completely self-sufficient, producing both goods for itself, and has no trade with H_1 at all.

If $\tau_0 \equiv \left(\frac{(1-\alpha)a_y^* L_1}{k \alpha a_y L^*}\right)^{1/2} \leq \tau < \frac{L_2 + \sqrt{L_2^2 + 4\alpha k a_y L^* L_1/[(1-\alpha)a_y^*]}}{2\alpha k a_y L^*/[(1-\alpha)a_y^*]} \equiv \tau_{1,,}$

the general equilibrium trade structure between H_1 and H_2 is Mode $(2a^d)$, in which H_2 produces both goods and sells good x to H_1 in exchange for good y (originally produced in F) from H_1.

If $\tau_1 \equiv \frac{L_2 + \sqrt{L_2^2 + 4\alpha k a_y L^* L_1/[(1-\alpha)a_y^*]}}{2\alpha k a_y L^*/[(1-\alpha)a_y^*]} \leq \tau < 1$, then the general equilibrium trade structure between H_1 and H_2 is Mode (1^d), in which H_2 exclusively produces good x and sells good x to H_1 in exchange for good y (originally produced in F) from H_1.

Comparative statics

Keeping all of our earlier assumptions concerning the value of k in mind, we can now carry out a comparative static analysis of individual utility levels in H_1, H_2, and F with respect to the value of τ.

When $0 < \tau \le \left(\dfrac{(1-\alpha)a_y^* L_1}{k\alpha a_y L^*} \right)^{1/2} \equiv \tau_0$ the trade structure of the general equilibrium between H_1 and H_2 is Mode (3^d). The corresponding individual utility levels in H_1, H_2, and F are shown in Eqs. 9.41. Obviously, when τ increases within the interval $(0, \tau_0]$, U_1, U_2, and U^* all remain unchanged.

When

$$\tau_0 \equiv \left(\frac{(1-\alpha)a_y^* L_1}{k\alpha a_y L^*} \right)^{1/2} \le \tau < \frac{L_2 + \sqrt{L_2^2 + 4\alpha k a_y L^* L_1/[(1-\alpha)a_y^*]}}{2\alpha k a_y L^*/[(1-\alpha)a_y^*]} \equiv \tau_1$$

the trade structure of the general equilibrium between H_1 and H_2 is Mode ($2a^d$). The individual utility levels in H_1, H_2, and F are shown in Eqs. 9.39. First, at $\tau = \tau_0$, it can easily be seen that there is no discontinuous jump for U_1, U_2, and U^*. Then, when τ increases continuously within the interval $[\tau_0, \tau_1)$, we can see that U_1 decreases continuously, U_2 remains unchanged, and U^* increases continuously.

Finally, when $\tau_1 \equiv \dfrac{L_2 + \sqrt{L_2^2 + 4\alpha k a_y L^* L_1/[(1-\alpha)a_y^*]}}{2\alpha k a_y L^*/[(1-\alpha)a_y^*]} \le \tau < 1$, the trade structure of the general equilibrium between H_1 and H_2 is Mode (1^d). The individual utility levels in H_1, H_2, and F are shown in Eqs. 9.31. First, it can easily be seen that, at $\tau = \tau_1$, there is no discontinuous jump for U_1, U_2, and U^*. Then, when τ increases continuously within the interval $[\tau_1, 1)$, we can see that U_1 decreases continuously, U_2 increases continuously, and U^* increases continuously.

It is also possible to carry out a comparative static analysis of the individual utility levels in H_1, H_2, and F with respect to the trade pattern between H_1 and F. Suppose the transaction efficiency coefficient k between H_1 and F is initially so low that, in equilibrium, no trade is possible between H_1 and F (i.e., Mode (3) between H_1 and F). It is further possible to study how the individual utility levels in H_1, H_2, and F change if

k jumps from such a low value of $\underline{k}$ to a sufficiently high value of $\overline{k}$ (which meets all our earlier assumptions and with which the general equilibrium mode of trade between H_1 and F is Mode (1)).

The initial low value $\underline{k}$ means there is no trade between the two countries, and obviously there is no domestic trade between H_1 and H_2. Therefore, with any $\tau \in (0, 1)$, we always have

$$U_1 = U_2 = \left(\frac{\alpha}{a_x}\right)^{\alpha} \left(\frac{1-\alpha}{a_y}\right)^{1-\alpha}, \quad U^* = \left(\frac{\alpha}{a_x^*}\right)^{\alpha} \left(\frac{1-\alpha}{a_y^*}\right)^{1-\alpha} \quad (9.49)$$

Let us now suppose the transaction efficiency coefficient k between H_1 and F jumps to a sufficiently high value of $\overline{k}$ (one that meets all our earlier assumptions). With this high value of $\overline{k}$, if τ happens to be such that $0 < \tau \le \left(\frac{(1-\alpha)a_y^* L_1}{\overline{k}\alpha a_y L^*}\right)^{1/2} \equiv \overline{\tau_0}$, then the individual utility levels in H_1, H_2, and F follow Eqs. 9.41. It can easily be shown that with this upward jump in k from $\underline{k}$ to $\overline{k}$, if $0 < \tau \le \overline{\tau_0}$, then U_1 unambiguously jumps upward, U_2 remains unchanged, and U^* unambiguously jumps upward.

Let us suppose instead, at the new level of the transaction efficiency coefficient $\overline{k}$, if τ happens to be such that

$$\overline{\tau_0} \equiv \left(\frac{(1-\alpha)a_y^* L_1}{\overline{k}\alpha a_y L^*}\right)^{1/2} \le \tau < \frac{L_2 + \sqrt{L_2^2 + 4\alpha\overline{k}a_y L^* L_1 / [(1-\alpha)a_y^*]}}{2\alpha\overline{k}a_y L^* / [(1-\alpha)a_y^*]} \equiv \overline{\tau_1}$$

that the individual utility levels in H_1, H_2, and F follow Eqs. 9.39. It can also be easily shown that with the upward jump in k from $\underline{k}$ to $\overline{k}$, if $\overline{\tau_0} \le \tau < \overline{\tau_1}$, then U_1 unambiguously jumps upward, U_2 remains unchanged, and U^* unambiguously jumps upward.

Finally, at the new level of the transaction efficiency coefficient $\overline{k}$, if τ happens to be such that $\overline{\tau_1} \equiv \dfrac{L_2 + \sqrt{L_2^2 + 4\alpha\overline{k}a_y L^* L_1 / [(1-\alpha)a_y^*]}}{2\alpha\overline{k}a_y L^* / [(1-\alpha)a_y^*]} \le \tau < 1,$
then the individual utility levels in H_1, H_2, and F follow Eqs. 9.31. It can easily be shown that with the upward jump in k from $\underline{k}$ to $\overline{k}$, if $\overline{\tau_1} \le \tau < 1$, then U_1 unambiguously jumps upward, U^* unambiguously jumps upward, and U_2 remains unchanged (if $\tau = \overline{\tau_1}$ exactly) or jumps upward (if $\overline{\tau_1} < \tau < 1$).

Moreover, another related fact can easily be seen: if k is now sufficiently high so that the trade mode of the general equilibrium between H and F is Mode (1), then a marginal increase in k (one that does not cause the general equilibrium between H_1 and H_2 to shift from one mode to another) will leave individuals in F strictly better off, and individuals in H_1 and H_2 at least no worse off than before the increase in k.

Let us now study the model from another perspective. Suppose, as before, k meets all our earlier assumptions so that the trade structure of the general equilibrium between H and F is Mode (1). The domestic transaction efficiency coefficient may fall into any one of the three intervals, $(0, \tau_0]$, $[\tau_0, \tau_1)$, and $[\tau_1, 1)$. Now suppose both k and τ are fixed, but the border between H_1 and H_2 shifts so that H_1 is now larger and H_2 smaller (i.e., L_1 increases and L_2 decreases, with the total population of H fixed at $L = L_1 + L_2$).

Let us now study the effects of an increase in L_1 on the individual utility levels of H_1, H_2, and F, holding both k and τ fixed. First, it should be noted that a change in L_1 shifts the dividing points τ_0 and τ_1. It can easily be shown that

$$\left.\begin{array}{l} \dfrac{\partial \tau_0}{\partial L_1} = \dfrac{1}{2}\left(\dfrac{(1-\alpha)a_y^*}{k\alpha a_y L^*}\right)^{1/2} L_1^{-1/2} > 0, \\[4mm] \dfrac{\partial \tau_1}{\partial L_1} = \dfrac{1}{M}\{-1 + [(L - L_1)^2 + 2ML_1]^{-1/2}(-L + L_1 + M)\} > 0 \end{array}\right\} \quad (9.50)$$

where $M \equiv 2\alpha k a_y L^* / [(1-\alpha)a_y^*]$. With our earlier assumption that $k > \dfrac{1-\alpha}{\alpha} \cdot \dfrac{L/a_y}{L^*/a_y^*}$, it can easily be shown that $M > 2L$, which in turn can easily be shown to imply that $[(L - L_1)^2 + 2ML_1]^{-1/2}(-L + L_1 + M) > 1$, hence $\dfrac{\partial \tau_1}{\partial L_1} > 0$.

If a marginal increase in L_1 is such that it does not shift the trade structure of the general equilibrium between H_1 and H_2, then it can straightforwardly be seen that this marginal increase in L_1 will make individuals in F strictly better off (if Mode (1^d) or Mode (3^d) is the structure of the general equilibrium between H_1 and H_2) or at least no worse off (if Mode $(2a^d)$ is the structure of the general equilibrium between H_1 and H_2), make individuals in H_1 strictly worse off (if Mode (1^d) or Mode (3^d) is the structure of the general equilibrium between H_1 and H_2) or no better off (if Mode $(2a^d)$ is the structure of the general equilibrium between H_1 and H_2), and make individuals in H_2 strictly worse off (if Mode (1^d) is the structure of the general equilibrium between H_1 and H_2) or no better off (if Mode $(2a^d)$ or Mode (3^d) is the structure of the general equilibrium between H_1 and H_2).

At a sufficiently high level of k and a given level[6] of τ, let us now suppose there is such a discontinuous upward jump in L_1 that the equilibrium structure between H_1 and H_2 shifts from Mode (1^d) to Mode ($2a^d$). It can easily be seen that U_1 unambiguously decreases, U_2 unambiguously decreases, and U^* unambiguously increases as a result. Let us suppose instead that this upward jump in L_1 causes the equilibrium structure between H_1 and H_2 to shift from Mode ($2a^d$) to Mode (3^d). In this case, U_1 unambiguously increases, U_2 does not change, and U^* unambiguously decreases.

Table 9.1 summarizes the comparative static analysis undertaken in this chapter. Table 9.1 shows, for example, if the transaction cost between the developed part of H_1 and the underdeveloped part H_2 is already low enough (we can roughly interpret this as there being little in the way of a transaction 'barrier' between the two parts of the country), then, *ceteris paribus*, further lifting the transaction barrier between the two parts will make residents in the 'underdeveloped' area better off at the expense of residents in the 'developed' area. This is one way through which changing transaction efficiency may affect the welfare of residents in different areas of the same country.

In developing and transition economies, transaction efficiency has a lot to do with infrastructure and institutions. The factors underlying transaction efficiency in a transition economy are usually fast changing. Therefore, the study of (changes in) transaction efficiency in a developing and transition country is very important for revealing and explaining the trade patterns of a country, as well as their effects on the country's economic growth and development.

A limit to our analysis in this section is that we have assumed exogenous transaction efficiency and exogenous comparative advantage in our model. However, both transaction efficiency and comparative advantage can be endogenously determined within the economy. For example, if we define 'full transaction efficiency' as zero transaction costs, then non-zero transaction costs will reduce the actual effects of one country's comparative advantage (as seen from the perspective of the other country). Non-zero transaction costs would affect not only exogenous (static) comparative advantage, but also the evolution path of endogenous (dynamic) comparative advantage. Moreover, transaction efficiency can be either exogenous or endogenous. If transaction efficiency is assumed to be given and fixed, then it is exogenous and not affected by comparative advantages, trade patterns, or other related factors. However, transaction efficiency can be endogenous as well. A country may acquire transaction efficiency just as it acquires endogenous comparative advantage by, say, knowledge accumulation. Then the patterns of comparative advantage and trade

Table 9.1 Summary of the comparative static analysis undertaken in this chapter

Fixed parameters	Changing variable		Mode H_1 & H_2	Mode H_1 & F	Utility levels		
					U_1	U_2	U^*
k, L_1, etc.	$\tau \nearrow$	$\tau \in (0, \tau_0)$	3^d	1	$=$	$=$	$=$
		$\tau \in [\tau_0, \tau_1)$	$2a^d$	1	$\searrow$	$=$	$\nearrow$
		$\tau \in [\tau_1, 1)$	1^d	1	$\searrow$	$\nearrow$	$\nearrow$
τ, L_1, etc.	$\tau \in (0, \overline{\tau_0}]$	$k \uparrow$ (upward jump from $\underline{k}$ to $\overline{k}$)	$3^d \to 3^d$	$3 \to 1$	$\uparrow$	$=$	$\uparrow$
	$\tau \in [\overline{\tau_0}, \overline{\tau_1})$		$3^d \to 2a^d$	$3 \to 1$	$\uparrow$	$=$	$\uparrow$
	$\tau \in (\overline{\tau_1}, 1)$		$3^d \to 1^d$	$3 \to 1$	$\uparrow$	$\uparrow$	$\uparrow$
	$\tau \in (0, \overline{\tau_0})$	$k \nearrow$ (marginal increase from $\overline{k}$ to $\overline{k}+\varepsilon$)	3^d	1	$\nearrow$	$=$	$\nearrow$
	$\tau \in (\overline{\tau_0}, \overline{\tau_1})$		$2a^d$	1	$=$	$=$	$\nearrow$
	$\tau \in (\tau_1, 1)$		1^d	1	$\nearrow$	$\nearrow$	$\nearrow$
k, τ, etc.	$\tau \in (0, \tau_0)$	$L_1 \nearrow$ (marginal increase from L_1 to $L_1 + \varepsilon$)	3^d	1	$\searrow$	$=$	$\nearrow$
	$\tau \in (\tau_0, \tau_1)$		$2a^d$	1	$=$	$=$	$=$
	$\tau \in (\tau_1, 1)$		1^d	1	$\searrow$	$\searrow$	$\nearrow$
	for some τ	$L_1 \uparrow$ (upward jump from L_1 to $\overline{L_1}$)	$1^d \to 2a^d$	1	$\downarrow$	$\downarrow$	$\uparrow$
	for some τ		$1a^d \to 3^d$	1	$\uparrow$	$=$	$\downarrow$

Notes: $\nearrow$ stands for increasing continuously, $\searrow$ stands for decreasing continuously, $=$ stands for keeping unchanged, $\uparrow$ stands for jumping upward discontinuously, and $\downarrow$ stands for jumping downward discontinuously. For simplicity, the possibility that $\tau = \overline{\tau_0}$ or $\tau = \overline{\tau_1}$ is not considered wherever necessary.

may have a lot to say about the evolution path of endogenous transaction efficiency. In this case, the effects of foreign trade on output, economic development, the welfare level, and regional disparities will depend heavily on the intricate interactions between static comparative advantage, dynamic advantage, and transaction efficiency. A thorough discussion of this issue, however, is beyond the scope of this chapter.

Concluding remarks

In this chapter we build a theoretical model that is diametrically different from the neoclassical growth framework to explain development and inequality in developing economies. Our model deliberately avoids modeling technological progress and capital accumulation, and looks at alternative mechanisms through which developing economies achieve their development. Following the inframarginal analysis framework of Cheng et al. (2000) based on the old Ricardian model, we have built an extended theoretical model founded on the concepts of comparative advantage and transaction efficiency to explain development and inequality in developing economies.

Our model allows us to make this general assertion: if domestic transaction efficiency, which can be viewed as a function of the domestic legal, institutional, and policy environment, is increased, the welfare (utility) level of H_1 households tends to decrease and the welfare level of H_2 households can be increased, thus reducing inequality between the two parts of a developing economy. By contrast, if international transaction efficiency, which can also be viewed as a function of the legal, institutional, and policy environment, is increased, then the welfare levels in both parts of a developing country can be increased. These and other basic results of our model, such as those in Table 9.1, may have important implications for developing economies in their policy-making.

Notes

1. Works on economics are often classified according to JEL classification codes, a system set up by the *Journal of Economic Literature*.
2. We omit the derivation procedure. Readers who are unfamiliar with this inframarginal analysis are referred to the 'Transaction efficiency and inequality' section (p. 100) where our model will provide a similar derivation procedure.
3. If $k_a = k_b$ happens to hold, then we will have $k_0 = k_1 = k_2$. This simply implies that under the condition $k_a = k_b$ the two countries will either be in complete autarky or in complete specialization, depending on the actual value of k: if $0 < k \leq k_0$, the two countries will remain in autarky; if $k_0 \leq k < 1$, the two countries will engage in complete specialization according to their respective comparative advantage. Mode (2) (i.e.,

Mode (2a) and Mode (2b)) simply cannot be the structure of the general equilibrium under the condition $k_a = k_b$.

4. The superscript d stands for 'domestic'.

5. The subscript d denotes the domestic market within country H. For example, $\hat{x}_{1d}$ denotes the quantity of good x a representative individual in H_1 buys from H_2.

6. For simplicity and without loss of generality, we do not consider the possibility that the given τ exactly equals one of the crucial values, τ_0 or τ_1.

References

Cheng, Wenli; Sachs, J.D.; and Yang, Xiaokai (1999) *An Inframarginal Analysis of the Heckscher–Olin model with Transaction Costs and Technological Comparative Advantage* (Working Paper No. 9), Cambridge, MA: Center for International Development at Harvard University.

Cheng, Wenli; Sachs, J.D.; and Yang, Xiaokai (2000) 'An inframarginal analysis of the Ricardian model,' *Review of International Economics*, 8, 208–20.

Ricardo, D. (1817) *The Principle of Political Economy and Taxation*, London: Gaernsey Press, 1973.

Sun, Guangzhen (2003) 'Identification of equilibrium structures of endogenous specialization: a unified approach exemplified,' in Y.K. Ng, H. Shi, and G. Sun (Eds.), *The Economics of E-Commerce and Networking Decisions: Applications and Extensions of Inframarginal Analysis*, London: Macmillan.

Sun, Guangzhen; Yang, Xiaokai; and Yao, Shuntian (1999) *Theoretical Foundation of Economic Development Based on Networking Decisions in the Competitive Market* (Working Paper No. 17), Cambridge, MA: Center for International Development at Harvard University.

Sun, Guangzhen; Yang, Xiaokai; and Yao, Shuntian (2003) 'Toward a theory of impersonal networking decisions and endogenous structure of the division of labor,' in Y.K. Ng, H. Shi, and G. Sun (Eds.), *The Economics of E-Commerce and Networking Decisions: Applications and Extensions of Inframarginal Analysis*, London: Macmillan.

Wen, Mei (1998) 'An analytical framework of consumer-producers, economies of specialization and transaction costs,' in K. Arrow, Y.K. Ng, and X. Yang (Eds.), *Increasing Returns and Economic Analysis*, London: Macmillan.

Yang, Xiaokai (1991) 'Development, structural changes, and urbanization,' *Journal of Development Economics*, 34, 199–222.

Yang, Xiaokai; and Zhang, Dingsheng (1999) *International Trade and Income Distribution* (Working Paper No. 18), Cambridge, MA: Center for International Development at Harvard University.

Yao, Shuntian (2002a) 'Walrasian equilibrium computation, network formation, and the Wen Theorem,' *Review of Development Economics*, 6, 415–27.

Yao, Shuntian (2002b) 'Privilege and corruption: the problems of China's socialist market economy,' *American Journal of Economics and Sociology*, **61**, 279–99.

Zhang, Dingsheng; and Shi, Heling (2006) 'A note on "An Infra-marginal Analysis of the Ricardian Model",' *Pacific Economic Review*, **11**(4), 505–12.

10

Economies of scale and industrial agglomeration

Abstract: In this chapter we explore economies of scale and industrial agglomeration, as well as their linkages with regional development and interregional disparity in China. We focus specifically on an empirical examination of the spatial distribution of manufacturing activity in China in the 2000s, a decade witnessing increased opening up to foreign trade and FDI. We set up our regression model and carry out a regression exercise to empirically examine the effects of openness to foreign trade and FDI on industrial distribution and agglomeration across China's provinces. Our regression results support our claim that openness to foreign trade and FDI do indeed play important roles in shaping the spatial pattern and distribution of industries.

Key words: economies of scale, industrial agglomeration, spatial concentration, regional development, industry mix, market integration.

JEL classification codes: F41; O11; O53.[1]

Introduction

In this chapter we explore economies of scale and industrial agglomeration and their relationship with regional economic development in China. We follow an approach that involves two main lines of attack. First, we present theoretical arguments explaining why we strongly expect to find a positive relationship between openness to foreign trade and FDI, industrial agglomeration, and economic growth in China. Second, we take a look at some of the empirical work that has been done in an effort to seek to document and support the expected positive relationship. We focus specifically on investigating the spatial distribution of manufacturing activity in China in an era of ever-increasing opening up to foreign trade and FDI.

Most research into industrial agglomeration and economic performance deals with empirical situations in developed economies (Fan and Scott, 2003). However, in this chapter we want to show that theory needs not only to take into account the economic bases of regional development but also socio-cultural factors such as the various institutions. We show that our approach is just as good at analyzing China's regions as it is at studying developed country situations. Like Fan and Scott (2003), we show that genuine industrial agglomeration is more characteristic of sectors and spaces that have undergone the greatest change as a result of economic reforms, market orientation, and opening up.

Substantial regional disparity, especially that between coastal and interior regions, stands out as one of the most significant features of China's development. Various factors such as regional infrastructure, investment, geographical location, regional policy, and human capital accumulation have been shown to have important impacts on regional development (Ge, 2006). There is a great deal of evidence supporting the claim that opening up to foreign trade and FDI played an important role in driving interregional disparity in the development of China's regions. This led researchers to delve more deeply into the mechanisms through which foreign trade and FDI may affect regional development. One such potential mechanism is industrial agglomeration.

In this chapter we mainly focus on the potential impacts of openness to foreign trade and FDI on spatial industrial agglomeration as a result of the effect they have in driving interregional disparity and facilitating economies of scale across China's provinces. The remainder of this chapter is organized as follows. In the second section 'Spatial agglomeration and regional development', we consider agglomeration and development in China from a theoretical perspective. In the third section 'Regional specialization and industrial agglomeration in China', we empirically examine patterns and trends in specialization and agglomeration in China in the 2000s. In the fourth section 'Spatial concentration of industries', we briefly discuss the measurement of spatial concentration of industries. In the fifth section 'Openness and industrial agglomeration', we carry out a regression exercise to empirically examine the effects of openness to foreign trade and FDI on industrial distribution and agglomeration across China's provinces.

Spatial agglomeration and regional development: theoretical considerations

In this section we take a theoretical look at spatial agglomeration and regional development. We mainly draw on the review of Ng and Tuan (2006) for our discussion of the issue. The central idea of Krugman (1990, 1998) emphasizes the spatial dimension of the economic interactions between firms and focuses on their behavior from a spatial perspective. The conceptualization of 'space' suggests that it exerts persistent effects on the behavior and interactions between firms, implying different drivers of agglomeration and sectoral specificities (Bottazzi et al., 2002). Krugman (1990, 1998) highlight the role played by agglomeration externalities in affecting the spatial pattern of investments through which geographic concentration is formed by means of interactions between increasing returns, transportation costs, and factor mobility. The existence of economies of scale in production tends to determine the pattern of spatial concentration and the locality of investments (Krugman, 1991a, b). Agglomeration economies as a result of the core–periphery relationship further act as the dominant force shaping specific regional investment and trade flows. This 'new economic geography' approach highlights the formation of industrial clustering through capital mobility and investment dynamics (Baldwin, 1997), industry spillovers through diffusion of manufacturing activities among regions (Puga and Venables, 1996), and the influences of forward and backward linkages among industries (Venables, 1996).

Historically, the existence of spatial concentration and diversity has been supported by early ideas about land use in city–suburban division (Alonso, 1964), the forces behind the urban system (Isard, 1956; Henderson, 1974), and what urban agglomeration economies mean for spatial development (Henderson, 1988; Richardson, 1995). Economies of scale are considered the incentives for agglomeration and concentration (Dixit and Stigitz, 1977; Fujita and Thissa, 1996; Krugman, 1991a, b, 1996). More recent research has emphasized the dynamism of economies of agglomeration, spatial agglomeration phenomena via location patterns, interactions between such economic activities (Authur, 1994; Bottazzi et al., 2002), and industrial districts and their interactions in a dynamic system (Curzio and Fortis, 2002). Fujita and Thissa (2002) and Fujita and Mori (2005) review developments in the 'new economic geography' and related aspects such as agglomeration of economic activities, agglomeration economies, location space, trade, transportation costs, and growth.

The concept behind Krugman (1991a)'s core–periphery system in China and the interrelationship between the city core and the periphery region has been examined from the perspective of the Hong Kong–PRD case (Tuan and Ng, 1995). The relations and effects as a result of the gravitational pull from the city core to the periphery market center were further investigated by Ng and Tuan (2003) and Tuan and Ng (2004). Recognition of the existence of agglomeration economies not only helps explain the spatial pattern of industries, but also envisages the dynamics of industrial activities that lead to regional growth. Recently, more extensive empirical research examining spatial agglomeration and its linkage to regional growth has emerged. Economies of scale are considered preconditions to the main centripetal force in determining the spatial pattern of firm locations. Empirical studies following Krugman's ideas on economies of scale have provided strong evidence to support such effects on the spatial pattern of firm locations. How this relates to FDI inflows has also been extensively examined since the 1990s. However, studies mostly emphasize the effects of FDI on regional growth through its role in technology transfer and market integration (Grossman and Helpman, 1991, 1995; Barro and Sala-i-Martin, 1995, 1997). The spillover effects of FDI on promoting regional or national economic growth in terms of human capital, employment, technology transfer, and trade were demonstrated by the ASEAN-5 economies (Bende, 1999). Inflows of FDI and imports were shown to promote economic growth in four ASEAN countries (Marwah and Tavakoli, 2004). Besides the role played by FDI in affecting local institutions, it also significantly benefited those countries by facilitating the formation of well-developed financial markets (Alfaro et al., 2004).

FDI-led economic growth has also been investigated (Borensztein et al., 1998; De Mello, 1999; Marwah and Tavakoli, 2004). FDI is considered the main transmission mechanism of advanced technology and thus fosters economic growth especially in developing countries. Cointegration and causality analyses of the long-run and short-run effects of FDI showed that both unidirectional and bidirectional causalities between FDI and economic growth exist (Nair-Reichert and Weinhold, 2001; Liu et al., 2002; Basu et al., 2003; Bengoa and Sanchez-Robles, 2003). The positive relationship between FDI and economic growth – in particular, the direction of causality from FDI to long-run economic growth – is well supported in the literature. However, little effort has been made so far to investigate the interrelationship between spatial industrial agglomeration, FDI inflows, and regional economic growth.

Inspired by these discussions, we follow Ng and Tuan (2006) in postulating four main research hypotheses to study the impacts of institutional characteristics on shaping firm location choices, spatial agglomeration patterns, and patterns of regional FDI inflows. The four hypotheses are: (H1) Foreign firms tend to exploit the advantages generated by business networking (agglomeration) and production-supporting facilities in order to increase efficiency and competitiveness. When choosing investment sites, firms are inclined to select locations with higher spatial agglomeration (i.e., spatial agglomeration by investment type positively affects FDI absorption). (H2) Strategic interactions between local and foreign investments contribute to agglomeration and economies of scale, which further attracts FDI into the region (i.e., strategic interaction positively affects FDI absorption). (H3) Forces generated by regional institutional characteristics significantly affect FDI inflows such that the frictional effect of the center core is crucial to directing FDI in a core–periphery economy. (H4) Spatial agglomeration promotes regional economic growth in that higher agglomeration not only directly induces higher output growth but also enhances regional output growth by absorbing FDI inflows (see Ng and Tuan, 2006).

Regional specialization and industrial agglomeration in China

Owing to data limitations, there have been few empirical studies on the patterns of regional industrial concentration and agglomeration in China. The patterns empirically investigated still remain ambiguous and controversial. One prevalent view is that local protectionism (barriers to interregional trade) impedes regional specialization and leads to duplication of the structure of regional production (Ge, 2006). For example, Young (2000) studied the structure of provincial production and concluded that the reform process in China led to fragmentation of the domestic market and duplication of the structure of regional production. Batisse and Poncet (2003) confirmed Young (2000)'s finding that local protectionism was responsible for duplication of the production structure at the provincial level. Bai et al. (2004) also found local protection had a negative effect on industrial agglomeration.

During China's industrialization, the most prominent change in economic structure was the movement of labor from the agricultural sector to the industrial and service sectors. In the 1990s, regional employment was still dominated by the traditional agricultural sector despite its importance declining over time. The labor share of the secondary industry in China, which includes mining, manufacturing, utility, and construction, increased in the early 1990s and declined in the late 1990s. Two possible forces underlie such a trend. First, state-owned enterprises, most of which were in manufacturing, were allowed to lay off workers in the late 1990s. Second, the expansion of the service sector in the late 1990s enabled it to absorb more workers from other sectors. Regional disparity existed in terms of sectoral labor shares across China's regions: the coastal regions had smaller agricultural labor shares than the western and central regions.

As the agricultural sector shrinks and the service sector expands, the overall regional industry mix in terms of labor shares is converging across China's different regions. Conflicting results in the literature may stem from the fact that different studies use different subsets of data covering different industries and sectors. Studies that use more aggregated data tend to reach the conclusion that the structures of regional production are becoming increasingly similar over time while studies that cover only the manufacturing sector tend to show regional specialization increasing in the 1990s. Like Ge (2006) we exclude the agriculture, mining, utility, and service industries and narrow our focus to the structure of regional production in the manufacturing industry. We do this because agriculture and mining rely heavily on local natural resource endowment while the utility and service industries rely heavily on local demand, leaving manufacturing as a footloose industry, within which we expect most industrial relocation and agglomeration to take place.

Like Ge (2006) we use production data on disaggregated manufacturing industries to examine the change in regional specialization in the 2000s. Two indicators are applied in this analysis. One is Hoover's coefficient of specialization (Hoover and Giarratani, 1984), which is defined as

$$HCS = \frac{1}{2}\sum_{k=1}^{K}\left|\frac{\sum_i E_i^k}{\sum_i \sum_k E_i^k} - \frac{E_i^k}{\sum_k E_i^k}\right| \qquad (10.1)$$

where HCS stands for Hoover's coefficient of specialization, and E_i^k represents employment in manufacturing industry k for region i. HCS measures the difference between the industry structure of a specific region and the structure of national production. The second indicator we apply in this analysis is the Krugman specialization index (Krugman, 1991b), which is defined as

$$KSI_{ij} = \sum_k\left|\frac{E_i^k}{\sum_k E_i^k} - \frac{E_j^k}{\sum_k E_j^k}\right| \qquad (10.2)$$

where *KSI* stands for the Krugman specialization index, and E_i^k and E_j^k are employment in manufacturing industry k for regions i and j, respectively. This index is used to compare the disparity in the production structure of two regions bilaterally.

The values of the Hoover's coefficient of specialization calculated from data on the 2000s show that there is an upward trend in regional specialization for each region. That is, the production structure of manufacturing of each region is increasingly different from that nationally. Compared with coastal regions, western regions have a higher degree of regional specialization. The levels of the Krugman specialization index calculated for the 2000s show the production structures of manufacturing in coastal and interior regions, and those of central and western regions diverging over time. These results basically show that over time regional specialization deepened and inland regions became more specialized than coastal regions. These results by and large mimic those of Ge (2006) for the 1990s. This indicates that regional specialization in China was on the rise between 1990 and 2010. Regions are becoming increasingly specialized as time move on.

Spatial concentration of industries

There are different ways of measuring the degree of industrial concentration, the most popular of which is the locational Gini coefficient (Krugman, 1991b). The Gini coefficient is defined with respect to the localization quotient of region i for industry k:

$$g^k = Gini^k(r_i^k) \tag{10.3}$$

where the localization quotient r_i^k is in turn defined as

$$r_i^k = \left[\frac{E_i^k}{\sum_k E_i^k}\right] \Bigg/ \left[\frac{\sum_i E_i^k}{\sum_i \sum_k E_i^k}\right] \tag{10.4}$$

where E_i^k is employment in manufacturing industry k for region i. It is a measure of regional specialization in industry k relative to the employment share of the industry for the entire nation. If r_i^k is greater than unity, region i has a higher percentage of industry k compared with its proportion of total industry employment. The higher the Gini coefficient, the stronger the locational divergence between the particular sector and the production structure of total manufacturing. Using the locational Gini coefficient as a measure of industry concentration and based on relevant data on the 2000s, we study the spatial concentration of employment in three aggregated sectors: agriculture, manufacturing, and service. It turns out that for all three sectors, the degree of concentration first decreased and then increased over the period of 2000–2010.

Openness and industrial agglomeration

Two broad theories explaining the impact of openness to foreign trade on the production distribution of a country concern comparative advantage and economies of scale. The first theory posits that trade arises as a result of regional comparative advantage, which originates from inherent regional characteristics such as resource endowment, institutions, technology, or policy. The second theory posits that trade arises in response to the distributions of regional production and regional demands, where production activities tend to cluster together in order to take advantage of economies of scale. The distinction between neoclassical trade models and new trade models is that the former are based on the assumptions of constant returns to scale and perfect competition. The most common model is the Heckscher–Ohlin–Vanek framework which predicts a linear relationship between trade volume and regional factor endowment. New trade models are based on the assumptions of increasing returns to scale, product differentiation, and the market structure of monopolistic competition.[2] In order to identify the various sources of increasing returns to scale, we have to distinguish between the two main types of increasing returns to scale. One is due to production externalities within the same industry ('localization') or across industries ('urbanization') while the other is due to pecuniary externalities modeled in new economic geography theories (Ge, 2006).[3]

To formulate our regression specification, we follow Midelfart-Knarvik et al. (2000) and Ge (2006) in assuming that the location of an industry depends on industry characteristics and regional characteristics, as well as interactions between them. There are three possible forms of interactions. First, in examining the effect of openness to foreign trade and FDI on industrial agglomeration, we consider the interaction between regional accessibility to foreign trade and FDI and the dependence of industry on foreign trade and FDI. Intuitively, industries that rely heavily on foreign trade and/or FDI tend to choose to locate in regions with easy access to foreign trade and FDI. Second, based on the theory of comparative advantage, we consider the interaction between a region's resource endowment and industry's requirement for resource endowment as we expect industries that are land based or labor based tend to choose to locate in regions where there is high land or labor endowment. Third, we also consider the interaction between domestic market potential and inter-industry linkage. When it comes to transportation costs, industries with strong backward or forward linkages tend to choose to locate close to their suppliers or customers.

Taking these interactions and the availability of practical data into account, the regression model can then be specified as

$$
\begin{aligned}
\ln(sha_{ik}) = {} & \delta + \varphi \ln(pop_i) + \beta_1 \ln(agr_i) + \beta_2 \ln(hum_i) + \beta_3 \ln(dom_i) \\
& + \beta_4 \ln(ope_i) + \gamma_1 \ln(agin_k) + \gamma_2 \ln(huin_k) + \gamma_3 \ln(doin_k) \\
& + \gamma_4 \ln(opin_k) + \theta_1 \ln(agr_i) \ln(agin_k) + \theta_2 \ln(hum_i) \ln(huin_k) \\
& + \theta_3 \ln(dom_i) \ln(doin_k) + \theta_4 \ln(ope_i) \ln(opin_k) + \varepsilon_{ik} \qquad (10.5)
\end{aligned}
$$

We have given all the variables in Eq. 10.5 as logs so that they bear percentage interpretation. At any given point in time (in a given year), the dependent variable on the left-hand side of Eq. 10.5 represents (the log of) the industrial share of region (province) i in the total national output of industry k. Therefore, the dependent variable pertains to each (province, industry) pair (i.e., (i, k) pair). Explanatory variables indexed by subscript i pertain to characteristics of the region (region i) while those indexed by subscript k pertain to characteristics of the industry (industry k). The first explanatory variable pop_i represents the provincial population, which is meant to represent the size of the region. Larger regions (in terms of the population) tend to have more economic activities and higher shares of the industry. The second explanatory variable agr_i is meant to represent the agricultural endowment of region i. Namely, agr_i is the share of agricultural production in region i's total provincial GDP. Inclusion of the variable agr_i in our regression model follows our expectation that the agriculture endowment of a province affects its share of the total national output of industry k through the level of dependence of industry k on agricultural endowment. The next explanatory variable hum_i is meant to represent human capital. Just like agricultural endowment, a province's human capital endowment also affects the size of the industry in the province. Therefore, the variable hum_i is designed to measure the stock of human capital in the province. How this variable of human capital stock can be constructed in practice will shortly be shown. The next explanatory variable dom_i (literally standing for 'domestic') is meant to measure the level of domestic market integration of a province in relation to all other provinces. Intuitively, if industry k is heavily dependent on other industries as a result of forward or backward linkages, then the degree of market integration of region i in relation to all the other provinces in China may play an important role in determining the size of industry k inside region i, provided the other industries to which industry k is forward or backward-linked are scattered in the other provinces. How this variable of market integration can be constructed in practice will shortly be shown. The next explanatory variable ope_i (literally standing for 'openness') measures the degree of provincial openness to foreign trade and FDI. Intuitively, we would expect a region with more openness to foreign trade and FDI to have a relatively larger share of industry k if this industry depends heavily on openness to foreign activities. How this variable of foreign openness can be constructed in practice will shortly be shown.

Before describing the remaining variables in Eq. 10.5, this is a good place to pause and explain how the provincial human capital stock variable hum_i, domestic market integration variable dom_i, and the foreign openness variable ope_i can be constructed.[4] The human capital stock variable can be constructed according to the simple decomposition

$$hum_i = \sum_j h^j L_i^j \qquad (10.6)$$

where $\sum_j L_i^j = L_i^{6+}$ $(j = a, b, c, d, e)$, in which L_i^{6+} denotes the population aged 6 and over in province i (at a certain point in time). L^{6+} can be divided into five groups by educational attainment, group a through group e. L_i^a is the total number of people aged 6 and over who have received zero schooling while L_i^b through L_i^e are, respectively, the total number of people aged 6 and over who have received schooling up to primary school level, junior secondary school level, senior secondary school level, and university level. We are obliged to perform this five-group decomposition on the regional population aged 6 and over because data on the distribution of educational attainment in regional total population, total employed population, or total working age population are unavailable. The values of h^j $(j = a, b, c, d, e)$ are then constructed as follows: $h^a = 1$, $h^b = 2.01$, $h^c = 2.60$, $h^e = 3.16$, and $h^e = 4.39$ (for every province in every year). These values are calculated according to piecewise linear rates of return to schooling based on the survey of Psacharopoulos (1994).[5]

We apply a price-based approach used by Parsley and Wei (2001) and Sheng and Mao (2011) to construct the domestic market integration variable dom_i for province i. The central idea behind this approach is that the dispersion of common currency price differentials of identical goods between two provinces can be an inverse indicator of the degree of market integration between the two provinces. Let $p(i, t, \pi)$ be the price of good π in province i at time t and $p(j, t, \pi)$ the price of good π in province j $(j \neq i)$ at time t. We define

$$D(ij, t, \pi) \equiv \ln\left[\frac{p(i, t, \pi)}{p(i, t-1, \pi)}\right] - \ln\left[\frac{p(j, t, \pi)}{p(j, t-1, \pi)}\right] \qquad (10.7)$$

Eq. 10.7 measures percentage change in the price of good π between provinces i and j during the interval $(t-1, t)$.[6] We then remove the time mean of $D(ij, t, \pi)$ for each good π separately to filter out good-specific effects from our dispersion calculation. Mathematically, we define

$$D(ij, t, \pi) \equiv D(ij, t, \pi) - \bar{D}(t, \pi) \qquad (10.8)$$

where $\bar{D}(t, \pi)$ denotes the mean of $D(ij, t, \pi)$ across province pairs. After $\ddot{D}(ij, t, \pi)$ is constructed by de-meaning $D(ij, t, \pi)$, we then calculate the variance (our measure of dispersion) of $\ddot{D}(ij, t, \pi)$, rather than that of $D(ij, t, \pi)$, across all goods for each province pair (i, j) and time period t. We denote this variance as $\text{var}[\ddot{D}(ij, t)]$. To construct the domestic market integration variable dom_i (for province i at a given point in time), we need to sum up all such variances $\text{var}[\ddot{D}(ij, t)]$ for any given i over all the j's. To do this, we define

$$V(i, t) \equiv \sum_j \text{var}[\ddot{D}(ij, t)] \qquad (10.9)$$

Finally, we construct our domestic market integration variable dom_{it} as

$$dom_{it} \equiv \frac{1}{\sqrt{V(i, t)}} \qquad (10.10)$$

What we need to do in practice to construct Eqs. 10.6–10.10 is select a specific set of π (types of) goods. Data availability obliges these goods to be (a) grain; (b) oil and fat; (c) meat, poultry, and related processed products; (d) eggs; (e) aquatic products; (f) vegetables; (g) fresh and dried fruit (including melons); (h) tobacco; (i) liquor; (j) garments; (k) clothing fabric; (l) footwear and hats; (m) durable consumer goods; (n) daily use household articles (cleaning products, etc.); and (o) cosmetics.

The variable measuring provincial openness to foreign trade and FDI, ope_i, can be constructed in the following way. First, the basic openness indicator normally used in the literature is the ratio of foreign trade to output. That is

$$f_{it} \equiv \frac{F_{it}}{GRP_{it}} \qquad (10.11)$$

where F_{it} and GRP_{it} are, respectively, the total real value of foreign trade (exports plus imports) and the total value of real GRP in region i at time t. However, we adjust the openness indicator in Eq. 10.11 to take account of differences in region size and the level of development. To correct for differences in province size and the level of development, we follow Low et al. (1998) and consider this regression

$$\ln f_{it} = \vartheta_0 = \vartheta_1 GRP_{it} + \vartheta_2 GRP_{it}^2 + \vartheta_3 pop_{it} + \vartheta_4 pop_{it}^2$$
$$+ \vartheta_5 (GRP_{it}/pop_{it}) + \vartheta_6 (GRP_{it}/pop_{it})^2 + u_{it}^f \qquad (10.12)$$

where u_{it}^f is the error term, and pop_{it} stands for regional population. We run a pooled OLS regression based on the specification in Eq. 10.12 and construct the fitted value such that

$$\ln \hat{f}_{it} = \hat{\vartheta}_0 + \hat{\vartheta}_1 GRP_{it} + \hat{\vartheta}_2 GRP_{it}^2 + \hat{\vartheta}_3 pop_{it} + \hat{\vartheta}_4 pop_{it}^2$$
$$+ \hat{\vartheta}_5 (GRP_{it}/pop_{it}) + \hat{\vartheta}_6 (GRP_{it}/pop_{it})^2 \qquad (10.13)$$

where the $\hat{\vartheta}$'s are the values of intercepts and slopes estimated from a pooled OLS regression.[8] $\hat{f}_{it}$ calculated according to Eq. 10.13 indicates the 'normal' or average degree of openness of a Chinese region, given the level of regional GRP and the size of regional population. Following this idea, the adjusted openness variable for use in the regression model in Eq. 10.13 can then be constructed as

$$ope_{it} \equiv \frac{f_{it}}{\hat{f}_{it}} \qquad (10.14)$$

This adjusted openness variable indicates the openness deviation of province i (at time t) relative to the 'normal' level of openness of a province of the same size regarding output and production.

The remaining explanatory variables in Eq. 10.5 pertain to the industry, rather than the province. The variable $agin_k$ represents the agricultural intensity of industry k (i.e., the share of total agricultural inputs used in total industrial output for industry k). Intuitively, the larger the share of agricultural inputs used in the output of industry k, the more likely industry k would choose to locate in a province that is rich in agricultural endowment. The variable $huin_k$ represents the human capital intensity of industry k, and can be approximated by the fraction of non-manual workers among industrial employees. Again, intuitively, the larger the fraction of non-manual workers in industry k, the more likely the industry would choose to locate in a province that is rich in human capital. The variable $doin_k$ measures the degree of dependence of industry k on inter-provincial domestic market integration within

China, through its forward and backward linkages to other industries. This variable can be proxied for by the percentage of output sold to other domestic industries as intermediates and capital goods. Intuitively, an industry that heavily relies on other domestic industries as its customers or suppliers would tend to choose to locate in a province having a higher level of domestic market integration with other provinces. The variable $opin_k$ measures the degree of dependence of industry k on foreign markets. Obviously, an industry that heavily sells its output to or buys its inputs from foreign markets would tend to choose to reside in a province that is more open to foreign activities. This variable can be constructed either as the percentage of total output sold to foreign markets or as the share of foreign capital in total capital, or as a combination of the two.

Eq. 10.5 captures the potential interdependence of the effects of variables in both the region's characteristics and industry characteristics.

Ideally, Eq. 10.5 should take advantage of the structure of panel data in order to control for time-constant province-specific factors. However, as data are not always available for every year, especially for variables pertaining to industries, it is then difficult to run regressions of the structure of panel data. We have little choice but to run an OLS regression based on cross-sectional data. Therefore, we run our regression based on Eq. 10.5 and summarize the major results in Table 10.1. Interestingly, estimated coefficients on all four interaction terms are not significant at the usual 5% significance level, suggesting that there are no significant interaction effects between region characteristics and the corresponding industry characteristics. Estimated coefficients on the variables in both the region's characteristics and the industry characteristics all have the expected positive sign, suggesting the appropriateness of the theoretical basis for the model. However, not all these estimates are significant. Our results suggest that openness to foreign trade has an important role to play in shaping the spatial pattern and distribution of industries across China's provinces.

Concluding remarks

In this chapter we have explored economies of scale and industrial agglomeration, as well as their linkages with regional development in China. Our focus was empirical examination of the spatial distribution of manufacturing activity in China in the 2000s, a time of ever-increasing opening up to foreign trade and FDI. We first provided some theoretical considerations on spatial agglomeration and regional development, then

Table 10.1   Regression results based on Eq. 10.5

Dependent variable: $\ln(sha_{ik})$ Number of observations: 420		
Coefficient	**Estimated value**	**P-value**
β_1	0.309*	0.001
β_2	0.183*	0.022
β_3	0.035	0.068
β_4	0.259*	0.041
γ_1	0.302	0.071
γ_2	0.124*	0.011
γ_3	0.048	0.308
γ_4	0.394*	0.039
θ_1	−0.034	0.872
θ_2	0.234	0.482
θ_3	−0.121	0.397
θ_4	0.210	0.245

Relevant p-values are reported. The asterisk * indicates significance at the 5% level.

empirically examined the pattern and trend of regional specialization and industrial agglomeration in the 2000s, and briefly discussed ways of measuring the spatial concentration of industries. Finally, we set up our regression model and carried out a regression exercise to empirically examine the effects of openness to foreign trade and FDI on industrial distribution and agglomeration across China's provinces. Our regression results supported our earlier claim that openness to foreign trade does indeed play an important role in shaping the spatial pattern and distribution of industries across China's provinces.

Notes

1. Works on economics are often classified according to JEL classification codes, a system set up by the *Journal of Economic Literature*.

2. For detailed reviews of the two lines of theories, see, for example, Helpman (1999), Davis and Weinstein (2001), and Bernstein and Weinstein (2002).

3. For more discussions related to this topic, see, for example, Quigley (1998), Eberts and McMillian (1999), Hanson (1998), Henderson et al. (2001), Overman et al. (2001), and Rosenthal and Strange (2003).

4. Essentially the same approaches to constructing the three variables were applied in Chapter 5. However, for the sake of chapter self-containedness, we repeat the description of the approaches here, too.

5. When calculating h^e, we assume that a person who has completed university has on average 17 years of schooling.

6. Inter-provincial market integration can be studied by examining cross-sectional dispersion (across goods) of $D(ij, t, \pi)$ for each province pair and time period. Any particular realization of $D(ij, t, \pi)$ can be either positive or negative without triggering arbitrage as long as the absolute value of $D(ij, t, \pi)$ is lower than the cost of arbitrage. The existence of arbitrage cost implies that $D(ij, t, \pi)$ must fall within a range, not that it must equal or trend toward zero. Any reduction in barriers to inter-provincial trade should thus reduce the no-arbitrage range. Therefore, the dispersion of $D(ij, t, \pi)$ across goods can be an inverse indicator of the degree of market integration between provinces i and j at time t.

7. It has often been argued that a large country (or region) in terms of output or population tends to have (relatively) less foreign trade, as there is a larger scope for trade within the country (or region). It has also been argued that a country (or region) with a high level of per-capita output may be biased toward having a lower trade-to-output ratio, because the share of the service sector tends to increase as the country (or region) develops, while the service sector is largely non-tradable (Low et al., 1998).

8. Note that the regression equation (Eq. 10.12) does not contain a time-variant intercept on its right-hand side. Note also that we have not opted for other regression methods, such as the within estimator. This is because a pooled OLS regression considers explicitly neither a time-variant intercept nor region heterogeneity, and contains all these in the error term of the regression.

References

Alfaro, L.; Chanda, A.; Kalemli-Ozcan, S; and Sayek, S. (2004) 'FDI and economic growth: the role of local financial markets,' *Journal of International Economics*, **64**(1), 89–112.

Alonso, W. (1964) *Location and Land Use*, Cambridge, MA: Harvard University Press.

Authur, W.B. (1994) *Increasing Returns and Path-Dependency in Economics*, Ann Arbor, MI: University of Michigan Press.

Bai, Chong-En; Du, Yingjuan; Tao, Zhigang; and Tong, S.Y. (2004) 'Local protectionism and regional specialization: evidence from China's industries,' *Journal of International Economics*, **63**(2), 397–417.

Baldwin, R.E. (1997) 'Agglomeration and endogenous capital,' *European Economic Review*, **43**(2), 253–80.

Barro, R.; and Sala-i-Martin, X. (1995) *Economic Growth*, New York: McGraw Hill.

Barro, R.; and Sala-i-Martin, X. (1997) 'Technology diffusion, convergence, and growth,' *Journal of Economic Growth*, **2**, 1–26.

Basu, P.; Chakraborty, C.; and Reagle, D. (2003) 'Liberalization, FDI, and growth in developing countries: a panel cointegration approach,' *Economic Inquiry*, **41**(3), 510–16.

Batisse, C.; and Poncet, S. (2003) *Protectionism and Industry Localization in Chinese Provinces* (ERSA Conference Papers No. ersa03p147), Louvain-la-Neuve, Belgium: European Regional Science Association.

Bende, N.A. (1999) *FDI, Regionalism, Government Policy, and Endogenous Growth: A Comparative Study of the ASEAN-5 Economies, with Development Policy Implications for the Least Developed Countries*, Farnham, UK: Ashgate Publishing.

Bengoa, M.; and Sanchez-Robles, B. (2003) 'Foreign direct investment, economic freedom and growth: new evidence from Latin America,' *European Journal of Political Economy*, **19**(3), 529–45.

Bernstein, J.R.; and Weinstein, D.E. (2002) 'Do endowments predict the location of production? Evidence from national and international data,' *Journal of International Economics*, **56**, 55–76.

Borensztein, E.; De Gregorio, J.; and Lee, J.W. (1998) 'How does foreign direct investment affect economic growth?' *Journal of International Economics*, **45**, 115–35.

Bottazzi, G.; Dosi, G.; and Fagiolo, G. (2002), 'On the ubiquitous nature of agglomeration economies and their diverse determinants: some notes,' in A.Q. Curzio and M. Fortis (Eds.), *Complexity and Industrial Clusters*, New York: Physica-Verlag.

Curzio, A.Q.; and Fortis, M. (Eds.) (2002) *Complexity and Industrial Clusters*, New York: Physica-Verlag.

Davis, D.R.; and Weinstein, D.E. (2001) *What Role for Empirics in International Trade* (NBER Working Paper No. 8543). Cambridge, MA: National Bureau of Economic Research.

De Mello, L. (1999) 'Foreign direct investment led growth: evidence from time series and panel data,' *Oxford Economic Papers*, **51**, 132–51.

Dixit, A.K.; and Stigitz, J.E. (1977) 'Monopolistic competition and optimum product diversity,' *American Economic Review*, **67**, 297–308.

Eberts, R.W.; and McMillian, D.P. (1999) 'Agglomeration economies and urban public infrastructure,' in P. Cheshire and E.S. Mills (Eds.), *Handbook of Urban and Regional Economics*, Vol. 3, New York: North Holland, pp. 1455–95.

Fan, C.C.; and Scott, A.J. (2003) 'Industrial agglomeration and development: a survey of spatial economic issues in East Asia and a statistical analysis of Chinese regions,' *Economic Geography*, **79**(3), 295–319.

Fujita, M.; and Mori, T. (2005) *Frontiers of the New Economic Geography* (Discussion Paper No. 27), Chiba, Japan: Institute of Developing Economies (IDE-JETRO).

Fujita, M.; and Thissa, J.F. (1996) 'Economics of agglomeration,' *Journal of the Japanese and International Economics*, **10**, 339–78.

Fujita, M.; and Thissa, J.F. (2002) *Economics of Agglomeration: Cities, Industrial Location, and Regional Growth*, Cambridge, U.K.: Cambridge University Press.

Ge, Ying (2006) *Regional Inequality, Industry Agglomeration and Foreign Trade, the Case of China* (Working Paper RP2006/105), Helsinki, Finland: World Institute for Development Economic Research (UNU-WIDER).

Grossman, G.; and Helpman, E. (1991) *Innovation and Growth in the World Economy*, Cambridge, MA: MIT Press.

Grossman, G.; and Helpman, E. (1995) 'Technology and trade,' in G.M. Grossman and K. Rogoff (Eds.), *Handbook of International Economics*, Vol. 3, New York: North Holland.

Hanson, G.H. (1998) 'Regional adjustment to trade liberalization,' *Regional Science and Urban Economics*, **28**, 419–44.

Helpman, E. (1999) 'The structure of foreign trade,' *Journal of Economic Perspectives*, **13**, 121–44.

Henderson, J.V. (1974) 'The sizes and types of cities,' *American Economic Review*, **64**, 640–56.

Henderson, J.V. (1988) *Urban Development: Theory, Fact, and Illusion*, New York: Oxford University Press.

Henderson, J.V., Shalizi, Z.; and Venables, A.J (2001) 'Geography and development,' *Journal of Economic Geography*, **1**, 81–105.

Hoover, E.; and Giarratani, F. (1984) *An Introduction to Regional Economics*, New York: Knopf Doubleday.

Isard, W. (1956) *Location and Space Economy*, Cambridge, MA: MIT Press.

Krugman, P. (1990) *Rethinking International Trade*, Cambridge, MA: MIT Press.

Krugman, P. (1991a) 'Increasing returns and economic geography,' *Journal of Political Economy*, **99**, 483–99.

Krugman, P. (1991b) *Geography and Trade*, Cambridge, MA: MIT Press.

Krugman, P. (1996) *The Self-Organizing Economy*, Cambridge: Blackwell.

Krugman, P. (1998) 'Space: the final frontier,' *Journal of Economic Perspectives*, **12**(2), 161–74.

Liu, X., Burridge, P.; and Sinclair, P.J.N (2002) 'Relationships between economic growth, foreign direct investment and trade: evidence from China,' *Applied Economics*, **34**, 1433–40.

Low, P.; Olarreaga, M.; and Suarez, J. (1998) *Does Globalization Cause a Higher Concentration of International Trade and Investment Flow?* (WTO Staff Working Paper ERAD-98-08), Geneva, Switzerland: Economic Research and Analysis Division, World Trade Organization.

Marwah, K.; and Tavakoli, A. (2004) 'The effect of foreign capital and imports on economic growth: further evidence from four Asian countries (1970–1998),' *Journal of Asian Economics*, **15**(2), 399–413.

Midelfart-Knarvik, K.H., Redding, S.J., and Venables, A.J. (2000) *The Location of European Industry* (mimeo), London: London School of Economics.

Nair-Reichert, U.; and Weinhold, D. (2001) 'Causality tests for cross-country panel: a new look at FDI and economic growth in developing countries,' *Oxford Bulletin of Economics and Statistics*, 63, 153–71.

Ng, Linda Fung-Yee; and Tuan, Chyau (2003) 'Location decisions of manufacturing FDI in China: implications of China's WTO accession,' *Journal of Asian Economics*, **14**(1), 51–72.

Ng, Linda Fung-Yee; and Tuan, Chyau (2006) 'Spatial agglomeration, FDI, and regional growth in China: locality of local and foreign manufacturing investments,' *Journal of Asian Economics*, **17**, 691–713.

Overman, H.G., Redding, S.; and Venables, A.J. (2001) *The Economic Geography of Trade, Production, and Income: A Survey of Empirics* (mimeo), London: London School of Economics/Center for Economic and Policy Research.

Parsley, D.C.; and Wei, Shang-Jin (2001) *Limiting Currency Volatility to Stimulate Goods Markets Integration: A Price Based Approach* (NBER Working Paper No. 8468), Cambridge, MA: National Bureau of Economic Research.

Psacharopoulos, G. (1994) 'Returns to investment in education: a global update,' *World Development*, **22**, 1325–43.

Puga, D.; and Venables, A.J. (1996) *The Spread of Industry: Spatial Agglomeration in Economic Development* (CEPR Discussion Paper Series No. 1354), London: Center for Economic and Policy Research.

Quigley, J. (1998) 'Urban diversity and economic growth,' *Journal of Economic Perspective*, **12**, 127–38.

Richardson, H.W. (1995) 'Economies and diseconomies of agglomeration,' in H. Giersch (Ed.), *Urban Agglomeration and Economic Growth*, Berlin: Springer-Verlag.

Rosenthal, S.S.; and Strange, W.C. (2003) 'Evidence on the nature and sources of agglomeration economies,' in J.V. Henderson and J.F. Thisse (Eds.), *Handbook of Urban and Regional Economics*, Amsterdam, The Netherlands: Elsevier.

Sheng, Bin; and Mao, Qilin (2011) 'Trade openness, domestic market integration, and provincial economic growth in China: 1985–2008,' *The Journal of World Economy*, November 2011, 44–66 [in Chinese].

Tuan, Chyau; and Ng, Linda Fung-Yee (1995) 'Hong Kong's outward investment and regional economic integration with Guangdong: process and implications,' *Journal of Asian Economics*, **6**(3), 385–405.

Tuan, Chyau; and Ng, Linda Fung-Yee (2004) 'FDI and industrial restructuring in post-WTO greater PRD: implications on regional growth in China,' *The World Economy*, **27**(10), 1609–30.

Venables, A.J. (1996) 'Equilibrium locations of vertically linked industries,' *International Economic Review*, **37**, 341–59.

Young, A. (2000) 'The razor's edge: distortions and incremental reform in the People's Republic of China,' *Quarterly Journal of Economics*, **115**, 1091–135.

11

Higher education and human capital mobility

Abstract: Knowledge as an intangible production input not only promotes economic growth but also facilitates structural change in a developing economy. Education is the major means of knowledge accumulation. Higher education in China plays an important role not only in promoting knowledge accumulation, but also in facilitating human capital mobility. This chapter empirically investigates the relationship between regional disparities, college preferences, and admissions under the National College Entrance Examination (NCEE) system, and potential interregional human capital mobility in China. Our empirical results show that examinees from western provinces tend to have a strong preference for coastal universities, compared with examinees from central provinces. In this sense, we expect college admissions in China under the NCEE system to exert a stronger impact on potential human capital movement from the western region to the coastal region than from the central region to the coastal region.

Key words: higher education, National College Entrance Examination, human capital mobility, regional disparity, openness, knowledge.

JEL classification codes: F41; O15; O53.[1]

Introduction

Knowledge as an intangible production input not only promotes economic growth but also facilitates structural change in a developing economy. In today's world, knowledge and other intangible assets have become progressively important creators of wealth for nations and the world. Increasingly, countries are creating more wealth from knowledge through services than from traditional industry and agriculture. Global trade in services has been growing faster than that in tangible commodities.

The market values of most firms consist more and more of intangible knowledge assets, and the knowledge contents of goods and services are increasing. The World Bank has introduced a knowledge-based framework at the national level called the 'knowledge-based economy', which consists of four pillars: education, science, technology, and innovation.

Education is the major means of knowledge accumulation. Higher education in China plays an important role not only in promoting knowledge accumulation, but also in facilitating human capital mobility. This chapter focuses on China's higher education system and its impact on interregional human capital mobility across China. As mentioned many times in previous chapters, China's rapid economic growth has been accompanied by increasing income inequality.[2] At the same time, there has been growing spatial inequality in educational resources across China's different regions. In this chapter, we address two issues: how factors such as spatial income disparities affect and shape the educational preferences of individuals in their choice of higher education institutions, and how spatial disparities in openness to foreign trade and FDI impact the preferences and choices of individuals.

This chapter specifically deals with college admissions under the National College Entrance Examination system (NCEE) and the potential implications of these admissions for cross-region human capital mobility in China. The chapter differs from previous research on the NCEE by measuring and accounting for the attractiveness of coastal universities to inland examinees, using data on college admissions under the NCEE system. This chapter is organized as follows. In the second section 'The issue and the model', we present the basic framework within which we conduct our empirical work in this chapter. In the third section 'The sample, data, and variables', we describe the factors considered in our empirical analysis. In the fourth section 'Empirical results and discussions', we report and discuss our findings.

The issue and the model

China regulates internal migration through a 'household registration system', known as the *hukou* system. However, it is possible to jump from rural to urban *hukou* status by getting a degree. Higher education thus facilitates human capital migration by helping individuals overcome the *hukou* barrier. First, college education provides undergraduates with the knowledge and skills required to get a better-paying city job, vital to covering the extra living costs in the host city. Second, having a degree contributes toward meeting the criteria set by the host city in granting the local urban *hukou*.

The NCEE is an academic exam held annually in China and is a prerequisite for entrance into almost all higher education institutions at the undergraduate level.[4] Although most high-school students are admitted to a university as a result of passing the NCEE, requirements for admission vary from province to province. This can be seen from the large variation in first-tier cut-off scores across different provinces. The provincial first-tier cut-off score targets matching the number of provincial examinees eligible for admission to first-tier universities with the corresponding provincial first-tier admission quota.[5] However, the provincial first-tier cut-off score is only a minimum requirement for admission to a first-tier university. The provincial cut-off score differs greatly from that of a university. The university sets the minimum required score for admission of an examinee from this specific province.

The wider the gap between the provincial cut-off score and the university cut-off score (for the corresponding province) the greater the appeal of this university to examinees from this province. The more attractive a university is to the examinees of a province, the more likely it will get high-score examinees from this province. As a result the university can set a higher cut-off score for this province and get the brightest students to fulfill the admission quota that has been allocated to this province. There are far more first-tier universities in the 11 coastal provinces than in the 20 inland provinces of China. Therefore, each year large numbers of inland examinees are admitted to coastal universities. In this chapter we measure and explain the appeal of coastal universities to inland examinees. To do this we set up our baseline regression model as

$$A_{ik,t} = \eta_t + \sum_{g=1}^{G} \beta_g \cdot x_{g,ij,t} + \sum_{h=2}^{H} \delta_h \cdot DV_h + \sum_{m=2}^{M} \varphi_m \cdot DP_m + \varepsilon_{ik,t} \quad (1.1)$$

where the subscripts i, k, and t index an inland province i, a coastal university k, and the time period t, respectively. $A_{ik,t}$, measures the attractiveness of university k to examinees from province i at time t. The explanatory variables fall into three categories. The first category, $\sum_{g=1}^{G} \beta_g \cdot x_{g,ij,t}$, contains the number of G variables related to each (i,j) pair at each time period t, where j in $x_{g,ij,t}$ indexes the coastal province where university k is located. The $x_{g,ij,t}$'s measure the provincial characteristics of inland province i with reference to coastal province j.

The second category, $\sum_{h=2}^{H} \delta_h \cdot DV_h$, contains dummy variables associated with a single coastal university, where the total number of coastal universities is H, and $DV_h = 1$ when $h = k$ and $DV_h = 0$ otherwise. The third category, $\sum_{m=2}^{M} \varphi_m \cdot DP_m$, contains dummy variables associated with an inland province, where the total number of inland provinces is M, and $DP_m = 1$ when $m = i$ and $DP_m = 0$ otherwise.

The sample, data, and variables

Our sample includes 46 first-tier universities located in 10 coastal provinces.[6] The home provinces of inland examinees number 19.[7] Our sample period is 2005–2011. The explained variable $A_{ik,t}$ is constructed as follows

$$A_{ik,t} = \ln Av_{ik,t} - \ln Cs_{ik,t} \tag{11.2}$$

where $Cs_{ik,t}$ denotes the first-tier cut-off score of province i for its science examinees in year t and $Av_{ik,t}$ denotes the average NCEE score of all the science examinees admitted to university k from province i in year t.

The $x_{g,ij,t}$'s in Eq. 11.1 measure regional gaps between the home province of inland examinees (inland province i) and the coastal province j where university k is located. We include the following three variables in the vector of $x_{g,ij,t}$'s. The first variable, denoted by $Ry_{ij,t}$, is the log of the ratio of per-capita GDP of the two provinces (lagged for one year), which measures the income gap between the two provinces. The second variable, denoted by $Rf_{ij,t}$, which measures relative regional openness, is defined as the gap in the trade-to-GDP ratio between the two provinces (averaged over the past five years). The variable $Rf_{ij,t}$ measures how much more open province j is compared with province i. Besides these two variables, we also include one time-invariant variable in the vector of $x_{g,ij,t}$'s in Eq. 11.1. This measures the geographical distance between provinces j and i. This distance variable, which we denote by $Dist_{ij}$, is constructed as the log of the spherical distance between the capital cities of the two provinces.

Finally, to take account of the time-variant intercept η_t in Eq. 11.1, we use period (year) dummies (along with a common intercept) in the regression equation. The six we use are denoted $d06$, $d07$, $d08$, $d09$, $d10$, and $d11$, respectively, and relate to a year between 2005 and 2011 other than 2005. With all the variables in Eq. 11.1 clearly defined and described, we can now run regressions based on this equation. The next section reports the principal results of our regression analysis.

Empirical results and discussions

We run regressions based on Eq. 11.1, using the three variables defined above (and subsets of them) as elements in the $x_{g,ij,t}$ vector. Tables 11.1, 11.2, and 11.3 summarize the principal findings. We use our entire sample in the regressions in Table 11.1, , where i indexes all the 19 home provinces of inland examinees. As we have 46 selected universities and seven years in our sample period, we should have 6118 (i.e., $19 \times 46 \times 7$) observations altogether. However, we actually have only 5954 observations owing to missing data. We use a subset of our entire sample in the regressions shown in Table 11.2, a subset only concerned with the western home provinces of inland examinees, where i indexes the 11 western home provinces of inland examinees. We end up with 3407 observations in this group of regressions. We use the subset of the sample associated with the central home provinces of inland examinees in the regressions in Table 11.3, where i indexes the eight central home provinces of inland examinees. We therefore have 2547 observations in this group of regressions. It should be noted that in all the regressions shown in Tables 11.1, 11.2 and 11.3, a full set of university dummies, inland province dummies, and year dummies (as well as a common intercept) is included in the regression equation. However,

Table 11.1 Regressions based on Eq. 11.1 (with i = all inland provinces)

	Dependent variable: $A_{ik,t}$						
	Regression No.						
Variable	(A1)	(A2)	(A3)	(A4)	(A5)	(A6)	(A7)
$Ry_{ij,t}$	−0.016* (0.004)	—	−0.014* (0.004)	−0.016* (0.004)	—	—	−0.014* (0.004)
$Rf_{ij,t}$	−0.003 (0.003)	−0.003 (0.003)	—	−0.003 (0.003)	—	0.003 (0.003)	—
$Dist_{ij}$	−0.005* (0.001)	−0.005* (0.001)	−0.006* (0.001)	—	−0.005* (0.001)	—	—
$\bar{R}^2$	0.863	0.862	0.863	0.861	0.862	0.861	0.861
Obs	5954	5954	5954	5954	5954	5954	5954

Standard errors are in parentheses. The sign * denotes significance at the 1% level. For the sake of brevity, the estimated common intercept and all estimated coefficients on university dummies, inland province dummies, and year dummies are not reported in this table.

Table 11.2 Regressions based on Eq. 11.1 (with i = western provinces)

				Dependent variable: $A_{ik,t}$			
				Regression No.			
	(B1)	**(B2)**	**(B3)**	**(B4)**	**(B5)**	**(B6)**	**(B7)**
$Ry_{ij,t}$	−0.013* (0.006)	—	−0.021* (0.005)	−0.013* (0.006)	—	—	−0.021* (0.005)
$Rf_{ij,t}$	0.012* (0.0050	0.017* (0.004)	—	0.012* (0.005)	—	0.017* (0.0040	—
$Dist_{ij}$	−0.005* (0.001)	−0.005* (0.001)	−0.005* (0.001)	—	−0.005* (0.001)	—	—
$\bar{R}^2$	0.863	0.863	0.862	0.862	0.862	0.862	0.862
Obs	3407	3407	3407	3407	3407	3407	3407

Standard errors are in parentheses. The sign * denotes significance at the 1% level. For the sake of brevity, the estimated common intercept and all estimated coefficients on university dummies, inland province dummies, and year dummies are not reported in this table.

Table 11.3 Regressions based on Eq. 11.1 (with i = central provinces)

				Dependent variable: $A_{ik,t}$			
				Regression No.			
	(C1)	**(C2)**	**(C3)**	**(C4)**	**(C5)**	**(C6)**	**(C7)**
$Ry_{ij,t}$	0.003 (0.004)	—	0.013* (0.004)	0.003 (0.004)	—	—	0.013* (0.004)
$Rf_{ij,t}$	−0.031* (0.003)	−0.032* (0.003)	—	−0.031* (0.003)	—	−0.032* (0.003)	—
$Dist_{ij}$	−0.007* (0.001)	−0.007* (0.001)	−0.007* (0.001)	—	−0.007* (0.001)	—	—
$\bar{R}^2$	0.881	0.881	0.877	0.875	0.877	0.875	0.871
Obs	2547	2547	2547	2547	2547	2547	2547

Standard errors are in parentheses. The sign * denotes significance at the 1% level. For the sake of brevity, the estimated common intercept and all estimated coefficients on university dummies, inland province dummies, and year dummies are not reported in this table.

for the sake of brevity, we neither report estimated coefficients on these dummies nor the estimated common intercept in these tables.

All three tables show the estimated coefficients as being either statistically insignificant (at the usual 5% significance level) or statistically very significant (even at the 1% significance level). In Table 11.1, where i indexes all the 19 home provinces of inland examinees, estimates of the coefficient on the income gap variable $Ry_{ij,t}$ are very close to one another (around -0.015) across the different regressions, probably owing to our large sample size. The estimates are also very statistically significant in all the regressions shown in this table (the relevant p-values are zero to three decimal places). These estimates suggest that an increase in $Ry_{ij,t}$ by, say, 0.2 would normally lower the level of $A_{ik,t}$ by about 0.003, *ceteris paribus*. In our sample, the maximum, minimum, and average values of the explanatory variable $Ry_{ij,t}$ are 2.574, -0.502, and 1.050, respectively, while the maximum, minimum, and average values of the explained variable $A_{ik,t}$ are 0.442, -0.066, and 0.109, respectively. Therefore, it can be seen that our estimates of the coefficient on $Ry_{ij,t}$ in these regressions do not in practice indicate a large partial effect of $Ry_{ij,t}$ on $A_{ik,t}$, despite the estimates being very significant statistically. All estimates of the coefficient on the openness gap variable $Rf_{ij,t}$ are insignificant (at the 5% level) in these regressions. This result implies that once all the other explanatory variables (including the dummies) are controlled for, the openness gap between the home and university provinces does not seem to exert a significant partial effect on university appeal. Estimates of the coefficient on the distance variable $Dist_{ij}$ are very close across the regressions (around -0.005), and they are very statistically significant in all these regressions (the relevant p-values are zero to three decimal places). These estimates suggest that, *ceteris paribus*, a 10% increase in the (spherical) distance between (the capital cities of) the two provinces i and j would lower the ratio of $Av_{ik,t}$ to Cs_{it} (i.e., $Av_{ik,t}/Cs_{it}$) by roughly 0.05 (see Eq. 11.2). Therefore, we do not in practice see a large partial effect of the distance variable on university appeal, despite the estimates being very statistically significant.

The regressions shown in Tables 11.2 and 11.3 run parallel to those in Table 11.1, but do so with respect to two sub-groups of the entire sample. The reason for splitting the entire sample into two sub-groups and investigating them separately is because we suspect that examinees from western and central provinces may be fundamentally different in the way they perceive the appeal of a coastal university. If this is the case, then pooling the data together (such as in Table 11.1) may lead to ambiguous and misleading results. Table 11.2 contains regressions that are based on the subset of the sample associated with the western home provinces of inland examinees. A prominent feature of the regressions shown in Table 11.2 is that all the estimated coefficients in these regressions are very statistically significant (even at the 1% significance level). Table 11.2, for examples, shows estimates of the coefficient on the openness gap variable are all significantly positive (at the 1% level). Table 11.3 contains regressions that are based on the subset of the sample associated with the central home provinces of inland examinees. Interestingly, the regressions shown in Table 11.3 produce estimated coefficients on the gap variables $Ry_{ij,t}$ and $Rf_{ij,t}$ with signs that are exactly opposite to those of the corresponding estimates obtained in Table 11.2. For example, the negative partial effect of $Ry_{ij,t}$ obtained in Table 11.2 suggests that, for western province examinees, a wider income gap between the province in which the university is located and an examinee's home province tends to reduce the attractiveness of the university. By contrast, the positive partial effect of $Ry_{ij,t}$ obtained in Table 11.3 suggests that, for central province examinees, a wider income gap between the province in which the university is located and an examinee's home province tends to increase the attractiveness of the university. Similarly, the positive partial effect of the openness gap variable obtained in Table 11.2 suggests that, for western province examinees, a wider openness gap between the university's home province and an examinee's home province tends to increase the attractiveness of the university. In contrast, the negative partial effect of the openness gap variable obtained in Table 11.3 suggests that, for central province examinees, a wider openness gap between the university's home province and an examinee's home province tends to reduce the attractiveness of the university. Estimates of the coefficient on the distance variable $Dist_{ij}$, like those obtained in Table 11.1, are significantly negative (at the 1% level) in all the regressions shown in Tables 11.2 and 11.3.

Finding a plausible explanation for the directions (i.e., the signs) of the estimated partial effects of gap variables in the regressions shown in Tables 11.2 and 11.3 deserves further scrutiny. However, according to the regressions shown in Tables 11.1, 11.2, and 11.3, the estimated partial effects of these three variables are in practice all very small despite their statistical significance. Therefore, although further investigation into the directions of the effects of these variables may be an important and interesting issue in itself, it is by no means urgent for the purpose of the present study, as we have in practice detected only very small effects of these variables from our regression results, no matter their direction.

In sum, the regression results shown in Tables 11.1, 11.2, and 11.3 lead to the conclusion that, once the university dummies, inland–province dummies, and year dummies are controlled for (i.e., netted out) none of the three explanatory variables – the income gap, the openness gap, and the distance – matters when it comes to accounting for university attractiveness.

Therefore, we need to look elsewhere to explain university attractiveness. The attractiveness of a university of course primarily lies in intrinsic factors of the university such as the quality and usefulness of the courses it offers. Unfortunately, lack of data prevents us from carrying out further study in this direction. In addition, as most 'good' universities (such as Tsinghua University and Fudan University) are located in 'good' regions (such as Beijing and Shanghai) in China, it is sometimes difficult to separate out influencing factors that belong to the university from those that belong to the region. Therefore, further study concerning potential influencing factors related to disparities in provinces hosting universities (the coastal provinces in this study) is also likely to be challenging. Given these difficulties, we can do little more than focus on disparities in the home provinces of inland examinees to explain university attractiveness.

Estimated coefficients on inland–province dummies (i.e., dummies for the different home provinces of inland examinees not reported in Tables 11.1, 11.2, and 11.3) can be exploited for our current purpose. According to the regressions shown in Table 11.1, western inland provinces have higher levels of province effects (i.e., higher estimated coefficients on their dummies) than central inland provinces. For example, according to regression (A7) in Table 11.1 (the last column), Qinghai comes first in having the highest level of province effects, followed by Xinjiang, Guizhou, Yunnan, Ningxia, Inner Mongolia, Shaanxi, Chongqing, Guangxi, Gansu, Jilin, Sichuan, Anhui, Heilongjiang, Jiangxi, Hunan, Hubei, Shanxi, and Henan: all western provinces have higher levels of province effects than central provinces, except for the Jilin–Sichuan inversion. This shows that coastal universities are generally more attractive to examinees from western provinces than those from central provinces. We suspect that this is due to there being generally fewer local universities in western provinces than central provinces, where universities located in an inland examinee's own province can be viewed as substitutes, to a certain degree, for universities in coastal provinces. In fact, a correlation test reveals that the numbers of local first-tier universities in these inland provinces are indeed negatively correlated with the levels of their province effects (where the correlation coefficient is -0.507).

Systematic disparities between the two groups of inland provinces (i.e., western provinces and central provinces), rather than disparities across all the individual inland provinces, can be examined by modifying our regression model (Eq. 11.1) by replacing all inland province dummies with a 'west' dummy, denoted by $West_i$, which equals unity when inland province i is a western province, and zero otherwise. The regression results are shown in Table 11.4. Moreover, we insert one or both of the two 'local university' dummies, $Lu1_{it}$ and $Lu2_{it}$, into these new regressions. The variable $Lu1_{it}$ is constructed as follows: $Lu1_{it} = 1$ if the number of first-tier universities in inland province i in year t, denoted by $u1_{it}$, is such that $u1_{it} \geq \bar{u}1_i$, and $Lu1_{it} = 0$ if $u1_{it} < \bar{u}1_t$, where $\bar{u}1_t$ denotes the mathematical average of the $u1_{it}$'s across all the i's. The variable $Lu2_{it}$ is defined in a similar fashion: $Lu2_{it} = 1$ if the total number of first-tier universities in inland province i *and* all bordering *inland* provinces in year t, denoted by $u2_{it}$, is such that $u2_{it} \geq \bar{u}2_t$, and $Lu2_{it} = 0$ if $u2_{it} < \bar{u}2_t$, where $\bar{u}2_t$ denotes the mathematical average of the $u2_{it}$'s across all the i's.

When we run all possible variants of the new round of regressions (not reported here for brevity's sake), it turns out that estimates of the coefficient on $West_i$ are all significantly positive (at the 1% level) with magnitudes around 0.05. This result suggests that, when the effects of the other explanatory variables are netted out, a western home province of examinees is associated with a ratio of $Av_{ik,t}$ to Cs_{it} that is about 5% higher than a central home province of examinees (see Eq. 11.2). Therefore, the variable $West_i$ can be shown to have in practice a large partial effect on the explained variable. The result implies that examinees from western provinces and those from central provinces are systematically different in the way they perceive the appeal of a coastal university. The estimated coefficients on $Lu1_{it}$ and $Lu2_{it}$ are all significantly negative (at the 1% level), even if in some cases both variables are simultaneously included in the regression. Apart from their statistical significance, the partial effects of $Lu1(i,t)$ and $Lu2(i,t)$ on the explained variable are also large in practice. The negative signs of the estimates provide evidence for our earlier conjecture that the number of universities in an inland province (and in neighboring inland provinces) affects the attractiveness of coastal universities to examinees of this inland province. It is interesting to see from these regressions that, even after the effects of $Lu1(i,t)$ and $Lu2(i,t)$ are netted out, the variable $West_i$ still has a large effect on the explained variable. This result implies that factors other than the different numbers of local universities (which implies an uneven spatial distribution of higher education resources in China) may also account for western–

central disparities with respect to the attractiveness of coastal universities. Finally, it can be shown that the estimated partial effects of gap and distance variables, despite their statistical significance, are all practically negligible. In sum, the major conclusion of our empirical analysis in this chapter is that examinees from western provinces tend to have a stronger preference for coastal universities than examinees from central provinces. Therefore, for reasons discussed in the 'Introduction' to this chapter, we expect college admissions in China under the NCEE system to exert a stronger impact on potential human capital movement from western to coastal regions than from central to coastal regions.

Concluding remarks

Increasing spatial disparities in income lead to human capital flows in China. Higher education in China may play an important role in promoting such cross-regional human capital mobility. This study is concerned with college admissions in China's regions under the NCEE system and their potential implications for cross-regional human capital mobility. Employing an advanced regression method and exploiting rich data, this study is the first attempt in the NCEE literature to empirically address the issue of regional disparities, college admissions under the NCEE system, and potential interregional human capital mobility in China. Our empirical results show that examinees from western provinces tend to have a stronger preference for coastal universities than examinees from central provinces. Therefore, for reasons discussed at the beginning of this chapter, we expect college admissions in China under the NCEE system to exert a stronger impact on potential human capital movement from western to coastal regions than from central to coastal regions.

Notes

1. Works on economics are often classified according to JEL classification codes, a system set up by the *Journal of Economic Literature*.
2. See, for example, Sisci (2005), WB (2005), Fan and Sun (2008), Fan et al. (2009), Yin (2011), and Zhu et al. (2012).
3. Some recent studies on the CEE include Wang (2006), Bai and Chi

(2011), Hannum et al. (2011), Wu and Zhong (2011), and Zhang (2013).

4. See, for example, Wang (2006), Bai and Chi (2011), Wang (2011), and Wu and Zhong (2011), for a general introduction to the NCEE system in China.

5. The provincial second-tier cut-off score (i.e., the provincial cut-off score for entry to second-tier universities), is decided in an analogous manner.

6. The ten coastal provinces are Beijing, Tianjin, Hebei, Liaoning, Shanghai, Jiangsu, Zhejiang, Fujian, Shandong, and Guangdong. One coastal province, Hainan, is excluded because of data unavailability.

7. The 19 inland provinces are Shanxi, Inner Mongolia, Jilin, Heilongjiang, Anhui, Jiangxi, Henan, Hubei, Hunan, Guangxi, Chongqing, Sichuan, Guizhou, Yunnan, Shaanxi, Gansu, Qinghai, Ningxia, and Xinjiang. Owing to missing data, one inland province, Tibet, is not included.

References

Bai, Chong-en; and Wei, Chi (2011) *Determinants of Undergraduate GPAs in China: College Entrance Examination Scores, High School Achievement, and Admission Route* (MPRA Paper No. 32797). Available from: *http://mpra.ub.uni-muenchen.de/32797/1/MPRA_paper_32797.pdf*

Fan, C.C.; and Sun, Mingjie (2008) 'Regional inequality in China, 1978–2006,' *Eurasian Geography and Economics*, **49**(1), 1–20.

Fan, Shenggen; Kanbur, R.; and Zhang, Xiaobo (2009) 'Regional inequality in China: an overview,' in Shenggen Fan, R. Kanbur, and Xiaobo Zhang (Eds.), *Regional Inequality in China: Trends, Explanations and Policy Responses*, London: Routledge.

Hannum, E.; An, Xuehui; and Hua-Yu, S.C. (2011) 'Examinations and educational opportunity in China: mobility and bottlenecks for the rural poor,' *Oxford Review of Education*, **37**(2), 267–305.

Sisci, F. (2005) 'Is China headed for a social red alert?' *Asia Times Online*, 20 October 2005. Available from: *http://www.atimes.com/atimes/China_Business/GJ20Cb01.html*

Wang, Li (2011) 'Social exclusion and inequality in higher education in China: a capability perspective,' *International Journal of Educational Development*, **31**(3), 277–86.

Wang, Xiang Bo (2006) *An Introduction to the System and Culture of the College Entrance Examination of China* (Research Note RN-28, November). New York: The College Board.

WB (2005) *World Development Report 2006: Equity and Development.* New York: Oxford University Press [World Bank].

Wu, Binzhen; and Zhong, Xiaohan (2011) *College Admissions Mechanism and Matching Quality: An Empirical Study in China* (SSRN Working Paper Series, August 11). Available from: *http://dx.doi.org/10.2139/ssrn.1909515*

Yin, Heng (2011) 'Characteristics of inter-regional income disparities in China,' *Social Sciences in China*, **32**(3), 123–44.

Zhang, Yu (2013) 'Does private tutoring improve students' National College Entrance Exam performance? A case study from Jinan, China,' *Economics of Education Review*, **32**(1) 1–28.

Zhu, Nong; Luo, Xubei; and Zou, Heng-Fu (2012) *Regional Differences in China's Urbanization and Its Determinants* (CEMA Working Paper No. 535), Beijing: China Economics and Management Academy, Central University of Finance and Economics.

12

Environmental factors and sustainable development

Abstract: This chapter empirically examines the linkages between pollution emission, output growth, and openness to foreign trade and FDI. Our regression results suggest that the 'gains from openness' hypothesis, which posits that openness to foreign trade and FDI has a positive impact on the environment, dominates the 'race to the bottom' hypothesis in the current case for China's regions. Our regressions do not provide evidence to support the race to the bottom hypothesis. As openness to foreign trade and FDI is likely to contribute to a better environment for China, policy-makers should remove barriers to foreign trade and FDI when it comes to environmental technology, goods, and services to allow further gains from openness.

Key words: openness to foreign trade and FDI, total factor productivity, pollution emission, sustainable growth, the 'race to the bottom' hypothesis, strategic interaction.

JEL classification codes: F41; O11; O53.[1]

Introduction

Achieving miraculous economic growth over the past 35 years, China has become the world's second largest single-country economy. Since the initiation of market-oriented reforms in 1978, economic growth has been the central task of the Chinese government. However, subsequent social and environmental problems have increasingly become a serious concern. Since 2007, China has surpassed the United States to become the world's largest greenhouse gas emitter. In 2008, according to the World Bank, China's economic losses due to pollution and environmental degradation were estimated to be over 10 percent of total national GDP. Along with China's spectacular economic growth as measured in GDP, various environmental challenges have dramatically increased in the past few decades. Rapid industrial development in China has relied heavily on increasing inputs of natural resources and environmental services. Resource depletion and environmental pollution have thus become serious problems that call for rethinking of government policies (Zhang, 2012).

Market-oriented reforms in China, especially those related to investment, economic construction, and opening up, may exert profound impacts on the environment. Expanded economic activities may put mounting pressure on natural resources and environmental quality. Research, however, suggests that economic development does not necessarily lead to environmental problems. This implies China needs not slow its development process or return to a closed economy to avoid environmental deterioration. However, a strategy for environmentally sustainable development is needed because it does not necessarily follow that the environment improves as the country becomes richer. Realizing the unsustainability of current growth, the Chinese government has made great efforts to address environmental deterioration and resource degradation in recent years.

China's environmental performance during its 11th Five-Year Plan (2006–2010) was a significant improvement over that of the previous Five-Year Plan (2001–2005). In fact, nearly half (9 of 20) of the environmental objectives under the 10th Five-Year Plan were not met, while the 11th Five-Year Plan failed to meet only 2 of its 13 quantitative objectives.[2] Environmental targets set under the 11th Five-Year Plan contributed to remarkable environmental achievements compared with the preceding plan. With regard to environmental protection, the 12th Five-Year Plan (2011–2015) continues the strategies that were successfully implemented under the previous plan, stressing the promotion of green development with environmental protection and further improvements in living quality by strengthening environmental management (see, for example, Zhang and Crooks, 2011). China faces severe pollution and environmental degradation for many reasons: rapid industrialization, reliance on coal as an energy source, a relatively large and energy-intensive manufacturing industry, and lax environmental protection enforcement. The 12th Five-Year Plan, whose environmental focuses are on reducing pollution, increasing energy efficiency, and ensuring a stable, reliable, and clean energy supply, shows the Chinese government determination to make a great effort in calling for more energy-saving and environmentally friendly methods of production in order to lower environmental costs in the future.

An important aspect of China's economic reform is the way in which it has embraced globalization by increasingly opening up to foreign trade and foreign investment. China's economic boom has benefited greatly from ever-increasing inflows of FDI and foreign trade. However, opening up is also blamed as a major cause of resource depletion and environmental degradation. According to the race to the bottom hypothesis, foreign trade and FDI may pose downward pressure on environmental regulations in host regions. Different jurisdictions may compete to attract foreign investment, so they tend to lower their environmental standards to cut their costs of production. As a result, foreign trade and FDI can lead to deterioration of the environment. In the case of China, though environmental standards are set at the national level, local Chinese governments can achieve differential *de facto* regulations by tightening or relaxing environmental enforcement (Zhang, 2012). Therefore, local jurisdictions in China have the incentives to attract FDI into their local regions by loosening environmental enforcement. On the other hand, foreign trade and FDI may also have positive effects on the environment as openness to foreign trade and FDI enables the regions to secure cleaner technologies and more environmental goods. Therefore, the net effect of openness to foreign trade and FDI on the environment depends on which of the two forces dominates. The literature provides very little evidence that foreign trade and FDI necessarily lead to worsening pollution and a deteriorating environment (Antweiler et al., 2001; Frankel and Rose, 2005).[3]

Globally, raised concerns about the seriousness of environmental degradation and the urgent need for environmental protection in the process of economic development have motivated the creation of models of green growth, or environmentally sustainable growth, for developing countries. In the language of the production function, output growth can be broken down into its various constituent parts (which are the inputs of various factors and so-called 'total factor productivity'). Although the concept of total factor productivity growth has been devised to measure the portion of output growth not accounted for by growth in the inputs of various factors, researchers argue that more substance needs to be filled into the amorphous term 'total factor productivity' (Easterly and Levine, 2001). In an unregulated market, environmental resources are used as unpaid factor inputs as the cost of pollution is not internalized (Brock, 1973). Taking environmental inputs into consideration, output growth previously ascribed to TFP growth may actually be due to an increasing use of environmental resources. The use of environmental resources as production inputs can be accommodated by incorporating an environmental measure (such as pollution) as an additional production input into the aggregate production function (Tzouvelekas et al., 2006).[4]

The rest of this chapter is structured as follows. In the second section 'The green Solow model', we present a model to illustrate the concept of green growth, or environmentally sustainable growth, and discuss the necessary conditions for balanced green growth. In the third section 'Potential impacts of foreign trade and FDI on the environment', we discuss the potential impacts of foreign trade and FDI on pollution and the environment. In the fourth section 'Strategic interaction in environmental protection efforts', based on one of the author's previous works (Jiang, 2013a), we review and update the spatial strategic interaction among provincial governments with respect to pollution abatement efforts. In the fifth section 'Output growth, TFP growth, and pollution emission', we discuss the linkages between output growth, TFP growth, and pollution emission. In the sixth section 'Pollution and openness to foreign trade and FDI', we empirically examine the potential impacts of regional openness to foreign trade and FDI on regional pollution emission and the environment.

The green Solow model

Before we turn to empirical analysis later in this chapter, we first present a version of the green Solow growth model which will help us illustrate the necessary conditions for long-run environmentally sustainable growth of the economy. This extended Solow growth model, for the sake of simplicity and tractability, assumes exogenous technological progress in both goods production and pollution abatement. We will see that on a balanced growth path technological progress in both goods production and pollution abatement will lead to continuous economic growth with rising environmental quality. We follow the procedure of Brock and Taylor (2004) and present the simplest version of the model where the saving rate and abatement intensity are both exogenously determined.[5]

We consider a standard one-sector Solow model with a fixed investment rate s. Output is ascertained through a production function that is strictly concave with constant returns to scale with respect to its two arguments: physical capital and effective labor. Physical capital accumulates via investment and depreciates at constant rate δ. Raw labor and labor-augmenting technology are assumed to grow exogenously at the constant rates n and g, respectively. All these imply that

$$Y = F(K, BL) \qquad (12.1)$$

where $\dot{K} = sY - \delta K$, $\dot{L} = nL$, and $\dot{B} = gB$, with B representing labor-augmenting technology. To model the impact of pollution we follow Copeland and Taylor (1994) and Brock and Taylor (2004) and assume that every unit of economic activity F produces Ω units of pollution as a joint product of output. We further assume that pollution abatement is a constant returns to scale activity and write the amount of pollution abated as an increasing and strictly concave function of total economic activity F and abatement effort F^A. Pollution emitted equals pollution created minus pollution abated. If abatement at level A removes ΩA units of pollution from the total created, we have

$$E = \Omega F - \Omega A(F, F^A) = \Omega F[1 - A(1, F^A/F)] = \Omega Fa(\theta) \qquad (12.2)$$

where E represents pollution emitted, and $a(\theta)$ is defined as $a(\theta) = 1 - A(1, F^A/F)$, in which $\theta = F^A/F$ (i.e., that part of economic activity devoted to pollution abatement). The second equality in Eq. 12.2 comes from the linear homogeneity of A. We assume $a(0) = 1$ and by concavity $a'(\theta) < 0$ and $a''(\theta) > 0$. Pollution abatement has a positive but diminishing marginal impact on pollution reduction. Once pollution abatement is taken into account, that part of total economic activity devoted to consumption and investment, Y, is then written as $Y = F(1 - \theta)$.

We further assume a form of exponential dissipation of pollution so that the stock of pollution X is determined by

$$\dot{X} = E - \eta X \qquad (12.3)$$

where $\eta > 0$ is the natural rate of regeneration. Finally, we assume that exogenous technological progress in pollution abatement lowers Ω at a rate $g^A > 0$. Combining all the assumptions and transforming the measures into the intensive form, we end up with the green Solow model:

$$y = f(k)[1 - \theta] \qquad (12.4)$$

$$\dot{k} = sf(k)[1 - \theta] - (n + g + \delta)k \qquad (12.5)$$

$$e = f(k)\Omega a(\theta) \qquad (12.6)$$

where $k = K/(BL)$, $y = Y/(BL)$, $e = E/(BL)$, and $f(k) = F(k, 1)$. Starting from any $K(0) > 0$, the economy converges to a unique k^* exactly as happens in the traditional Solow model. On a balanced growth path, aggregate measures such as output, capital, and consumption all grow at rate $n + g$ while corresponding per-capita measures grow at rate g.

The growth rate of aggregate emissions on a balanced growth path, G_E, can be either positive or negative:

$$G_E = n + g - g_A \qquad (12.7)$$

Therefore, if we define long-run environmentally sustainable growth (green growth) as representing a balanced growth path that generates rising consumption per capita and improves the environment, then long-run green growth is guaranteed by

$$g > 0 \quad \text{and} \quad g_A > n + g \qquad (12.8)$$

That is, technological growth in the production of goods is needed so as to generate growth in per-capita income while technological growth in pollution abatement must always proceed at a faster rate than growth of aggregate output so that pollution can be alleviated and the environment improved.

Potential impacts of foreign trade and FDI on the environment

In the preceding section we demonstrated that long-run environmentally sustainable growth of the economy can only happen if technological progress in pollution abatement runs at a faster rate than total output growth.[6] To offset the adverse impacts of population and income growth on the environment, we have to rely on technological progress and the market system. Technological progress has a positive impact on pollution abatement and resource conservation while the market mechanism dictates that the explicit or implicit price of environmental goods will rise in accord with deterioration of the environment (Zhang, 2012).

How does openness to foreign trade and FDI impact pollution and the environment? As mentioned earlier, key to China's economic reform is its increased openness to foreign trade and foreign investment. Economic growth, openness, and the environment are interrelated. Opinions diverge on whether openness to foreign trade and FDI is beneficial to the quality of the environment. The race to the bottom hypothesis posits that with more and more openness and ever-increasing opportunities for securing FDI, China's regions may engage in a race to the bottom (i.e., compete to attract and retain foreign investment that likely is pollution intensive). Such investment may result in the lowering of regions' environmental standards (see, for example, Smarzynska and Wei, 2001; King, 2011).

In other words, in order to attract and retain FDI, different jurisdictions may interact strategically to compete for investment by reducing their environmental standards. This interaction between regions is the consequence of foreign investment looking to relocate to regions with weaker environmental standards (i.e., the pollution haven hypothesis).[7] The possibility of such interactive behavior is particularly worrisome for less developed regions, which lack other capacities to attract and retain foreign investment. The least developed regions are mostly located in the west of China and are ecologically sensitive, which makes the race to the bottom even more detrimental. However, the literature provides little empirical evidence to support the pollution haven hypothesis (Jeppesen et al., 2002). Nevertheless, things like bureaucratic corruption may actually deter FDI, despite being positively correlated with lax environmental standards. Thus omitting this information from empirical analyses may give rise to misleading results (Smarzynska and Wei, 2001).

On the other hand, openness to foreign trade and FDI may exert positive impacts on the quality of the environment because technological spillovers facilitated by foreign trade and FDI may enable China's regions to gain access to cleaner technologies in a more cost-effective manner. In this sense, openness to foreign trade and FDI contributes to a better environment. Therefore, the net effect of openness to foreign trade and FDI on the environment hinges on which of the abovementioned two opposing forces has the stronger impact (Frankel, 2003; Zhang, 2012). Recent empirical studies find that foreign investment in China is not significantly influenced by weak environmental standards in choosing firm locations (Dean et al., 2009). Such results suggest that environmental standards have little impact on investment decisions, and the impact of openness to foreign trade and FDI on the environment is unlikely to be negative. In certain cases, openness could lead to an improved environment.

Strategic interaction in environmental protection efforts

In this section we look at strategic interaction among China's provincial governments in environmental protection efforts. In a country where information flows easily and people and resources move frequently across regions, local governments need to consider environmental decisions made by neighboring local governments as well as their own. This gives rise to a situation where local environmental decisions are affected not only by characteristics of the home region, but also by decisions taken by other regions.

The literature on strategic interaction is generally built on two broad types of theoretical models. The first type is called the 'resource flow model' or 'competition model'. Such a model is often used as a theoretical basis to empirically analyze tax or welfare competition among different jurisdictions. The second type is called a 'spillover model'. Such a model is usually used as a theoretical basis to empirically study strategic interaction among jurisdictions associated with inter-jurisdictional spillovers. Examples include spillovers of certain benefits (i.e., pollution abatement), or spillovers of information of use to local residents in evaluating decisions made by their local government. Despite their differences, the two types of models ultimately lead to the same empirical specification (Edmark, 2007).[8]

There exist at least three channels through which China's regions are incentivized to engage in strategic interaction with respect to their pollution abatement efforts. First, there exist potential interregional spillovers of benefits from pollution abatement across regions. This implies that local governments make decisions on pollution abatement interactively (strategically) on the basis of decisions made by other local governments. This is because pollution abatement decisions made elsewhere have spillover effects on any single jurisdiction. Second, even if there are no spillover effects, interregional strategic interaction in environmental protection efforts may still be present as a result of 'information spillover'. Residents of a region are able to compare their local government's efforts in environmental protection with those of surrounding regions. This may drive a local government to mimic the environmental policy of a neighboring region, in order not to look bad in the comparison. Third, strategic interaction may involve competition for resources. As already mentioned, regions may compete by lowering their environmental standards (i.e., by engaging in a race to the bottom) to attract and retain investment that runs the risk of being pollution intensive (Jiang, 2013a).[9]

In this section, we review and update the empirical results of one of the author's previous works (Jiang, 2013a). To do this we estimate a reaction function of the form

$$z_{it} = \beta \sum_{j \neq i} w_{ij} z_{j,t-1} + \mathbf{X_{it}} \boldsymbol{\theta} + \delta_t + \pi_i + v_{it} \qquad (12.9)$$

where β (a scalar) and $\boldsymbol{\theta}$ (a vector) are the unknown parameters to be estimated, ε_i is an error term, and w_{ij} are nonnegative weights that are specified *a priori*. z_i is the regional decision variable indicating the level of the government's environmental protection efforts in region i. In Jiang (2013a), z_i is constructed as the ratio between environmental protection expenditure of the provincial government and provincial GDP. The weights w_{ij} in Eq. 12.9 indicate the relevance of other provinces j with respect to interregional strategic interaction. In Jiang (2013a) two weighting schemes are used. One is a 'smooth distance decay' scheme in which we assign weights by letting $w_{ij} = 1/d_{ij}$ for $j \neq i$, where d_{ij} is the distance between the capital cities of province i and province j.[10] The second weighting scheme is a 'contiguity' scheme where $w_{ij} = 1$ for provinces j that share a border with province i, and $w_{ij} = 0$ otherwise.

In Eq. 12.9 $\mathbf{X}_{it}$ is intended to capture the time-varying exogenous provincial characteristics that affect z_{it}. The following variables are chosen: provincial GDP, percentage value added by secondary industry to GDP in the province, provincial population, general budgetary revenue of the provincial government, total developed urban area in the province, population density (i.e., population per square kilometer) in urban areas of the province, percentage illiterate people in the population aged 15 and over in the province, percentage urban population in the province, registered urban unemployment rate, total value of foreign trade (exports plus imports) in the province, and energy consumption per-unit GDP in the province.[11]

Using panel data of China's provinces over 2007–2011, we update the results of Jiang (2013a). Our results suggest that provincial governments in China engage in strategic interaction when deciding how much effort to allocate to environmental protection. The significantly positive estimates of the reaction slope suggest that environmental protection efforts of provincial governments are strategic complements. However, contiguity weighting seems better at capturing the pattern of interregional strategic interaction: direct interregional strategic interaction in environmental protection efforts seems to occur only among contiguous provinces.

Output growth, TFP growth, and pollution

In line with the spirit of the green Solow growth model presented earlier, let us first see if it is true that increased production generates higher levels of pollution. In Jiang (2013b) the linkage between per-worker output and per-worker pollution across China's provinces was empirically examined using a regression approach. Jiang (2013b) used the total provincial volume of industrial waste gas emission (in units of 100 million cubic meters) to proxy for total provincial pollution from China's provinces. The sample comprised 28 province-level divisions over the period 1997–2011, but excluded Tibet, Chongqing, and Hainan as a result of incomplete data. Most relevant data are either directly available from or can be calculated from the various editions of the *China Statistical Yearbook* (1997–2012). The *China Statistical Yearbook* does not directly record data on physical capital stocks for China's regions. Therefore, as in previous chapters, we followed the basic procedure of Zhang et al. (2007) and Zhang (2008) and use the perpetual inventory method (PIM) to construct physical capital stock data for China's provinces, assuming that the annual depreciation rates of physical capital are uniformly 9.6 percent for all provinces throughout the sample period.

Jiang (2013b)'s regression results showed by and large that an increase in the level (or growth) of real per-worker GDP leads to a significant increase in the level (or growth) of per-worker pollution. More importantly, these results showed it was variation in TFP growth that was mainly responsible for variation in pollution emission – not variation in extensive growth. As a result our attention turned to the linkage between TFP and pollution. The focus was then whether TFP growth in China's regions was being achieved at the cost of increasing pollution, and whether China's economic growth could be considered environmentally sustainable. Regression analysis of Jiang (2013b)'s empirical results showed that during China's economic growth over the sample period, even when the effect of capital accumulation is netted out, output growth is still seen as being achieved at the cost of increasing pollution. This finding showed that growth of regional TFP in China's regions goes hand in hand with ever-increasing regional per-worker pollution. Therefore, TFP growth in China's provinces traditionally estimated in most of the literature has not been totally 'green'. Jiang (2013b)'s regressions enabled us to effectively chip from the traditional concept of TFP a chunk of 'environmental resource' that is an additional factor input contributing to the production of output. A byproduct of Jiang (2013b)'s regression analyses was an implicit value for the structural parameter α of the aggregate production function, which at 0.5 agreed well with its empirically accepted value.[12]

Pollution and openness to foreign tradeand FDI

Having completed a review of the literature on the linkages between pollution, output growth, and TFP growth, we are now in a position to

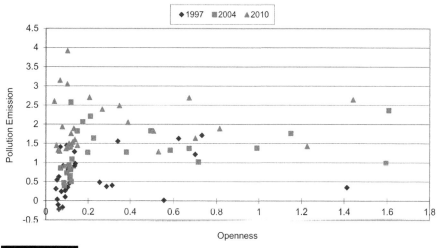

Figure 12.1 | **Regional openness versus regional pollution**

The regional trade-to-GDP ratio is depicted on the horizontal axis while the log of regional per-worker industrial waste gas emission is depicted on the vertical axis.

empirically examine the relationship between regional openness to foreign trade and FDI and regional pollution. To get an intuitive idea of what we have in mind, let us first graph the relationship between the two in Figure 12.1 for three representative years (1997, 2004, and 2010). For simplicity, we use the ratio between total regional foreign trade (i.e., total exports plus total imports) and regional GDP as our measure of regional openness. What we see from the graph is that for any specific level of regional openness to foreign trade, regional per-worker pollution tends to increase over time. The positive correlation between pollution emission and output can clearly be seen.

Further scrutiny shows the effects of output have to be netted out so that the potential impact of regional openness to foreign trade and FDI on regional pollution emission can be studied. To do this we run regressions of regional per-worker pollution (proxied for by regional per-worker industrial waste gas emission) on regional per-worker GDP and the regional trade-to-GDP ratio. Different regression methods are applied and the regression results are summarized in Table 12.1. Estimated coefficients on the first explanatory variable, regional per-worker GDP, are unsurprisingly all significantly positive, suggesting regional pollution is indeed positively related to the size of regional output. Estimated coefficients on the second explanatory variable, the regional trade-to-GDP ratio (a variable that supposedly measures the degree of regional

Table 12.1 Various regressions

	Dependent variable: ln m Number of observations: 420				
	Regressions				
Variable	**OLS**	**FD**	**FE**	**Between**	**RE GLS**
ln y	0.862* (0.033)	1.504* (0.189)	1.115* (0.024)	0.738* (0.131)	1.101* (0.025)
TR	−0.737* (0.743)	0.030 (0.121)	−0.069 (0.085)	−0.656* (0.273)	−0.215* (0.083)
_cons	−5.886 (0.268)	−0.039 (0.020)	8.259 (0.197)	−4.847 (1.065)	−8.093 (0.214)

The regressions are of ln m (the log of provincial per-worker pollution) on ln y (the log of provincial per-worker output) and TR (provincial trade-to-GDP ratio). Standard errors are in parentheses. The asterisk * indicates significance at the 5 percent level.

openness to foreign trade and FDI), are either significantly negative or insignificant. This means we have failed to find evidence showing that regional openness to foreign trade and FDI has a positive impact on regional pollution. Replacing the trade-to-GDP ratio variable with another variable that measures either the stock or the flow of regional FDI does not change the results of these regressions in any important way.

This section's empirical results suggest that the gains from openness hypothesis, which posits that openness to foreign trade and FDI has a positive impact on the environment, dominates the race to the bottom hypothesis in the current case. Openness to foreign trade and FDI enables China's regions to attain cleaner technologies and more environmental goods in a cost-effective manner (Zhang, 2012). Openness thus contributes to a better environment. To allow further gains from openness, policy-makers should remove barriers to foreign trade and FDI from environmental technology, goods, and services.

Concluding remarks

China's economic growth in the past 35 years has been seen as a miracle. However, such rapid growth may have been accomplished at the cost of severe resource degradation and environmental deterioration. This chapter, based on previous work of the author, empirically examines the linkages between pollution, output growth, and openness to foreign trade and FDI. The race to the bottom hypothesis posits that regional openness to foreign trade and FDI may pose downward pressure on environmental regulations in China's regions, as they may be tempted to lower their environmental standards to cut the costs of production in order to attract foreign investment. The gains from openness hypothesis, on the contrary, posits that openness to foreign trade and FDI may have positive impacts on the environment as this openness enables host regions to adopt cleaner technologies and more environmental goods and services. As a result, the net effect of openness to foreign trade and FDI is yet to be determined, depending on which of the two forces is stronger. This chapter's empirical results suggest that the gains from openness hypothesis, which posits that openness to foreign trade and FDI has a positive impact on the environment, dominates the race to the bottom hypothesis regarding China's regions. Our regressions in this chapter do not provide evidence to support the race to the bottom hypothesis. As openness to foreign trade and FDI is likely to contribute to a better environment for China, policy-makers should remove barriers to foreign trade and FDI from environmental technology, goods, and services to allow further gains from openness.

Notes

1. Works on economics are often classified according to JEL classification codes, a system set up by the *Journal of Economic Literature*.
2. China failed in reaching two major environmental targets in its 10th Five-Year Plan: SO_2 emission increased by 27 percent rather than the target 10 percent reduction, and gross chemical oxygen demand (COD) discharge decreased by 2 percent rather than the target 10 percent reduction (UNEP, 2008).
3. See also Jeppesen et al. (2002) and Dean et al. (2009).
4. Brock (1973), Becker (1982), Tahvonen and Kuluvainen (1993), Bovenberg and Smulders (1995), Smulders and Gradus (1996), Mohtadi (1996), Brock and Taylor (2004, 2005), Xepapadeas (2005), and Considine and Larson (2006) are a few examples in which the aggregate production function has been specified to incorporate environmental measures into the production process.

5. Assuming the intensity of pollution abatement does not vary allows us to focus on the central idea of the model. On the other hand, assuming a constant saving rate, as commonly used in different versions of the Solow growth model, is little more than uninteresting.

6. The green Solow model generates a path for income per capita and environmental quality that traces out an environmental Kuznets curve (see Brock and Taylor, 2004).

7. The pollution haven hypothesis posits that dirty industries migrate from developed countries (regions) to less developed countries (regions) as a result of lower environmental regulatory costs.

8. Among the early theoretical literature analyzing interaction spillovers were Williams (1966), Pauly (1970), Oates (1972), and Boskin (1973). Many later studies focused on interaction due to tax base mobility, generating what has become known as the 'tax competition' literature. See also Besley and Case (1995), Wilson (1996, 1999), and Brueckner (2000) for reviews. Murdoch et al. (1997) and Fredriksson and Millimet (2002) are two examples that examine strategic interaction in pollution abatement efforts among European countries and individual states of the U.S.A., respectively.

9. For more detailed discussions see Chapter 12 of Jiang (2013a).

10. The unit of measurement for distances is irrelevant because the weights assigned for each region will be normalized to make their sum equal one.

11. See also Chapter 9 of Jiang (2013a) for further explanations.

12. See Jiang (2013b). For further discussions of the possible value of the structural parameter see also Klenow and Rodriguez-Clare (1997), Hall and Jones (1999), CBO (2001), Chow and Li (2002), Musso and Westermann (2005), Chow (2008), Zheng et al. (2009), Brandt and Zhu (2010), Jiang (2011, 2012).

References

Antweiler, W.; Copeland, B.R.; and Taylor M.S. (2001) 'Is free trade good for the environment?' *American Economic Review*, **91**, 877–908.

Becker, R. (1982) 'Intergenerational equity: the capital environment trade-off,' *Journal of Environmental Economics and Management*, **9**, 165–85.

Besley, T.J.; and Case, A.C. (1995) 'Incumbent behavior: vote seeking, tax setting and yardstick competition,' *American Economic Review*, **85**, 25–45.

Boskin, M.J. (1973) 'Local government tax and product competition and the optimal provision of public goods,' *Journal of Political Economy*, **81**, 203–10.

Bovenberg, A.L.; and Smulders, S. (1995) 'Environmental quality and pollution augmenting technological change in a two sector endogenous growth model,' *Journal of Public Economics*, **57**, 369–91.

Brandt, L.; and Zhu, Xiaodong (2010) *Accounting for China's Growth* (Working Papers tecipa-394), Toronto, Canada: Department of Economics, University of Toronto.

Brock, W.A. (1973) 'Polluted Golden Age,' in V.L. Smith (Ed.), *Economics of Natural and Environmental Resources*, New York: Gordon & Breach.

Brock, W.A.; and Taylor, M.S. (2004) *The Green Solow Model* (NBER Working Paper No. 10557), Cambridge, MA: National Bureau of Economic Research.

Brock, W.A.; and Taylor, M.S. (2005) 'Economic growth and the environment: a review of theory and empirics,' in P. Aghion and S. Durlauf (Eds.), *The Handbook of Economic Growth*, Amsterdam, The Netherlands: Elsevier.

Brueckner, J.K. (2000) 'Welfare reform and the race to the bottom: theory and evidence,' *Southern Economic Journal*, **66**, 505–25.

CBO (2001) 'CBO's method for estimating potential output: an update,' August. Available from: *http://www.cbo.gov/ftpdocs/30xx/doc3020/PotentialOutput. pdf* [Congressional Budget Office].

Chow, G.C. (2008) 'Another look at the rate of increase in TFP in China,' *Journal of Chinese Economic and Business Studies*, **6**(2), 219–24.

Chow, G.C.; and Li, Kui-Wai (2002) 'China's economic growth: 1952–2010,' *Economic Development and Cultural Change*, **51**(1), 247–56.

Considine, T.J.; and Larson, D.F. (2006) 'The environment as a factor of production,' *Journal of Environmental Economics and Management*, **52**(3), 645–62.

Copeland, B.R.; and Taylor, M.S. (1994) 'North–south trade and the global environment,' *Quarterly Journal of Economics*, **109**, 755–87.

Dean, J.E.; Lovely, M.E.; and Wang, H. (2009) 'Are foreign investors attracted to weak environmental regulations? Evaluating the evidence from China,' *Journal of Development Economics*, **90**(1), 1–13.

Easterly, W.; and Levine, R. (2001) 'What have we learned from a decade of empirical research on growth? It's not factor accumulation: stylized facts and growth models,' *The World Bank Economic Review*, **15**(2), 177–219.

Edmark, K. (2007) *Strategic Competition in Swedish Local Spending on Childcare, Schooling and Care for the Elderly* (Working Paper Series No. 21), Uppsala, Sweden: Uppsala University, Department of Economics.

Frankel, J.A. (2003) *The Environment and Globalization* (NBER Working Paper). Available from *http://www.nber.org/papers/w10090.pdf*

Frankel, J.A.; and Rose, A. (2005) 'Is trade good or bad for the environment? Sorting out the causality,' *Review of Economics and Statistics*, **87**, 85–91.

Fredriksson, P.G.; and Millimet, D.L. (2002) 'Strategic interaction and the determinants of environmental policy across US states,' *Journal of Urban Economics*, **51**, 101–22.

Hall, R.E.; and Jones, C.I. (1999) 'Why do some countries produce so much more output per worker than others?' *Quarterly Journal of Economics*, **114**, 83–116.

Jeppesen, T.; List, J.A.; and Folmer, H. (2002) 'Environmental regulations and new plant location decisions: evidence from a meta-analysis,' *Journal of Regional Science*, **42**(1), 19–49.

Jiang, Yanqing (2011) 'Understanding openness and productivity growth in China: an empirical study of the Chinese provinces,' *China Economic Review*, **22**(3), 290–8.

Jiang, Yanqing (2012) 'Technology diffusion, spatial effects and productivity growth in the Chinese provinces,' *International Review of Applied Economics*, **26**(5), 643–56.

Jiang, Yanqing (2013a) *Openness, Economic Growth and Regional Disparities in China*, Berlin, Germany: Springer-Verlag.

Jiang, Yanqing (2013b) 'Total factor productivity, pollution, and "green" economic growth in China,' *Journal of International Development*, available online July 31, 2013.

King, J. (2011) 'Foreign direct investment and pollution havens,' *Journal of Economics and Econometrics*, **54**(1), 39–47.

Klenow, P.; and Rodriguez-Clare, A. (1997) 'The neoclassical revival in growth economics: has it gone too far?' *NBER Macroeconomics Annual*, **12**, 73–103.

Mohtadi, H. (1996) 'Environment, growth and optimal policy design,' *Journal of Public Economics*, **63**, 119–40.

Murdoch, J.C.; Sandler, T.; and Sargent, K. (1997) 'A tale of two collectives: sulphur versus nitrogen oxide emission reduction in Europe,' *Economica*, **64**, 281–301.

Musso, A.; and Westermann, T. (2005) *Assessing Potential Output Growth in the Euro Area: A Growth Accounting Perspective* (ECB Occasional Paper No. 22), Frankfurt, Germany: European Central Bank. Available from *http://www.ecb.int/pub/pdf/scpops/ecbocp22.pdf*

Oates, W.E. (1972) *Fiscal Federalism*, New York: Harcourt Brace.

Pauly, M.V. (1970) 'Optimality, "public" goods, and local governments: a general theoretical analysis,' *Journal of Political Economy*, **78**, 572–85.

Smarzynska, B.K.; and Wei, S.J. (2001) *Pollution Havens and Foreign Direct Investment: Dirty Secret or Popular Myth?* (NBER Working Paper No. 8465), Cambridge, MA: National Bureau of Economic Research.

Smulders, S.; and Gradus, R. (1996) 'Pollution abatement and long term growth,' *European Journal of Political Economy*, **12**, 505–32.

Tahvonen, O.; and Kuuluvainen, J. (1993) 'Economic growth, pollution and renewable resources,' *Journal of Environmental Economics and Management*, **24**, 101–18.

Tzouvelekas, E.; Vouvaki, D.; and Xepapadeas, A. (2006) *Total Factor Productivity Growth and the Environment: A Case for Green Growth Accounting* (Working Paper No. 0617), Heraklion, Greece: University of Crete, Department of Economics.

UNEP (2008) *Green Accounting Practice in China*, Shanghai, China: UNEP-Tongji Institute of Environment for Sustainable Development, College of Environmental Science and Engineering Tongji University. Available from: *http://www.caep.org.cn/english/paper/Green-GDP-Accounting-Pratice-in-China-Draft-by-UNEP-Tongji-Team.pdf* [United Nations Environment Programme].

Williams, A. (1966) 'The optimal provision of public goods in a system of local governments,' *Journal of Political Economy*, **74**, 18–33.

Wilson, J.D. (1996) 'Capital mobility and environmental standards: is there a theoretical basis for the race to the bottom?' in J. Bhagwati and R. Hundee (Eds.), *Fair Trade and Harmonization: Prerequisites for Free Trade?*, Vol. 1, Cambridge, MA: MIT Press.

Wilson, J.D. (1999) 'Theories of tax competition,' *National Tax Journal*, **52**, 269–304.

Xepapadeas, A. (2005) 'Economic growth and the environment,' in K.G. Mäler and J. Vincent (Eds), *Handbook of Environmental Economics: Economy Wide and International Environmental Issues*, Amsterdam, The Netherlands: Elsevier.

Zhang, Jun (2008) 'Estimation of China's provincial capital stock (1952–2004) with applications,' *Journal of Chinese Economic and Business Studies*, **6**(2), 177–96.

Zhang, Jun; Wu, Guiying; and Zhang, Jipeng (2007) *Estimating China's Provincial Capital Stock* (Working Paper Series), Shanghai, China: China Center for Economic Studies, Fudan University.

Zhang, Junjie (2012) *Delivering Environmentally Sustainable Economic Growth: The Case of China*, Asia Society Report. Available from: *http://asiasociety.org/policy/environmentally-sustainable-economic-growth-possible-china*

Zhang, Qingfeng; and Crooks, R. (2011) 'Environmental strategy for the 12th Five-Year Plan period: what can the People's Republic of China learn from the 11th Five-Year Plan?' *ADB Briefs*, **8**, June. Available from: *http://www.adb.org/sites/default/files/ADB-Briefs-2011-8-PRC-5Year-Plan.pdf*

Zheng, Jinghai; Hu, Angang; and Bigsten, A. (2009) 'Measuring potential output in a rapidly developing economy: the case of China in comparison with the US and EU,' *Federal Reserve Bank of St. Louis Review*, July/August, 317–42.

13

Knowledge economy and knowledge-based development: a tentative discussion

Abstract: This chapter briefly discusses the knowledge economy and knowledge-based development in China. Despite its long tradition of respect for knowledge, China's development is still based much more heavily on the advantages of low-cost labor. A central challenge posed by the global knowledge economy for China is to develop an industrial structure to better exploit rapidly growing global knowledge with a view to accelerating its own economic development and facilitating its transition to becoming a knowledge-based economy. For this purpose, China should further leverage its FDI inflows and focus more on attracting FDI with a higher degree of knowledge content. Foreign trade is another channel through which Chinese enterprises can tap into global knowledge and technology. While importing capital goods is a major way of acquiring foreign technology, management and knowledge support should also be acquired in order to maximize technology investment productivity.

Key words: knowledge-based development, knowledge economy, sustainability, knowledge transmission, knowledge management, learning by doing.

JEL classification codes: F41; O11; O53.[1]

A knowledge economy creates, distributes, and uses knowledge to generate value and gives rise to 'a network society, where the opportunity and capability to access and join knowledge and learning intensive relations determines the socio-economic position of individuals and firms' (OECD, cited in Clarke, 2001; Laszlo and Laszlo, 2007). China's knowledge economy called for the need to manage intangible assets that do not depreciate but increase in value over time. To meet this need, the field of knowledge management began to take shape. Thanks to advances in information and communication technologies in the 1990s, China's knowledge economy and knowledge management were able to develop. The initial usefulness of the knowledge economy was that it was a source of competitive advantage for firms. 'Knowledge management provides the means to generate, distribute, and use knowledge in ways that add value to business activity and provide new opportunities for enterprise' (Clarke, 2001).

Knowledge-based development has its roots in the knowledge management agenda (Laszlo and Laszlo, 2007). 'As knowledge management comes of age, it is evolving into a strategic management approach, applicable to purposeful human organizations in general' (Carrillo, 2002). Knowledge-based development therefore involves applying knowledge management to development issues. Education and training, activities associated with knowledge transmission and application, are the two core elements of development strategies. The application of more sophisticated knowledge strategies to industries, regions, countries, or any other social systems can be seen as a natural extension of the applicability of knowledge management (Laszlo and Laszlo, 2007). According to the literature, two interrelated objectives of knowledge-based development can be recognized. First, knowledge-based development is a powerful strategy for nations or regions to seek economic prosperity. Technical, market, financial, and human knowledge are all useful in bringing about economic returns (Lever, 2002). Second, knowledge-based development also aims to foster the knowledge and skills of people as a means for individual and social development (Ovalle et al., 2004). Evidently, the two main objectives of knowledge-based development are mutually supportive. An increase in intellectual and human capital brings about more creativity, innovation, and entrepreneurship promoting economic outcomes whereas economic prosperity offers individuals more opportunities to accumulate knowledge and skills.

The growing importance of knowledge in economic activities is seen in many aspects of private and public behavior in modern economies. Investment in knowledge, such as expenditure on education, training, and research, now exceeds 10 percent of total GDP of OECD countries. One defining characteristic of the knowledge economy is the increasing incorporation of knowledge into economic activities concerned with both goods and services. Knowledge became embedded in productive activities in many different ways, ranging from workers learning by doing in workshops to formal processes of labor training, of investment in advanced technology, and of knowledge application. Similarly, services education and training, business consulting, and medical diagnosis and treatment rely increasingly heavily on embodied knowledge. Increasing knowledge intensity in economic activities is associated not only with increasing knowledge intensity in individual goods and services, but also with the growing importance of goods and services that rely on embodied knowledge. Therefore, the advent of the knowledge economy is associated with significant changes in the economic structure of developed countries. The shift from goods industries to knowledge and person-based industries in terms of the composition of employment or output is a crucial characteristic of the knowledge economy (Sheehan, 1999).

Despite its long tradition of respect for and emphasis on knowledge, China's economic development is still based much more heavily on the advantages of low-cost labor than on the application of advanced knowledge. A central challenge facing China brought about by the global knowledge economy is to develop an industrial structure that could make fuller use of knowledge developed both abroad and within China. Moreover, growth in an open global knowledge-intensive economy generates continuous pressures on increasing inequality within China (Sheehan, 1999). This short chapter provides a tentative discussion of the knowledge economy and knowledge-based development and their implications for China.

The success of China's economic reform since the 1980s and the growth of the country's innovation capacity can partly be attributed to the policy of attracting foreign direct investment (Buckley et al., 2002; Liu and Wang, 2003). However, some researchers point out that as a result of the huge influx of FDI China has become overly dependent on foreign technology and that the rapid expansion of China's exports is largely boosted by the growth of China's low-wage manufacturing industries (Gilboy, 2004). In the last few decades, China attracted FDI by providing fiscal incentives as well as institutional and physical infrastructure. Over time, the Chinese government has gradually shifted its preferential fiscal policy from low-tech labor-intensive industries to high-tech manufacturing and service industries. In 2007, the Ministry of Commerce and Central Administration of Customs amended the list of low-tech goods whose production should be restricted. This restricted the establishment of foreign firms wanting to produce low-tech goods in China's coastal provinces, but encouraged the development of domestic manufacturers in its interior provinces. The amendment signaled the end of low-tech FDI in China (Huang and Soete, 2007). Along with regulating FDI, the Chinese government also increased its support of innovation in enterprises. To finance innovation, China also aimed to establish a well-functioning financial system, especially a venture capital system, to support technology-based enterprises. Local governments and state-owned organizations contributed to establishment of a fund to facilitate venture capital investments.

In sum, China needs to exploit rapidly growing global knowledge with a view to accelerating its own economic development and facilitating its transition toward a knowledge-based economy. The challenge is to strike a proper balance between knowledge creation and knowledge acquisition (Dahlman and Aubert, 2001). This means adapting foreign knowledge to the contexts of China's economy and in the meantime budgeting for research and development activities to create knowledge within China. Transnational corporations are usually considered the main drivers of the rapid expansion of global knowledge. As mentioned in earlier chapters, attracting FDI is one of the most effective means for China to gain access to foreign technology. FDI not only helps promote free flows of labor and build high-quality teams of personnel, but also stimulates domestic firms through competition and promotes economic and technological exchange and cooperation at home and abroad.

Even a cursory analysis shows China's current FDI stock is impressive. However, more detailed analyses yield important insights that are likely to have significant policy implications. What stands out here is that most of China's FDI is concentrated in manufacturing and related industries. Despite being underdeveloped, the service industries have the greatest potential for creating jobs and absorbing FDI in the short and medium term, but much depends on the government's determination to deregulate them and introduce more competition by opening them up to foreign participation. There are many restrictions preventing foreign enterprises currently operating in China from getting involved in such service industries as banking, insurance, transport, and the legal sector. The Chinese government needs to tap foreign expertise in the service industries and thereby gain experience of operating in open environments (Dahlman and Aubert, 2001). What also stands out is that China should leverage its FDI further by focusing on attracting FDI that has a high knowledge content. For this to happen, China has to improve its intellectual property rights. The lax intellectual property rights in China threatens the long-term viability of foreign enterprises and discourages further FDI, foreign trade, and technological cooperation and other forms of knowledge sharing. In addition to attracting FDI (especially FDI that has a high knowledge content), the Chinese government needs to provide incentives to stimulate Chinese enterprises to invest in foreign countries. Operating on the international stage will help

Chinese enterprises keep up with advances in modern technology and management.

FDI aside, foreign trade is another channel through which Chinese enterprises can tap into global knowledge and technology. First, high-tech products and capital goods embody a tremendous amount of knowledge and technology. Second, active engagement in foreign trade also brings beneficial spillovers to Chinese firms and the Chinese economy. However, while China has been active in importing technology embodied in tangible goods, it has been less active in importing disembodied technology, which normally incurs royalties or licensing fees. Low imports of disembodied technology have a negative effect on the utilization of technological knowledge. While importing capital goods is a major way of acquiring foreign technology, the management and knowledge support that go hand in hand with it should also be acquired in order to maximize technology investment productivity. For example, more resources should be spent training workers and hiring foreign experts to make the best use of imported equipment.

Note

1. Works on economics are often classified according to JEL classification codes, a system set up by the *Journal of Economic Literature*.

References

Buckley, P.J.; Clegg, J.; and Wang, C. (2002) 'The Impact of inward FDI on the performance of Chinese manufacturing firms,' *Journal of International Business Studies*, **33**(4), 637–55.

Carrillo, F.J. (2002) 'Capital systems: implications for a global knowledge agenda,' *Journal of Knowledge Management*, **6**(4), 379–99.

Clarke, T. (2001) 'The knowledge economy,' *Education + Training*, **43**(4/5), 189–96.

Dahlman, C.J.; and Aubert, J-E. (2001) *China and the Knowledge Economy: Seizing the 21st Century* (WBI Development Studies), Washington, D.C.: World Bank.

Gilboy, G. (2004) 'The myth behind China's miracle,' *Foreign Affairs*, **83**(4), 33–48.

Huang, C.; and Soete, L. (2007) *The Global Challenges of the Knowledge Economy: China and the EU* (UNU-MERIT Working Paper Series No. 2007-28}, Maastricht, The Netherlands: Maastricht Economic and Social Research and Training Centre on Innovation and Technology, United Nations University.

Laszlo, K.C.; and Laszlo, A. (2007) 'Fostering a sustainable learning society through knowledge based development,' *Systems Research and Behavioral Science*, 24(5), 493–503.

Lever, W.F. (2002) 'Correlating the knowledge-base of cities with economic growth,' *Urban Studies*, 39(5/6), 859–70.

Liu, Xiaohui; and Wang, Chenggang (2003) 'Does foreign direct investment facilitate technological progress? Evidence from Chinese industries,' *Research Policy*, 32(6), 945–53.

Ovalle, M.D.R.G.; Marquez, J.A.A.; and Salomon, S.D.M. (2004) 'A compilation of resources on knowledge cities and knowledge-based development,' *Journal of Knowledge Management*, 8(5), 107–27.

Sheehan, P. (1999) *The Global Knowledge Economy: Challenges for China's Development* (CSES Working Paper No. 15), Melbourne, Australia: Victoria University.

Index

Printed and bound by CPI Group (UK) Ltd, Croydon, CR0 4YY

08/05/2025

01864974-0001